THE
HUSBANDS
AND WIVES CLUB

A Year in

the Life of

a Couples

Therapy Group

LAURIE ABRAHAM

A Touchstone Book
Published by Simon & Schuster
New York   London   Toronto   Sydney

 Touchstone
A Division of Simon & Schuster, Inc.
1230 Avenue of the Americas
New York, NY 10020

First Touchstone hardcover edition March 2010

TOUCHSTONE and colophon are registered trademarks of Simon & Schuster, Inc.

For information about special discounts for bulk purchases, please contact Simon & Schuster Special Sales at 1-866-506-1949 or business@simonandschuster.com.

The Simon & Schuster Speakers Bureau can bring authors to your live event. For more information or to book an event contact the Simon & Schuster Speakers Bureau at 1-866-248-3049 or visit our website at www.simonspeakers.com.

Designed by William Ruoto

Manufactured in the United States of America

10   9   8   7   6   5   4   3   2   1

Library of Congress Cataloging-in-Publication Data
Abraham, Laurie
    The husbands and wives club : A year in the life of a couples therapy group/ Laurie Abraham.
        p.   cm.
    "A Touchstone Book."
    1. Marriage—Psychological aspects—United States. 2. Marital conflict— United States. I. Title.
    HQ536.A223 2010
    155.9'24—dc22
        2009023303

ISBN 978-1-4165-8550-3

CONTENTS

PROLOGUE

F or some years now, I've read with an eye, or ear, to who gets it
"right" about marriage. This wasn't conscious much of the time,
other than perhaps in my predilection for fiction that is character
driven, spinning on the axis of human relationship rather than plot. But
as a result, a fair number of my books, the novels mostly, have at least
one or two scribbled effusions like, "My God, that's it!" Or, "Exactly
right." Or just "✓," check marks being, in the world of magazine editing
from which I come, the indication of appreciation for a particular word,
sentence, or idea—restrained, but no less the loving for it.

In magazines, my niche has become something like feminism, psychology, and sex, and the politics thereof. (My first big piece in that
realm, published in 1999 in the now-defunct *Mirabella* magazine, was
a ten-thousand-word opus on female sexual desire and the evolution of
sex and marital therapy.) When you cover such topics for magazines,
the "peg," or news hook, is usually the latest therapist-guru or how-to
book, and over time I began to see patterns in the way relationships were
conceived—and to be able to detect ideas that were richer, fresher, and
potentially more useful to readers. The more I delved into modern psychological thinking and research, the more, too, I was drawn to earlier
sources: to Freud and to other psychoanalysts, to family therapy pioneers
of the 1960s and 1970s.

Which brings me to this book. The idea for it, or rather for *The New*

York Times Magazine piece that inspired it, came now nearly five years ago. As I remember it, I'd just read Paula Fox's *Desperate Characters* and admired how she'd nailed the choppy river of dialogue, spoken and unspoken, that perpetually runs between spouses.

Oh, did I forget to mention it? I'm married, eleven years, and so an expert in how one couple constantly communicates—even when, or maybe especially when, we think we're not. I wanted to write nonfiction about marriage at different developmental stages the way Fox wrote fiction: close-up, textured, "real." I knew it wouldn't work to just interview husbands and wives. Even if I spoke to people repeatedly, so that they perhaps began to open up, it would be difficult to capture the feeling of their relationships, the split-second shifting of mood and intention. Although for an earlier book on health care and poverty I'd been a journalistic fly on the wall, hung out with various members of one family hour upon hour for several years, I couldn't imagine replicating that with couples. Too much downtime, which, granted, there was a fair amount of in my reporting for the health care book, but there also were relevant events, such as visits from home health nurses, hospital stays, and doctor's appointments. What was I going to do, ask some couple to call me before they fought, or made tender love?

In any event, I never seriously considered that. My mind quickly went to couples therapy because I specifically wanted to explore how couples live—and live *through* (or not)—their troubles. My husband and I saw a marriage therapist together and found it moderately helpful, and, as I've suggested, I was interested in therapy as an entity of its own, its theory and practice. Summing it up in a sentence, my overall question became: How does marriage work to tear people down—leaving them feeling bitter or diminished, dulled or lost—and if that process can be interrupted, if a therapist can lift spouses out of the muck of their own making, how does it work?

After I decided I wanted to follow a therapy group, I contacted several people who run them for couples, among them a Philadelphia therapist named Judith Coché. Over coffee near my office at *ELLE* magazine in Manhattan, I told Coché I wanted to spend a year attending her group and also have permission to interview her and the couples outside of it, possibly in their homes. I'd try to faithfully represent the members and her thinking and technique, but neither she nor her group would have any say over what I wrote. If I was at all confused about what she was trying to do with the group, I'd ask her about it. Coché was cautiously excited. Confidentiality is an ethical mandate for therapists, and to decide to stretch it for an outside observer, certainly a journalist, wasn't something she could do lightly. Yet here was an opportunity to educate the public about the benefits of marriage therapy, and the group form in particular. (I'm sure she didn't mind the attention, either, though after three decades as a therapist, she was professionally well established.)

After reading much of my work—and, without telling me, contacting former subjects of my magazine pieces—Coché broached the project with the new group she was forming. It was to include three couples who were continuing from the year before and two new ones. They'd meet one weekend a month, for one or two six-hour sessions. The groups used to meet biweekly, but Coché increasingly found that getting both members of five separate couples, many with children, to show up so frequently was impossible. The monthly sessions would also allow people to enroll who lived beyond the immediate Philadelphia area, and in the group I'd follow, the couples drove as long as three hours to get to Coché's office in Center City Philadelphia or one she has near her summer cottage on the Jersey shore.

Some members were enthusiastic about my observing, others agnostic, a few quite nervous, Coché told me. All were willing to entertain the idea. Coché then arranged a conference call in which the group could ask me questions. Their main concerns, not surprising, hinged on confidentiality, and I agreed to use middle names or nicknames, according to the *New York Times* protocol. I told them I'd protect their identities as much as possible, but I wouldn't make up details about them. I might leave a few things out—for example, I don't say in the book where anyone lives—but with one exception (which I'll explain later), I do not concoct alternate professions or other personal information. I continue to believe that when I'm writing nonfiction, it shouldn't be fictional, so in this book I followed fairly conventional journalistic standards. I didn't compress or otherwise alter the chronology of events, and the quotes are actual. I audiotaped and later transcribed all of the group sessions (and did the same for outside interviews).

Okay, after all my lofty assurances, the exception: My agreement with the group was that anything they said during the sessions or in interviews was fair game for the magazine article. One of the five couples refused to participate, however, unless I left out a central conflict. I told my *Times* editor, and we agreed to the condition, partly because I hadn't expected the pair to play a major role in the article. And in fact, I only ended up having space to tell *one* couple's story in the magazine. That led to the writing of the book. Usually, when I publish a magazine piece, even though I've moaned to my editor all along about needing more space, I feel finished—I've used all the good stuff and left the rest on the cutting-room floor. This time that wasn't the case. The dynamics and problems of the other couples were equally fascinating. Each seemed to represent a distinctive shade on the wide spectrum of discontent that periodically darkens marriage.

A book also would offer a chance to tease out the thinking of the people whom I consider, in their insight and command of the nuances of human experience, to be philosophers of monogamy, as well as to expand on the critique of couples therapy begun in the *Times*. Vast amounts of social science about therapy's effectiveness—and marriage in general—have accumulated in the past thirty to forty years, so there was plenty to scrutinize. (To this end, I told Coché she wasn't the only therapist I'd be interviewing.) I was curious, in particular, about the reliability of highly publicized studies that predict which marriages will succeed or fail based on observing couples interact for short periods of time.

So, to do the book, I returned to the couple whose problem I'd agreed to redact. Could I write more fully about them now? This time they agreed, sort of. They'd participate but only if I changed some identifying details. I did so, deciding that their struggle was more important to a book on marriage than an absolutely accurate biographical portrayal.

One question I've been asked frequently is how I affected people in the group—if at all—and how they affected me. To begin with, I was rather quiet. Analogizing my role to that of a student intern, Coché urged me to ask questions or make observations in the moment, but I was slow to take her up on that. I didn't want the group members to mistake me for one of their own as opposed to someone who would ultimately write about them; I assumed any factual confusion I had would clear up with time, anyway. And while my head buzzed with reactions and thoughts based on my forays into the psychology of marriage and my relationship with my husband, I wasn't at all sure my comments would be welcome or helpful.

Gradually, however, the group and I became more comfortable with each other. I began to ask questions, make jokes, and let my emotions show somewhat. Which is not to say I had myself under perfect control: One time, I burst into tears, stricken by a story recounted by a woman in the group. Coché later told me not to be worried by my crying; the group was a little low on the "affect side," she said, and I'd added a jolt of feeling.

The members themselves, I sensed, were happy to have me join in a little, and some eventually said that they appreciated my questions, even my bluntness. When the *Times* story was published, one member (who was mentioned only briefly in the magazine) was upset because something I'd written hurt her relationship with a relative. But apart from that, no one ever told me or Coché that my participation was a liability. That doesn't mean no one privately believed this: Once the group agreed to have me there, they were pretty much stuck. I guess someone could have started a campaign to oust me, but that probably would have been more trouble than it was worth. As yet another member told me, "You weren't my focus. My marriage was."

I also related an occasional anecdote from my own life. Early on, I did it mostly when I thought somebody could use an ally; for example, once it seemed like a certain man was being left to believe that no one in the group ever became explosively angry, and I let it be known that I could be a terror. Later, I offered a few revelations about myself and my marriage that, while expressing solidarity, also betrayed vulnerability. While we never dwelled on me, it was a relief, I suppose, to unburden myself.

The usual concern for journalists, or anthropologists, when they become part of the action is that their report may end up being skewed because their presence influenced the subjects. For a therapy group, the matter seems tricky to gauge, however. Each group is idiosyncratic and the measurement of cause and effect relatively murky and subjective. It's true that part of what I try to do in the book is trace the arc of the couples' changes, so I don't reject the idea that there are turning points. Few, if any, of them, however, could be traced to the intervention of a single member—except perhaps Coché—and all were rooted in what came before.

Since I cried at one point, it's probably obvious that I came to care about the people I sat with each month—for a year, then two. I told them when I started that even though their real names weren't being used, they might hate the way they were portrayed. I wouldn't put words in their mouths, but what I chose to concentrate on, what I noticed, would say as much about me as them. Yet I wasn't the one who was to be laid out on the page; they were. The group accepted this, but I don't think you can understand what it feels like to be written about until it happens.

So I really, really don't want to hurt anyone in the group, to have them suffer because of anything I've written. I am deeply grateful to them for allowing me into their circle. But I'm not giving them veto power over the book's contents, either. Reporting requires a measure of ruthlessness. When the playwright Horton Foote died in 2009, *Times* reviewer Ben Brantley had this to say about him: "I think he loved all his characters . . . but he was too honest to let any of them off the hook." Yes, I'm writing nonfiction, not fiction—and yes, I'm no Horton Foote—but the best I can hope is that Coché and the ten people in the group will know, because of what I've written or in spite of it, that I feel love for them.

CHAPTER 1

——————

Who Would Submit to This?

"The emotional intimacy," Marie is telling her husband, Clem, and, unavoidably, the therapist and three other couples in the room, "needs to come *before* the physical intimacy."

"Okay," Clem says. His tone is chipper—so much of marriage is in the tone. This is the first meeting of a couples therapy group that will convene one or two days a month for the next year, and Clem doesn't sound discouraged by this seemingly unoriginal request from his wife. (Women need to feel close before they can have sex, blah, blah, blah.) To the contrary: Clem is hearing it as a revelation, something he can *do* to make things better. His wife of twenty-two years is sitting catty-corner to him in a turquoise T-shirt with a tropical fish swimming across her chest; but her slim ankles are demurely crossed, the resting pose of one of those fifties starlets who swished around on-screen in full skirts, sheer hose, and kitten heels. So what if Marie is only wearing a loose T-shirt, cotton shorts, and white Keds? Clem first met her in college, when she was eighteen, and her legs are good, long for a woman of her modest height and round figure.

The therapist who runs the group, Philadelphia psychologist Judith Coché, opened the proceedings by instructing each of the four couples (there is a fifth, but they had to miss the first session for a long-scheduled vacation) to huddle together and tell each other what they wanted to accomplish in the next year. Quiet murmuring, periodically ripped by a seagull's screech, filled the room. Located in a town called Stone Harbor on the Jersey shore, this is what Coché calls her "beach office," or "The Weekend Retreat," according to the hand-painted, hand-carved sign hanging on the front door. In Philadelphia, she works from the "Coché Center." Both offices are retrofitted condos whose names confer a bit more grandeur than is evident, in part because hearty self-promotion seems reflexive for Coché. A few colleagues have criticized her for it in the past, she once told me. Then she shrugged, as if indifferent to their attitude or just puzzled by it.

Stone Harbor's business district consists of five blocks of ice cream parlors and souvenir emporiums, and Coché's office is just off the main strip, on the third floor of an anonymous low-rise with a cleaning service at the street level. The building backs up against a small bay, lined with vacation homes and a bustling boat-and-float-rental business. Standing on the balcony during a break in the group, all the activity can make you wistful—those people are having so much fun!

Back inside the office, the decor is insistently pleasant. On the bookshelves, ersatz beach paraphernalia is interspersed with pop and academic psychology titles; the galley kitchen where Coché prepares lunch for the group is papered in factory-issue floral; and a small Zen sand garden sits on the coffee table in the room where the therapy is conducted, next to a box of tissues.

Cutting against the anodyne mood, Coché had cued up a crackly old recording of Cole Porter singing "I Get a Kick Out of You" as the couples trailed in for the 10 A.M. start time. Lighthearted inspiration? Maybe. But this is a couples therapy group, a setting in which one might expect to find the "gross, destructive mutual raids on personality that often form marriages," as the British writer Rebecca West observed. If you were so situated, Cole Porter's witty professions of infatuation might sting rather than amuse, remind you of the adoration you were unrequitedly craving.

Marie and Clem, both in their mid-forties, are the first pair to volunteer to report their goals back to the group, who've settled into a rough circle. I'm on the periphery, my eyes darting among the couples, except when someone meets my gaze. Then I quickly look away. I feel voyeuristic, intrusive—and definitely disinclined to take Coché's advice to speak when I have something to say. There are five couples—ten separate people—who have one or two days a month to get their say, at a cost of about $6,000 for the year. That may sound like forever, but troubled marriages are small countries of love and hate, of confusion and icy clarity, of guilt and recrimination, of running to and from. Picking across the rugged terrain takes time.

Surveying the circle, Marie is sitting with her back to the room's windows, which are cracked open to let in a chilly breeze off the bay. She's chosen one of two deep, upholstered chairs, and her arms are loosely crossed, resting on a pillow lying in her lap. Clem is a few feet away, sitting a little stiffly on one end of a couch. It could be that he's afraid to brush up against Rachael, whom he's just met. She and her husband, Michael, both in their mid-thirties, are sharing the couch with Clem. They're practically on top of each other—well, not really, but their thighs are touching and Michael's arm is thrown across the back of the couch, his hand resting companionably on his wife's shoulder.

In a chair next to Michael is Mark, the group's most emphatically grown-up member. An executive in his early fifties, he is six feet three inches tall and speaks in a deep baritone. When he opens his mouth, you want to sit up straight, smooth your skirt, and pay attention. His wife at his side, Sue Ellen, is about a foot shorter, and takes up space with her silence. The mother of three almost grown sons, she does not come off as angry so much as very, very contained. She's wearing a soft taupe sweater, trimmed in green velvet, and a pearl necklace; she spends the morning holding her small zebra-skin purse in her lap.

Having rolled her black leather desk chair over to the circle, Coché is perched just above everyone else, her preferred position since it gives her the best vantage point from which to conduct the group. *Conduct* is Coché's word for the way she approaches her job. A tall, broad-shouldered brunette with a taste in clothes that is a cross between tailored elegance and earth mother, she is commanding, almost showily confident. She has season tickets to the Philadelphia Orchestra, she has told me, and she always sits at the back of the stage behind the players, so she can watch the maestro work. "Creating a sense of performance, it's really inspiring to people," she says. "It gives them something to hold on to when everything else is falling apart."

What traces of vulnerability Coché does display in the group are oddly riveting. Like when she folds her five foot ten inch frame into one of the modern leather chairs in her Philadelphia office and her awkward adolescent self pops into view: one long leg splayed here, another there, her arms hanging loosey-goosey over the sides, fingertips grazing the floor. Or when she later will injure her hand in a boating accident and come to the group with a large white bandage wrapped around her authoritative index finger, chips in her wine-colored nail polish. Next to Coché is the last couple, Leigh and Aaron, who are in their early sixties. Couples "contract" to attend a year's worth of sessions and may re-up at the end of the time; Leigh and Aaron have kept coming back far longer than anyone else in Coché's nearly two decades of running couples groups. This is their *tenth* year—the typical stay is two, perhaps three years—and Aaron will preface many of his comments in the coming months with the cheerful declaration that this is it for him and Leigh. Leigh has agreed to that plan, but she doesn't seem nearly as thrilled about it.

Now Leigh looks encouragingly at Clem as he explains that he didn't understand that his wife wanted to put emotional intimacy before "other things," before sex, that is. "But now I'm thinking to myself, that's great. Really. That's great. Maybe I'll just start sending you e-mails or calling you more, leaving notes, trying, trying," Clem stutters, "to break through to that next level instead of just trying to be sexual first. It'll be a good goal. It sounds fun even."

"You're open to it," Coché says. He sounds more than open, though; he sounds mildly enthusiastic.

From the bowels of her chair, Marie is watching. She is watching Clem, watching *them* figure it all out. They haven't. "Sometimes I just want to be heard and nothing more," she says, pleading in her voice, and finger wagging. Marie's graying brown hair hangs to the middle of her back, and she wears it in a long side ponytail. Hair like that could be a girlish affectation in a middle-aged woman or a sign of indifference about her appearance. With forty-four-year-old Marie, I'll come to believe, it's both.

During the couple's tête-à-tête, Marie had not spelled out for Clem what she meant by "emotional intimacy" because, it seems, she herself doesn't know what she means. But she knows that Clem's translation, the soft seductions of notes and e-mails, isn't right. What Marie seems to want him to absorb at this point is her inchoate dissatisfaction—with him, with life—her lack. "If you're already at the fix-it level," Marie complains, "then you haven't really heard me."

"Say that again," Coché says, jumping off Clem's train and onto Marie's.

"I would like to just express myself so that Clem would fully understand who I am."

"That would be better than fixing it," Coché reiterates.

"Yes," Marie agrees. But she doubts whether Clem will be able to merely listen.

"Sometimes if I just listen," Clem says, like something straight out of *Men Are from Mars, Women Are from Venus,* "it seems like I didn't *do* anything."

"Try saying it this way," Coché coaches Clem. "When I listen, I feel helpless."

"When I listen, I feel helpless," Clem mimics. "I feel like I'm not making any progress. I get anxious, so I try to fix it." As his momentum increases, it seems like he's actually hearing what he's saying, and he's blinking as if he's been punched. "And that's what I've done for the twenty years I've known you."

"Which ends up being that you *don't* know me," Marie retorts.

"Oh, I think I *do*," Clem flares thinly. His introspective efforts have been turned against him. Before the squabble can continue, Coché breaks it up.

"See," Marie says to Coché, you have to intervene. Earlier Marie was joking, grimly, that the therapist was going to have to come live with them because this is their second year with the group, and they still can't apply what they learn here at home.

Clem tries again with Marie. "So you say I don't know you because I don't listen, and I try to fix things?"

"Yes," Marie replies. "Do you want me to take time to explain?"

"No," Coché cuts her off. "I want to move on." She is reflecting, surely, the will of the group, who can become at times like a single organism; the creature sucked in its breath when Marie offered to "take time to explain." She has a tendency to engage in what behavioral researchers who videotape couples in conflict call "self summarizing"— put less diplomatically, she repeats herself.

But the group, or rather Clem, is not going to get off that easy. Marie has some parting words for him. "I need for you to *actively* listen to me right now," she says. In addition to sharing information, the private one-on-one conversations are an opportunity for the couples to practice "active listening," Coché has told them, meaning that the listener doesn't challenge the speaker and checks in to make sure he or she understands what his or her partner is trying to communicate ("What I hear you saying is . . ."). Coché knows so-called active listening has become a cultural joke, shorthand for everything that is silly about our overly therapized world, but she thinks the concept can be useful.

"Phone calls," Marie goes on, "would *not* make me feel good." Clem protests that he knows, he knows . . . he knows his wife doesn't like to talk on the phone.

"Don't call me," she says. "Thank you for listening."

"Okay." Clem's tone is flat.

The offhand cruelty of this exchange is crushing (not to mention that it shows the limits of active listening; intention can matter as much as technique), but no one acknowledges it out loud in this, the first session. It's not just that these people are still shy together, or already cowed by Marie (though they are both). Sometimes it will be disconcerting how suddenly the subject changes in the group, how quickly the onrush of voices blots out a wrenching spill. Which is similar to how the ceaseless domestic demands operate in marriage: the scheduling and the meal making and the bill paying sopping up the feeling, fortunately, perhaps.

This is probably the time to say a bit more about my own situation: I've lived with my husband for fourteen years, eleven of them married, and we have two daughters. My marriage, like many I know, has had its problems, its head-banging frustrations. And like many spouses, I've wondered how I could act, or *re*act, differently, be it more constructively or simply more kindly, wondered how my husband and I might increase our allotment of peaceable—and passionate—coexistence.

I didn't spend a year with the group, however, to voyeuristically enhance my own marriage. I knew I might take home some new insight, but the impetus for attending was professional: I wanted to combine an intimate look at wedded malaise with the fruits of my formal and informal study over the years of the psychology of relationships. Initially, I checked into shadowing therapists who counsel couples individually, but then it occurred to me that a *group* of husbands and wives would be ideal. I'd not only get to observe multiple subjects at once, but they'd be interacting among themselves, itself revealing.

While marriage therapy is very common, *group* marriage therapy is not. Still, with just a little googling, I tracked down a handful of candidate group therapists. I chose Coché for three practical reasons: She was relatively nearby; she reconfigures her group annually and was about to start a new round; and she seemed like a competent therapist. I gleaned the latter by checking her credentials and interviewing her and people who knew her work. I could tell by how she talked about therapy—the people she'd studied with, the way she conceptualized marital problems—that she was familiar with the dominant approaches of couples counseling. I also watched Coché conduct a mock therapy session at a conference, and I liked her style. She seemed like a good combination of intellectually curious and emotionally perspicacious.

Who would submit to a couples group? I would, because I come from a family where the mind is treated as something that may periodically need attention and care, just like the body. But many people can't fathom it, and when I first met the couples, I was struck by how unprepossessing they were, at least on the surface. The five men and five women range in age from their mid-thirties to early sixties; several hold relatively high-powered or high-status jobs, the rest work in white-collar or retail middle management. About half of the group has been in therapy on and off for years, the others are fairly new to it. Three of the couples have children.

Coché culls clients for her groups from her conventional individual and couples therapy practice, as well as from referrals from colleagues. Groups are particularly helpful, she believes, for people who are rigid or keenly defensive, since the clamor of voices is harder to dismiss than a single, ever-so-reasonable therapist. Couples in which one spouse can barely speak up for herself are also prime candidates, she says: The meeker half will find a "subgroup" within the larger group to take his or her part. She excludes people who are seriously mentally ill, are of limited intelligence, or have some practical impediment to showing up every month. Coché also does not invite couples in which either spouse is having an affair, though there has been at least one instance, she says, when a man lied about it. (When anyone comes to her for marriage counseling, she asks straight out about adultery, if the subject doesn't arise naturally.) Other times, Coché says, people have had flings during their year with the group, and the infidelities were then addressed.

Among the ground rules for the group, which Coché imparts in screening interviews and again during the first session, are that people commit for one year and that they not socialize outside of the sessions (which may precipitate all manner of upheaval if, for example, someone has a party and invites certain members but not others). Participants also must agree to meet with Coché or another therapist at least once between meetings, to assimilate what they're learning and zero in on their own specific situations.

Coché started running couples groups in the mid-1980s with her then husband, Erich Coché, a German-born psychologist who'd made his reputation designing in-patient groups for the mentally ill. She was besotted with Erich, she says, from the moment they met. "Will you have a hamburger?" he asked, accosting her on the boardwalk in Atlantic City, where they both were attending a professional conference. (A colleague had told him this was the best way to ask an American girl for a date.) Only twenty-three years old, Judith was drawn to his European cosmopolitanism, his intellect, how different he was from anyone else she knew. "On our second date, we went to the zoo, and then we spent the next year talking about how it was impossible to get married," she says. "How could a Main Line only child of Jewish parents, some of whose family had been killed in the Holocaust, marry a Dutch German?"

Their careers were intertwined from the start—she had her first published article, about a boy she treated who chronically soiled himself, translated into German. The pair wrote an academic book about couples groups and together led the group until Erich died, in 1991, at age forty-nine, a year after being diagnosed with cancer. He's still a presence in her life—"according to Erich Coché . . ." she'll say to the group—and just this morning, before the group began, she rummaged around in a coat closet and pulled out a picture of him. It had been lying facedown in a basket. She didn't say anything, and it took me a split second to figure out who I was looking at. Then she returned the photograph to its place in the closet, facedown. Her second husband, John, whom she married in 1994, is a retired CEO in scientific publishing. She has one child, with Erich, a thirty-year-old daughter named Juliette, who is considering joining the family business. She is a psychiatric resident at the University of Pennsylvania—and took a required course on group therapy that her mother has taught there for years.

Although couples groups may be rare, professional-led groups for people with specific emotional or physical conditions are easy to find: Coché has run them for overweight adults and learning-disabled adolescents. And there is one kind of couples group that has registered on the national radar in the last decade: premarital education. Often run by religious organizations, the education groups were a darling of George W. Bush, whose administration funneled money to programs targeted at low-income couples who'd yet to tie the knot. The so-called marriage cure was intended to increase the wedding rate, the reasoning being that two-parent families are less likely to need welfare.

So what's unusual are groups like Coché's: ongoing, trafficking in emotion. (A brochure for one Bush-era couples-education seminar reassured, or warned, depending on your perspective: "Couples do *not* share personal issues or feelings.") Coché's groups are also experiential, meaning she mines the interactions among the members in the moment. "Sitting here for six hours you just know what it's like to be married to him," Coché muttered to me once, out of earshot of the offending spouse.

• • •

Being with Michael and Rachael is like sitting across from lovers on the subway; try as you might, you can't stop staring at them. When the pair went off on their own to talk about what they wanted to address over the next year, they held each other's eyes, giggled, grabbed hands. When they're back with the group on the couch, the vibe between them is kind of sexy, kind of friendly like brother and sister. Rachael is a thirty-four-year-old émigrée from Australia with fair, dewy skin, pale blue eyes, and chin-length curls, while Michael, four years her senior, has a slightly beaky nose and a floppy shock of brown hair, neither light nor dark, that he is regularly pushing out of his face. The similarity is not in their appearance but their presence: Rachael and Michael both project a comfortable ordinariness, a low-key, jokey affability. You can just see him chucking her on the shoulder, and her chucking him right back, grinning all the while.

Before she and Michael launch into their goals, Rachael pulls her hair back into a ponytail, like therapy is an aerobic sport. She looks to Michael to start, and he takes his cue. This is his second marriage, he says, and he's afraid of replicating the deleterious patterns from his first, of losing his independence, "sacrificing himself to the other person."

Rachael, too, was married before, and she's also worried about repeating the past, she says. She puts her hand on Michael's knee, and smiles reassuringly. "It's not that I think there's a great danger, but it's there."

"What specifically are you afraid of?" Michael says, turning to face her on the couch.

"Being lonely," she says quietly.

"Why were you lonely?"

"Because he was there, but not . . . attainable." Her words creak out.

"Is there anything else?" Michael is admirably adhering to the active-listening script.

"No, that's it."

Michael's face relaxes. She won't be lonely under his watch—no way.

Coché, who has counseled Rachael individually and with her first husband, tells the group that Rachael's girlhood might predispose her toward loneliness; the condition may not have been strictly about her first husband.

Tears redden Rachael's eyes.

"What are the tears?" Coché asks.

"That Michael and I can talk like this," Rachael says.

"So those are good tears?"

Rachael nods. She will be the only person in the group who's quick to cry, which is not because some of them don't have plenty of reason to. More than once, noticing the circle of immobile faces, I want to grab the group by its collective collar and shout, *Hey, does anyone here have a feeling?*

From the short introduction Rachael and Michael offer of themselves, it seems—and it will seem for some while—that the fault lines in their marriage are speculative rather than actual. Common sense says that people only gradually unveil themselves in therapy, and Coché believes the tentativeness is exacerbated in couples groups. Not only do spouses often have unspoken agreements about what's fit for public consumption, but certain topics are off-limits between husbands and wives themselves, such that "partners are often unaware of these taboo subjects as problems worth mentioning," as Coché put it in her book.

Per the agreement I made with her, I sometimes will stay after the group to ask Coché for clarification or question her on therapeutic strategy. She is pretty open during our talks, though mindful of not leaking information to which she is privy but that a couple has yet to disclose.

So following the first group, I'll mention that Michael was convincing when he announced that he and Rachael were there to "get things started off in the right way." Perhaps the couple is just looking for some basic education to prevent trouble down the line? After all, Coché herself has likened the group to a "mental health fitness club." But Coché, I will discover, was just speaking loosely. Before the year is out, the couple for whom I perhaps least expected it will be weighing divorce. Another pair will be confronting the husband's attraction to men, while a third will make a stunning turn for the better. There will be miscarriages and infertility to confront, job loss and betrayal. As for Michael and Rachael in particular, Coché has worked with each of them in the past, and she smiles ruefully at my suggestion that they're just here for some marital prophylaxis. "Believe me," she says, "nobody makes this kind of commitment just to get a few pointers."

The day of the first group, in mid-May, dawned blaringly bright but cool. So instead of having lunch at the table on Coché's balcony, or at the one she put on the building's bayside deck, the couples stick indoors. They eat Coché's chicken salad as a movable feast, perching for a few minutes at the kitchen table, then alone with a spouse in a corner of one of the condominium's three rooms, then back together, a bit awkwardly, again. They confine themselves to small talk—abiding by the group rule that members not extend "group business" beyond group time— and the halting conversations emphasize how little these people really know each other. The distance will gradually lessen, of course, but it raises one of the hesitations people have about group therapy in general: Isn't the setting dubiously artificial, tending more to "distort rather than reflect one's real behavior," as psychologist Irving Yalom—himself a founding father of the group method—writes. The answer to the question he rhetorically poses is, essentially, it depends on your definition of "real": "The group attempts to identify and eliminate social, prestige, or sexual games," Yalom writes. "[M]embers go through vital life experiences together; the reality-distorting facades are doffed." Compare *that* to Thanksgiving with your family.

To kick off the afternoon, Coché gives a speech about how an effective group must stay in the present. Which, after all, is a prerequisite for "intimacy," she tells the couples (the group's preferred euphemism for sex). Sure, she says bluffly, "You can make love with your partner and not pay any attention to them whatsoever." She looks around the room. "I expect more than one person has done that more than once." Marie is studying the pillow in her lap, playing with the fur.

Staying in the moment with a spouse in the distraction-free environment of the group may sound simple, she says, but what about when your anxiety is pricked? "Anxiety is catching; we give it to those we love," Coché likes to say, paraphrasing early-twentieth-century psychoanalyst Harry Stack Sullivan. He believed that our very existence, from infancy, is organized around avoiding "points of anxiety," such that we mount "security operations" to steer clear of the noxiously churning state. (It must be said that Sullivan's definition of anxiety was purposefully vague: Anxiety, he wrote, was whatever happened to the baby when his "zones of connection" with the outside world were impinged upon, whatever stopped him from doing what he was doing before.)

It follows that security operations in marriage are as rote as a morning cup of coffee. A common one, which Coché says is counterproductive to the group, is "storytelling," reconstructing past events as airy fortresses against any real suffering. Long-timer Aaron does this a lot, or at least tries to: He clears his throat to deliver a little lecture about his "repressive" family rather than meet the displeasure of his wife sitting next to him. Another waste of time, Coché tells her crowd, is severing the cable to your feelings and firing straight from the brain. "There are times when you'll need to talk about what you *think,* but a masterful way to avoid intimacy for the rest of your life is to remain cognitive at all times."

"Owww, you're hurting my hand," Leigh says, pulling away from Aaron's apparently viselike grasp.

"Turn your [wedding] ring around so it doesn't squeeze," Aaron says. (In other words, it's not my fault, Leigh, it's yours.) The ten-year group veterans are approaching their seventh wedding anniversary, meaning they started coming three years before they married. They joined to see *if* they could marry, in fact, or at least Leigh did. She was the prime mover behind their seeking help.

My first response to the couple's epic tenure in the group was: What's *wrong* with them—why didn't they just call it quits? When I later suggested as much to Coché, with the added implication that perhaps she was at fault for dragging this mess out, she matter-of-factly replied, "My job isn't to decide things for people. It's to help them figure out where they want to go, then help them get there."

This was a second marriage for both Leigh and Aaron. He was divorced in the late 1970s and has three children. Leigh's first husband, and the father of her four children, died suddenly, after two decades of marriage; he's been gone for close to fifteen years, but he is hardly forgotten. A successful, respected lawyer with an outsize personality, he was the love of her life, it will become clear, and they had a passionate sex life. Which obviously set the bar for Aaron quite high.

"I already *did* turn my ring around," Leigh replies, swiveling in her chair to catch her husband in her glare. She is a person whose smile transforms her appearance; you notice her intelligent eyes and ready warmth, her stylishly cut and highlighted hair. When she's annoyed (or just listening intently), her lips are pursed, and her chin juts out in a kind of ducklike pout.

"I'm guessing," Coché says lightly to Aaron, a gangly, self-employed surveyor, "that you're a little, uh, anxious." The group laughs. In this couple the security operations seem to be failing (a step toward or away from mental, or marital, health?).

Leigh, who went back to school to get her Ph.D. in anthropology after her first husband died, prompted Aaron's hand crush when she said that *she* was getting anxious as she conjured a persistent pattern in their marriage: Aaron treats her like his mother, ceding control to her instead of speaking up, and then "throws a tantrum" to reassert himself.

"So put both feet on the floor, and find your breath," Coché had instructed. Leigh closed her eyes and inhaled, shakily at first. Coché looked down at her hands. "There's something I'm going to ask you to do . . . when you're ready." After a pause, Coché caught Leigh's eyes. The therapist seems to have real tenderness for this woman, perhaps because they both lost beloved husbands far too young. "Turn to Aaron and say: 'I'm not your mother, I never will be your mother, so *get* me out of that place.'"

Leigh repeated Coché verbatim, except she added "*please* . . . get me out of that place."

"What I hear you saying, my dear," Aaron began avuncularly. "What I hear you saying is that I'm not your mother, I don't want to be your mother, and I want you to get me out of that place." Huh? Marie may have used active listening as a weapon, but Aaron barely seems to grasp it.

"Do you want to put me in that place sometimes?" Leigh asked— did her husband even know what he was saying? And then, the death grip: "Owww . . ."

"How are you feeling at this moment?" Leigh presses on. She has given her hand back to Aaron (he obviously wants it) but she is determined to have some kind of authentic dialogue with him—a man who, despite what seem the best of intentions, can resemble a ventriloquist's puppet, his mouth moving helplessly up and down, teeth chattering.

"Look at me, please. Please look at me," Leigh says. It's a command, edged with a beg.

"Yeah, yeah, I am," Aaron says, annoyed. "I'm thinking, I am." Thinking about his wife's question, that is: How does he feel? "I feel . . ."—he stops—"confident that I've made progress at trying to be more in control in our relationship." He will use this same line over and over again—"I'm confident I've made progress"—as if, if he says it enough times, it will be true, and he'll be released from the group, finally. He doesn't act resentful about being here; he's unfailingly pleasant. It's more that his sense of himself as a worthy human being seems bound up with getting a clean bill of health from Coché and a stamp of approval from his wife.

When Leigh ordered Aaron to look at her, she became, of course, the mother she doesn't want to be, and a few minutes later, Marie gently suggests that perhaps Leigh is "cueing" Aaron to be the "bad boy" more than she thinks?

"The—the way you said that to Aaron," Clem adds—he and Marie seem to recognize themselves in the other couple. "Do you sometimes feel like Aaron is your son?"

Leigh scratches her nose with the hand that is still twined with Aaron's. "Not really my son, but not an adult, either," she says dejectedly. There is more consonance between the substance of what Leigh says and her emotional demeanor than in anybody else in the group—her heart and head seem connected. "Not an adult," she repeats.

"So that means if the sex got better," Coché says, "it would feel like incest."

Ow . . . Now, that had to sink in, not to mention wake up the group, who are bobbing listlessly along as Aaron lurches toward addressing the mother-child arrangement he has going with his wife.

Aaron is a highly anxious guy, of the obsessive-compulsive variety—in his early years in the group, he constantly scribbled notes, Coché says, until the other members insisted he put down his pencil and *listen*. The main impetus for him and Leigh to join the group, in fact, was how this trait manifested in the couple's sex life. For the first four to five years they were together, Aaron suffered from performance anxiety so severe that he couldn't have intercourse. While some people their age might have settled for genial companionship, Leigh was not ready to give up on sex—and Coché told her it would be a mistake to think she could live without it. Leigh loves sex. Aaron went along, because, as he likes to say, and not without an objective basis, as I'll come to believe: "Leigh is the best thing that ever happened to me."

If Coché had stopped at that single sentence—stopped at incest—the knife might have gone too deep, or so she seems to think. Without pausing, she expands more innocuously on how if "the parent-child relationship wins, it's hard to enjoy sex," and then the group strays to another topic—to protect Leigh and Aaron, or themselves?

But Coché is not finished nicking Aaron on sex. While the couple's physical relationship has improved remarkably—Aaron has progressed from the penile pump, to Viagra, to being able to have sex with his wife without either—both began the new group just a few hours ago saying it was something they still wanted to work on. Well, actually Leigh said she still wasn't entirely satisfied with their sex life, and Aaron agreed. After ten years, Coché is not going to let it rest.

Rachael gives her the opening: How did it feel, she asks Aaron, when Leigh said that she didn't view him as a full adult?

"Well, I feel badly about that," he says, "but there's a certain immunity that I have, and it goes back to childhood. If you get beat over the head so many times, you get used to it, like a boxer." Anyway, he doesn't think that Leigh really means she sees him as a child.

"No," Leigh says. "I *do* fully mean it." You can end up sounding spiteful when your husband is coated in Teflon.

"So let's go somewhere else with this," Coché says to Aaron. "The numbing you learned when you were little, what might that have to do with sex?" Coché knows from her long years with Aaron that he was treated like the weirdo in his strict German Jewish family, continually denigrated by his mother, in particular. He mentally checked out to survive it.

"Anxiety, [lack of] trust," he says.

"You got it. Avoidance, keep me safe. Keep me numb."

The mood of a couple over the course of a single session of the group can change dramatically, and Clem seems to have rebounded from his thwarted attempt to brainstorm ways to establish emotional intimacy with Marie. There is a reason for his buoyancy: The pair actually *had* sex recently, he divulges. "I guess, in the last week, Marie has changed around—she's been more upbeat, she's wanted to do more things, she's been more interested in sex, and, uh, it's really just, uh, I'm just on cloud nine." He doesn't sound *that* ecstatic—verbally dexterous Clem is not—but he does sound like he's percolating with hope, based on a single good week.

This is Marie and Clem's second year with the group, and one of his major reasons for being here is, indeed, the sexlessness of his marriage (once a month at best, though the couple would disagree about the frequency in a perversely predictable way: Clem, who missed it most, believed they'd had it least, and vice versa). Resentment and anger, meanwhile, seep from Marie, the mother of their two teenage daughters, which sounds like the oldest story of marital disenchantment in the book. And to some extent, it is. But what I discover during the year with the group is that every family *is* unhappy in its own way—its own peculiar, layered, internally contradictory, often surprising way.

Under questioning from the group, Marie cryptically attributes her willingness to spend time with Clem and have sex with him to "some different phrases that I heard that made sense to me."

"Like what?" Coché asks.

"That, um . . . [it's important] to truly be a husband and wife and not just friends."

"Clem said that?" Coché asks. "You said that? Who said it?" Spit it out already.

"Well, it's something that I'm embarrassed about, um, uh . . ." It's usually Clem, not Marie, who falters. "Sometimes," Marie says, "I watch *Dr. Phil.*"

The group explodes in laughter. They're laughing because Marie is their most intellectual—and self-consciously intellectual—member. She scorns pop culture, especially the fairy-tale romance sort.

"I enjoy *Dr. Phil* sometimes, too," Rachael says lightly.

"Absolutely," Coché says, a smile in her voice.

Marie doesn't seem to mind that the joke's on her, but she has something else she wants to say. She's worried she can't keep up the sex, or "doing things" with Clem. Being more involved with her husband is "energy sapping," she says, "exothermic rather than endothermic," which, for those who weren't college biology majors like Marie, means her relationship with Clem releases heat, rather than generates it. Marie's rhetorical flights may seem ostentatious at times, but they're usually wincingly appropriate.

"I'm always trying new and different things, but eventually they won't work," she laments. Marie has taken medication for depression on and off for ten years. She isn't currently depressed, but that doesn't mean that she's found anything to affirmatively be happy about.

Coché describes her therapeutic orientation as "eclectic" (like an estimated 80 percent of U.S. therapists) but what's most prominent in her work is the influence of existentialist psychology, a theoretical framework that assumes people are driven, above all, to find meaning in their lives. Meaning is what Marie seems to be sorely missing.

"I've recently started every day, throughout the day, telling myself I'm happy," interjects Sue Ellen, her purse now at her feet. Like her husband, Mark, she has spoken relatively little so far. "It has changed how I feel, and what I do each day, and I'm not down like I used to be."

Sue Ellen does not seem like a frivolous person; in her late forties, she manages a small, family-owned motel in addition to raising her sons (while Mark routinely works fourteen-hour days at the office). So I wonder about Sue Ellen's regimen of positive affirmations, which have become the stuff of comedy thanks to Stuart Smalley on *Saturday Night Live*. Assuming she and her marriage do benefit from the internal soliloquy, why her and not Marie? Why can't Marie take Dr. Phil's pithy counsel—act like husband and wife, and not just friends—and run with it, ad infinitum?

Maybe, Aaron offers, Marie can't—or won't—stick with what's going well between her and Clem because she's afraid of success? It sounds plausible.

"No," Marie counters. "I still think it's a matter of running out of steam."

"Trust her," Coché says to the whole group.

"The only thing I have never run out of steam with my entire life is wanting to be alone and reading," Marie says. "And raising my children."

Later, after the group, Coché tells me why she thinks Marie was on her best behavior in and out of the bedroom the past week. Up until a few days before the new group began, Clem had been making noises about dropping out, and divorcing Marie.

CHAPTER 2

———

Sex Weekend

The theme of June's two-day group is "Keeping the Erotic Pot Bubbling," and Coché is wearing red. It's not racy red—she's wearing a knee-length dress, scarlet, with tiny sprigs of white flowers—but it's the kind of thing she'd do: choose a red dress, and hot pink sandals, to kick off the group's sex weekend. As the members take seats in the room similar to the ones they took last time (Rachael and Michael plunk down on the couch), everyone seems edgy, or at least curious. How far will crazy Judith take this titillating theme? The group members respect her, and most of them are pretty trusting of her, too, but they also know Coché has a provocateur's bent. You might be explaining how you barked at your boy-husband one afternoon, and before you know it, she's taken it to incest in the dark of night.

When Coché and her late husband ran the group, they had a good cop/bad cop routine going: She pushed while Erich reassured, stroked. Coché has had other coleaders since he died, and she's always kept the same role in the two-person setup. For this weekend, she has a guest coleader, but most of the rest of the year she's on her own, which complicates her job. She once pulled a picture from her shelf that shows her grinning out from under a mass of black curls, her daughter's white Siamese cat draped across her shoulders: "I keep this here because this is what the job is like to me. I look a little mischievous, like I'm having fun." Or, as she put it another time: "Causing the right amount of trouble is an art form."

This weekend trouble will practically start itself, coming from way out in left field. Or to use Coché's cliché instead, it will come from an empty erotic pot, one blackened and crusty with the remains of what had been cooking years before. To begin the morning, however, nothing seems terribly dire. Coché introduces her coleader for the next two days, Philadelphia sex therapist Julian Slowinski. He is the therapist to whom Coché referred Aaron ten years earlier, and he's written a book for men suffering from impotence and cohosted a series of educational videos for couples, the latest on sex toys. He also has a gig as a national speaker for the pharmaceutical maker Eli Lilly. He travels the country lecturing to doctors about the drug Cialis, as well as the psychological impact of erectile dysfunction on men and their partners. A former Benedictine monk, he's definitely the designated nice guy. He has a bearded, teddy-bear face, and swaddles people with talkiness.

To spark the conversation, Coché asks everyone to take a minute to jot down how they'd "like to improve sexual enjoyment with their partner." Think about your "wish list," she says, "what's actually in your heart, even if it's politically incorrect." Like the previous time, the couples go off on their own, to confide in their spouses, before letting the whole group in on it. As they break up, you can see an uncharacteristic current of apprehension behind Marie's eyes. For Leigh and Aaron, the mother-son angst of the last group is nowhere in evidence. This time she's the one reaching for his hand, and nudging him like a fawn to look into her eyes.

Mark cracks up at something Sue Ellen says, and she smiles wryly. Like Marie and Clem, Sue Ellen and Mark are in their second year with the group. They landed here after Mark grabbed his middle son in a stranglehold. "He had threatened to kill me, and I told him he should just do it now," Mark soberly explained in the last session, to hushed silence. "And we—*I* wound up grabbing him around the neck."

While Coché subsequently saw Mark and Sue Ellen with their son, then a seventeen-year-old with a drug problem, she also recommended that they join the group, believing that if their marriage improved, they'd be better parents. They made "huge progress" last year, Coché says, and they do seem easy together. Twenty-seven years of marriage seem like a soft cloak for them, rather than an itchy wool topcoat with rocks in the pockets. You wonder, too, if the malaise of some of the others in the group makes Mark and Sue Ellen's pleasure in each other that much more piquant. "One of the reasons couples like to be with other couples," Coché commented a moment ago, "is that they can sit back and breathe a sigh of relief: I thought *I* was in the worst shape in the room, but that other person really has it bad." Or, inversely, I imagine, aren't we a picture of marital harmony compared to them?

"Who wants to start—how would you improve sexual enjoyment?" Coché asks. The group has reconvened around her, except for the couple who was missing last month—they're driving in from several hours away, and they're late.

"I can shut down when I hear the children, so that's one thing," Sue Ellen answers immediately (only her youngest son, in his late teens, is still living at home). Coché has needled her and Mark about letting everyone else talk first, and Sue Ellen seems to want to show her mettle, or maybe just get this over with. Her reticence with the group seems a product of what an effort it's been for her to eke out words, period. The notion of women needing to "find their voices" isn't new, but with Sue Ellen it has a kind of literal accuracy. She was the youngest girl of ten children, with a violent, alcoholic father and an embittered mother; her emblematic memory is of her sisters hustling her down the hallway and pushing her into a closet to shield her from her parents' rows.

"Having more time to be intimate," Sue Ellen continues, "and to be more comfortable with my body, to reveal my body more often to Mark." At five two, Sue Ellen is petite and well-proportioned. This day, she's dressed in pale blue clam diggers and a white, short-sleeved polo shirt, which is less feminine than usual, I'll come to see. More typical are fine-gauge sweaters she knits herself, delicate necklaces and earrings.

"To reveal your body," Coché repeats.

"Well, I don't like to"—Sue Ellen pauses, regarding the therapist with deliberate dispassion, her thin lips clamped in a straight line—"walk around naked."

"No, I—I understand," Coché says, to laughter. Coché wasn't prodding Sue Ellen to be more graphic but more expansive. The therapist tries again with her, by calling on the rest of the group, what she calls her "Greek chorus." A virtue of groups over other kinds of therapy,

Coché has told me, is that members can affirm each other's struggles, or, equally important, harass each other about the habits corroding their marriages. "In a group, there's an experience of being held accountable for one's own behavior," Coché says, adding that it's more powerful to be called out—or cared for—by a civilian than by a professional. "I'm a job; I'm a role; I'm a paid consultant. I'm not a real person." This is not to suggest that the members bully each other, as in the encounter groups of the 1970s (the excesses of which are thought to explain some of the decline in the popularity of free-form groups). Coché sets the tone for her group, and while she is at times confrontational, she treats even the most trying clients with the utmost respect, as far as I can tell. It's not that she puts herself at an expert's chilly remove, either: She is voluble, just not *volatile*.

Now Coché wants to know if anyone else in the group shares Sue Ellen's concerns about weight and sex?

Rachael, the youngest woman in the room, says that she's put on some pounds, and whereas she's typically "quite happy to be seen naked in the light," she's covering up lately.

For you, Coché says, turning toward Sue Ellen, the urge to hide your body (after nearly three decades of marriage) is more constant than that?

"Yes." Sometimes I'll admire Sue Ellen's refusal to dilute her message by unnecessarily adorning it. Other times, her "yeses" and "nos" are merely clipped, a means of shutting down inquiry.

"Mark?" Coché asks, bustling on.

"One of the things I observed," he says, fixing his gold-rimmed glasses on the tip of his nose and peering down at his paper, "was that our goals were almost the same, which I was happy to see." His long legs are stretched loosely out in front of him, crossed at the ankles, flip-flops flapping against his feet. "So mine was to find more time when we can be together and both in the mood, which also has to do with privacy." And, "to talk more about what would be enjoyable for Sue, and, uh, don't let anything affect the good sex we have."

Slowinski offers that the busy Mark is probably going to have to schedule time to be with his wife, as unromantic as it sounds. Mark nods in agreement. Coché said earlier that this two-day group was a chance for the group to go "deeply inside of themselves," but so far no one's scratched skin.

"Should we go?" Michael asks Rachael, sitting beside him. She shrugs good-naturedly. If how people act on a couch is any indication of what goes on in bed, these two are doing fine, though Michael did murmur earlier that he was concerned about how "normal" he was, whatever that meant. "I'm a little more blunt," he says to the group. "I said I would want more oral foreplay." He turns to Rachael and she giggles.

"Are you embarrassed?"

"In a funny way," Rachael says.

"Do you want to give or receive or both?" Coché asks.

"Receive," Michael says. "I've given, but more receive. On the whole I think our sex life is actually very robust. Um, it's just that certain skills need to be improved on."

"Anybody," Coché says, a little like a carnival barker, "who else like Michael would enjoy more oral play?"

Thunderous silence.

"Who wants to *admit* it," Michael deadpans. Mark lifts his eyebrows conspiratorially. "Exactly," Michael says over the guffaws.

"So nobody would enjoy more oral play?" Coché repeats.

"I would like it," Leigh pipes up. "But I've just given it up."

"You would enjoy more?" Coché asks.

"Well, I'd like it to *happen*. That's one of the things I feel I've had to give up in this marriage."

"So 'more' isn't quite the right word."

"Just *some* would be wonderful," Leigh says, "but it's not going to happen."

"You're giving Aaron permission not to?" says Slowinski, with predictable therapeutic spin.

"I'm just resigned," Leigh says. "I don't want to pressure him or make him feel he has to." But, she says, pointedly to Slowinski, "I'm *not* giving him permission not to." She turns to Aaron: "Did you feel I was giving you permission not to?"

"No." It's the shortest answer he will give all year.

"I think I'd like some, too," Clem says, joining the oral-sex-deprived contingent. "But pressuring Marie isn't going to help." Clem is the personification of mild: fit and trim, with prematurely white hair that sets off his baby-blue eyes.

"Very similar to how Leigh feels," Coché says. "Do you *think* you'd like more oral sex, Clem, or are you fairly certain that you would?"

"Yes, I'm—I'm certain. So thank you for providing some leadership and being blunt." Clem scoots forward on the couch so he can see past Rachael to Michael, who's on the other end. Michael nods, smiling.

"Yeah," Mark says to Michael. "Thanks."

"How's the erotic pot?" It's Bella. She and her husband, Joe, have just arrived, blown in on a fresh wind. They're in their mid-thirties, attractive, well dressed: prom queen and king for the moment. They notice the two empty chairs waiting for them, and plop down. Bella crosses her legs. She's wearing a clingy royal blue dress and strappy gold sandals.

Do you want to continue with your wish list? Coché asks Rachael, who amiably agrees. She'd like to try more sexual positions, bring food into the bedroom, and dress more erotically, if she could shed a few pounds. Then she smiles at Bella and Joe, who are close in age to her and Michael. "Hi, I'm Rachael. Nice to meet you." The rest of the group follows suit.

"How does it feel to walk into this conversation?" Coché asks Bella and Joe.

"Actually it feels good," Joe says, like, no problem—he's cool with this therapy thing, with oral sex. He apologizes for being late, saying he feels like he let people down.

"Are you feeling at all like you missed anything for yourself?" Coché asks.

"I guarantee it," he says immediately.

To begin melding the reconfigured group, Coché says she wants to back up for a minute. "A group moves as quickly as its slowest member, and we were just joined by two people who didn't have the benefit of being with us last time. So we're moving backward, and then we'll move forward again." She wants to go from person to person, to find out how many total years of marriage are in the room. "We do this around the table at Thanksgiving with ages—it's fun," she says. The members matter-of-factly oblige her, with the exception of Mark. He speaks proudly of his marriage's long duration. Then Coché raises the intensity. "Of those years of marriage, how many have felt satisfying, successful?"

"Two months," Rachael says, which is how long she's been married to Michael. Her first marriage lasted ten apparently unremarkable years.

"A year and a half," says Michael, referring to *his* first five-year marriage (ten, if you count how long the couple lived together before walking down the aisle). "Then two months with Rachael."

"I'd say zero," Clem says. That's zero out of twenty-one.

"Three," Marie adds.

"Yours is higher than Clem's," Coché says to Marie. "Wow. I don't understand that very well, but that's something we ought to understand better."

"In this marriage," Aaron says, "all seven."

"I would say all twenty-three in my first marriage," Leigh says, "and in this marriage—two." The *tick, tock, tick* of the wall clock is deafening.

"So we begin to hear the disparity," Coché murmurs.

"Twenty-seven for me," Mark says.

"I'd say about fifteen," Sue Ellen says, so softly you can barely hear her. Her hand was resting on top of her husband's a few minutes earlier, but at some point, she took it back.

"I think there's like two days that haven't been blissful," Bella says, of her yearlong marriage to Joe.

"That was actually my answer," he says.

"So," Coché says. She hesitates. Bella and Joe notwithstanding, the mood is leaden.

"People change, in my opinion," the therapist says solemnly, "when there is nothing left to do." The corollary to that for Coché is one of her other favorite one-liners from the existentialist canon: "Despair is a great motivator." Existentialist despair is founded in the recognition of the ultimate meaningless of existence (there is no God to grant purpose), but Coché doesn't delve into the philosophy. She uses "despair" more broadly and tangibly, though not more lightly. For existentialists, the answer to this universal tragedy isn't for man to throw up his hands but to take responsibility for making meaning (while not losing sight of the ultimate absurdity of the endeavor). Coché sees herself as a guide for that task.

"The changes you're able to do easily you're not going to need our help for," she tells the group now. "We're here to work with what *doesn't* feel okay . . . and I think now we can go back and keep talking." The question the couples were considering, again, was how they'd like to increase their own sexual enjoyment, which sounds trifling in the current context. Except that sex has the potential to be deeply meaningful. (Even a Hobbesian like Freud believed it: "The union of mental and bodily satisfaction is one of life's culminating peaks. Apart from a few queer fanatics, all the world knows this and conducts its life accordingly.")

Aaron proffers that he wants to "verbally show" his love and feelings for Leigh. "It's something I can improve," he says.

Nuh-uh, Coché says. This is about what would add to *your* enjoyment, not your wife's.

"I feel like I'm enjoying things much more," he says.

"So much better than you thought you ever would that you can't imagine it could be better?" Coché asks.

"Absolutely, right, right," he says. He'd still like to focus less on his performance, but, "as I like to say with a little humor, I've gone from kindergarten to college to graduate school. From, uh, a skill deficit to I'm relatively okay."

"That's huge," Coché compliments him.

"That is huge," parrots Leigh. She is Coché's fellow cheerleader in the group, which is not to say that she isn't genuinely impressed by the change in her husband. "The first time we were in bed together," Leigh tells me outside of the group, "he just froze. He just became stiff, and he didn't touch me. He lay like this." She put her arms straight down at her sides, elbows locked. "He was petrified, absolute fear. And the next day he broke out in shingles." Leigh told him that their relationship was over unless he got professional help for his extreme anxiety, and he did, first in individual and couples counseling with Slowinski, then as part of the group.

"Would you have believed this much change would have been possible?" Coché asks Aaron. She's feeding him a setup line to keep him dwelling on his own accomplishment, a means to solidify the progress, she thinks.

"Probably not, no, no, no," Aaron says, warming to the topic, "I wouldn't have believed it. As we've said, Leigh and I would not have gotten married if we hadn't participated in the group, with the original Lewis and Clark explorers." He chuckles.

"We were reminiscing last night how he wouldn't even stay in the room [after sex]," Leigh says. "As soon as there was a session he was gone." The night before, however, "you were so loving and verbal," she says. Leigh is talking to Aaron, not the group, and it's as if she's willing him to look at her, to soak up the appreciation in her eyes. He turns his head. "It was really very, very wonderful," Leigh tells him.

When it comes to what she'd like sexually, Leigh doesn't mention the oral sex again. She is trying to ask for something she has a chance of getting. While the couple first had intercourse at about the same time they married, Aaron, as you might guess, still had a ways to go on sexual *relations,* and on close relations in general. Somewhere along the line, however, he stalled out, despite Slowinski, despite the couples group, or at least that was Leigh's opinion. "With his anxiety, it was like there was this wall," she says, again in private to me. "He didn't listen to what I was saying, didn't hear me crying." And their physical relationship had plateaued: Aaron never touched Leigh sexually; the couple always used a vibrator.

For whatever reason, nine years of this was Leigh's limit. (She wouldn't have lasted that long, she says, she would've felt too badly about herself, had sex and affection not been so "natural" in her first marriage.) So at the beginning of last year, Leigh told Aaron she'd divorce him if he didn't touch her. "Not *try,* do it," she says, remembering how fed up she was. "I decided I'd rather be alone—I'd gotten to that point."

Aaron took her seriously; never before had she raised the prospect of divorce, and she wasn't the type to make idle threats. With Slowinski, he reapplied himself to a desensitization program to lessen his almost phobic reaction to the female anatomy; he agreed to take antianxiety medication; and he did what his wife required: He started to touch her every now and again.

So now, a year later, Leigh is here to keep their gains from evaporating, and she asks Aaron to continue to "notice her." She wants to be admired, told she's pretty—basically, she wants to be seduced a little, feel less like a "mannequin." "I've done a lot of work on feeling [attractive] on the inside," Leigh tells the group, "but there's only so much I can—it still really makes me so happy when he tells me."

"Anybody else in here feel like your enjoyment would increase if you were more noticed or your partner was more verbal?" Coché asks.

Clem sticks up his hand. "I wrote down 'wish my partner would show interest in me, wish Marie had more interest in sex and touching.' It's been hard for me, after twenty years. At one point I probably lost twenty-five pounds and got in really good shape, and even *that* didn't make any difference."

Clem is wearing dock shoes with no socks, and you want him to cover his bare ankles, to stop making himself naked. This year, Clem continues, "It's just, uh, it's, uh, I'm trying to give Marie her space." A watched pot never boils, so to speak.

"You can't push it," Coché agrees. "But you can do what Leigh did, which is require that your partner keep working on it."

"Marie?" Coché asks. She's the last person up before lunch—Bella and Joe are going to address the question after the break.

"Um, I don't feel in the same place that any of y'all are," Marie says. She grew up in a rural area, and she hasn't entirely scrubbed the country from her speech.

"I think you're more where Aaron was," Coché replies. "That's part of why I asked him to speak out."

"Yeah, I get that," Marie replies curtly. "But right now I don't have a sexual need, because while you all are almost at the technique level, I'm at the inside-dead level."

"Sheesh," Coché says, impressed by Marie's insight into herself.

"So if I can't nurture or expand the parts that make up myself," Marie says, "it's like asking somebody if they're hungry while they're choking."

"Wow, you should write a novel," Slowinski gushes.

Marie smiles, and I think I see a hint of pride in her expression. Pride that she, "gimpy"—as Marie thinks she's perceived by Clem and the group—can outtalk the purveyors of the talking cure? Marie goes on to say that if she could "develop" herself, "I kinda think the sexual part would flow easily."

What Marie's development might look like is elusive. Her lack of professional fulfillment is clearly part of it. A medical administrator, she's been languishing in the same job for years. Her frustrating situation dates back to soon after she and Clem married, when he told her he wanted to move to the beach town where his family had had a summerhouse. He'd dropped out of college, and he was sure he could find a job there as a mechanic (he now works maintaining electronic systems for the federal government). Marie loved school, meanwhile, and graduated at the top of her class in biology. Settling in a small community would constrict her opportunities, Marie knew, but although she was the one with the bigger brain and ambition, she never really considered asking Clem to follow *her*. Now, twenty years later, with her daughters almost grown, what, if anything, could she do to change things?

Then there is her marriage. Marie grew up as the bookish only daughter in a household of men, two older brothers and a father who, according to her and Clem, can best be described as bullies: physically intimidating, crude, and derisive of the opposite sex. For years, she says, she believed that she didn't have the "right" to expect anything from a man other than what he chose to bestow—and she is only beginning to forthrightly make her preferences known to Clem. Not that what she describes as her "submission" appears very submissive. Nonetheless, she is always talking about her determination to stand her ground with Clem, to express her point of view. Holding on to a firm sense of herself within her marriage seems crucial to her.

She doesn't say any of this directly, however. After Slowinski compliments her writerly turn of phrase, she tosses out a welter of words about what she needs in order to "feel alive": "Something really has to be crossed first, and then as I discover those areas I will have a better idea of looking outside of the situation and figuring out what would be a mature way to approach it, so I can assign values . . ." She seems both confused and inauthentic, unwilling to state something she knows. She makes several comments that are dismissive of the group—how could these nimrods possibly understand where she's coming from—yet when Coché says that maybe the best the group can do at this point is to acknowledge her "chronic ennui" (the label Marie gave it), she is moved. "Yeah," Marie says, the tears breaking through that single word.

She is adamantly clear about one thing. Her dissatisfaction and quest for meaning should not be written off as symptoms of depression, even though she makes comments like, "So when you talk about oral sex, it's inconsequential if you're not sure you want to wake up tomorrow."

Coché nods, lips pursed. She is well acquainted with Marie's depressions and agrees she's not in the depths of it: "She's gone through these periods of clinical depression, they're *horrible.* It requires going into her bedroom and being brought meals, crawling into a hole—her kids can't get to her, nobody can."

The morning ends in notable weariness, not only because of Marie's formless disaffection; it's the formlessness of the group, too. How can a group devoted to sex be productive for anyone when one couple wants to master the fine points of fellatio; another is generally optimistic about their sex life (and too inhibited to talk about enhancing it in any case); one has spent a decade struggling with profound sexual dysfunction; and another has such a yawning gap between them—she can't be bothered by sexual desire, while he has staked it at the center of his existence?

After the lunch, the group members return to their former seats. Everybody is pretty quiet—are they thinking about where they'd rather be? Coché likes to extol the "community" in which the group enfolds couples, but so far I've haven't noticed much. People ask each other the occasional question, deliver short pep talks, but the interactions seem dully safe, their impact glancing. Could this be how community starts? Could the group really become the modern equivalent of the Puritan village that Michael Vincent Miller, a psychologist, depicts when bemoaning the isolation of the modern couple in his 1995 book, *Intimate Terrorism?* "What would it be like," he asks, "if as in the Puritan villages of old, representatives from the larger community were to step in, calm the two down, stress the larger social importance of their well-being, and offer support and help by redirecting the couple's energies away from mutilating each other toward something more cooperative?"

Beneath the group's postlunch lassitude, there is an unstated challenge to Coché: So how you gonna pull this one off, Judith? She responds by taking on, tactfully, those in the group who she believes are avoiding what is bedeviling them. "Now is the time for you to come into this room with what's going on sexually and let it rip," she says. "Talk about what you're uncomfortable with right on the level of your dealings, and watch it wake up."

There is a long pause. Yes, Michael mentioned worrying that he was "normal," but would he be willing to elaborate? Would Mark ever say anything about his nearly three decades of having sex with Sue Ellen that could be construed as even faintly critical? Was Aaron prepared to go beyond marveling at his progress? And assuming not, what options did Leigh really have? Did anyone want to hear Marie intellectualize her predicament again, or Clem stutter his longing?

"I feel inadequate," Joe blurts, "on a performance level." The new guy saves the therapeutic day, or so it seems. Perhaps everything isn't corsages and "Stairway to Heaven" for the husband who earlier seconded his wife's appraisal that their one-year marriage has been unmitigated bliss.

"You talkin' about frequency, you talkin' about what?" asks Slowinski, with studied informality.

"Length of session, everything, and, um, that's something I no longer generate in the relationship." Joe has the stocky, square body of the college athlete he used to be. He shifts in his chair, his mouth tight. Bella is looking on, curiously.

"It's a damn cycle. It's a self-fulfilling prophecy almost," he says. "It's like, oh, okay that was off, what was wrong with you? That was two days [off]; okay, that was three; now you're not actually showing up the way you used to."

"What does 'showing up' mean?" Coché asks blandly.

"Uh, bringing to the table what—" Joe says.

"Being aroused?" interrupts Slowinski.

"Getting aroused?" Coché continues.

"No," Joe says.

"Having a good erection, coming too soon, not at all?" Slowinski asks, trying again.

"One orgasm and that's it for me."

The room erupts in laughter. Later, I'll ask Coché the same question about Bella and Joe that I'd asked about Rachael and Michael. They seem like they're still in the honeymoon stage; are Bella and Joe just here for general marital education? She gives me much the same answer: "This is a therapy group. If couples don't have a reason to be here, they can find much better things to do on the weekends."

Once the jokes sputter out, Joe explains that it's not merely his own orgasm quota that is not being met; sometimes Bella doesn't come at all. That provokes a discussion among Bella, Rachael, and Leigh about how alienating it can be when their husbands get fixated on bringing them to orgasm to prove their own studliness. "It doesn't matter if I say this feels good or this doesn't because he's going to do whatever he's going to do," Bella says. "So I'm like, whenever you're done, let me know." She laughs.

"So you don't always care about the orgasm," Coché says.

"I don't all the time," Bella says. "That's not my reason for being with him."

"And have you said that to Joe?" Coché probes.

"Yeah, he'll make himself so crazy, go off in the corner because he didn't perform on some scale he invented that has nothing to do with me."

"The effect it had on me," Leigh says, "I felt like I didn't even need to be there."

"How do you feel *now,* though?" Aaron asks his wife. A few moments before, he acted the elder statesman with Joe, commiserating about what it's like to fasten oneself to strict performance standards. But Aaron described his affliction strictly in the past tense, and he wants Leigh to join his triumphal parade.

"I feel like I need to be there," she says, stepping in line—almost. "But not all the time. Not *all* the time do I need to be there." Aaron doesn't dare turn toward her—it's as if there is cotton in his ears—and the group plows on.

"I think I know just how you feel, Joe," Clem says, returning to the male end of the equation. "A while back I had a vasectomy, and it didn't feel like I would get an erection as long or as hard. And it took me two, three years until I finally relaxed about it, and it seemed to work better." Once again, Clem's unfiltered plainspokenness wrings the heart.

"I just realized where I veered off," Joe says, a "duh" in his voice. "It used to be sex was the opportunity to be with Bella, and somewhere along the line it became the opportunity to prove that it was as good or better than the last time." As the group will slowly learn, Joe's need to prove himself in bed may have risen inversely to his ability to prove himself outside of it.

After a rather meandering discussion about the various sexual pressures the group members put on themselves, Marie speaks up, for the first time all afternoon. She's been so quiet that it's been possible to forget that she's here, sunk in her chair.

"[The pressure for me] isn't about orgasm," she says, low and level. "Mine is the pressure for Clem to have a vasectomy."

"Pressure for Clem to have a vasectomy?" Slowinski asks.

"I feel like I was backed into a corner, put into a corner."

"Put into a corner about what?" Coché joins in.

"That I had to agree," Marie says.

"To?" Coché asks. They're having to drag it out of her.

"To the vasectomy," Marie replies.

"Want to talk to Clem about it? He's right here," Coché says.

"Well, actually the three of us talked about it," Marie says.

The bottom of the pot has been reached. Fourteen years before, after the birth of their second child, in 1991, Clem went to Marie to say he planned to get a vasectomy. She signed the required consent, but now she is saying she felt forced into it, that she told Clem she wanted more children, but he "disregarded" her. A strange twist in the matter is that the couple had an appointment with Coché to discuss whether to proceed with the surgery (she hadn't been seeing them regularly at the time), though she doesn't seem to remember it.

"We'd just had our second daughter, and I was laid off, and I couldn't make ends meet," pleads Clem. "[The procedure] was ten dollars, my insurance would pay for it, and at that point our relationship wasn't going that good, and I didn't want to add another child into the mix." Marie didn't want to use birth control pills, he says, and "I thought maybe we'd have more sex if we didn't have to worry about getting pregnant." The irony would be funny if it weren't so poignant. The lengths to which Clem went to get more sex may have actually gotten him less.

Coché addresses Marie: "How many times have you felt backed into a corner and had to give up part of yourself?"

"Pretty much since day one," Marie says, oddly cheerful. The therapist is digging into Marie's past to help explain how it was that she agreed to something that so devastated her, not to mention how she'd spent the next decade and a half uttering not a word of it to Clem.

"And how many times did it feel like it was men backing you in the corner?" Coché asks, knowing the answer.

"If it wasn't *by* men, it was *for* men," Marie says, referring to the contortions her mother put herself and Marie through to meet the demands of the men in the family.

"So will you turn to your husband and tell him that 'my assumption is that when push comes to shove, and you want something, I don't count . . . You will simply go out and do what you want, anyway'?"

Marie complies.

Clem's face is pink; he is not used to being seen as the heavy. "I didn't know she felt that strongly about it," he tells Coché, who for the rest of the session will act like Marie's lawyer, arguing her case before a rapt courtroom.

"I knew you weren't happy about it, but it's like . . . you signed it," Clem says to his wife's stern countenance. "I, uh, at the time I think I was taking charge, and I was angry. I was taking charge," he repeats.

The aggression of Clem's arguably unilateral decision to have a vasectomy flashes into view, but as Coché starts calling witnesses to aid in the prosecution, you can't help but feel that he's being tried in a kangaroo court. She asks the women to say how it would have felt if their husbands came to them and said, "I'm having a vasectomy—sign this." When Sue Ellen offers that it would have felt "very severe," Coché leads her witness. "Might it have felt abusive?"

"Yes," Sue Ellen says, terse, as usual.

A few minutes later, Coché lets loose with this: "Let me say something on Marie's behalf that she doesn't know how to say yet, because it would feel too harsh for her. So if I were Marie and wanted to talk to you about it, I might say something like"—the therapist slows down to enunciate each word— "'How dare you rob me of that birthright.'"

"If you were me in that situation," Clem rebuts, "I had every right. That's how I feel about it."

"I understand that," Coché says, not very understandingly, "and you look angry." No joke.

Coché explains that she's channeling Marie's resentment. Marie's everyday treatment of Clem is laced with this hatefulness, the therapist says, so the couple might as well get it out on the table—examine it like a pathologist searching a vital organ for the source of the disease.

Eventually, Coché gets around to asking Clem whether it would feel "appropriate" for him to ask for forgiveness from his wife.

"No," he says.

"Because?" Coché asks.

"Because Marie will think I'm just saying it, and not really meaning it." This is another of the issues to which they will regularly return: that Clem says he'll do this or that, agrees with Marie's take on one matter or another, but then doesn't follow through.

"If you thought she'd take you seriously, would it occur to you to ask for forgiveness?" Coché inquires.

"Yes."

"Marie, are you okay with taking responsibility for your part in this?" Coché asks.

"Definitely," Marie says quickly. Even she may be feeling that Clem is getting dumped on. Marie blames herself, she says, for not being strong enough to go to Clem and say, as Coché paraphrases it: "Look, Clem, I gotta talk this out, I can't do this . . . I'm giving you a no because I can't give you a yes."

If she'd been that direct, Clem says, he indeed would have put the surgery on hold.

"I believe you when you say that," Marie says.

And then Clem says he's sorry, for his cruelty, for not listening to his wife more.

"Thank you," Maries replies, her eyes softening. "I'm starting to believe you now."

"Okay, well, at least you're taking some part of it," Clem says. He still seems offended.

Leigh praises Marie for breaking her silence on the fifteen-year-old breach: "It is so incredible."

"I'm sorry, but I *have* to go to the bathroom," Marie interrupts, breaking into a grin. The group audibly exhales. That was rough.

She is going to have to hold on a bit longer, however, because before anybody can get up, Slowinski asks people how they're "feeling." It's as if he's trying to redeem himself by offering up the f-word. Earlier, Coché chided Slowinski for taking the group out of the moment with a mini sex-education lecture. Sex therapists, many trained in a more inhibited era, tend to want to bestow knowledge: about technique, about the other gender's peculiar anatomy and perspective. But in an age where surveys show lack of desire, not orgasms, is the most common sexual "dysfunction," for women at least, something beyond the how-to is obviously in order.

In any event, the group responds to Slowinski's question. Leigh says she's feeling "great," Aaron hails the "breakthrough" between Marie and Clem. "Yeah," Slowinski agrees, shaking his head in wonderment.

Coché frowns. She's going to have to correct her coleader (and Aaron), again. "I want to put a caution on breakthrough," she says, "because this took fifteen years to build up. It's gonna be slow."

With ten minutes left before the group ends, at 4 P.M., Coché gives her own speech, expounding on how Marie's openness was a kind of model for how the group should operate. "We didn't joke [her problem] away, we didn't tell stories to get away from it. We allowed the moment to happen. Now, it's not magical, and she's not going to leave here and her marriage will be fantastic. But this what intimacy is—it's allowing the truth between people to happen, in a way that's helpful rather than terrifying." She looks down at her hands, folded in her lap. "So Bella is going to get in touch with the truth about herself, and she knows I could tell her what that truth is, but she knows I wouldn't insult her by telling her." Bella first saw Coché in her late teens, when her parents were getting divorced, then contacted her again as she was preparing to marry Joe. Does she know what "truth" Coché is referring to, or is she as ignorant as the group? Coché's omniscience sounds presumptuous, but then it might act as a subtle force that keeps the group members coming back for more: *Yeah, what is Bella's deal?*

"Really all that happened today," Coché continues, "is that Marie talked about what she felt, and we helped Clem listen, and he talked about what he felt, and we helped her to listen."

"Well, you know, thanks," Marie says, "for letting us talk about this."

While Marie sounds grateful to have visited this piece of her and Clem's past, as the group leaves for the day, I'm thinking that her husband has been unjustly spanked. Yes, Marie eventually took responsibility for not exercising her prerogative to stop the vasectomy, but why did she refuse to use birth control in the first place? Didn't that force Clem's hand? And for Coché to equate what Clem did with abuse, and to say things like, "Why would anybody want to have sex with someone who would just go off and do what he wanted?"—wasn't that over-the-top? After all, hadn't she herself counseled the couple about the vasectomy and failed to realize how wrecked Marie would be by it? And hadn't the statute of limitations on Clem's "betrayal" expired, anyway?

The group will be back tonight—for ice-cream sundaes, coffee, and unspecified movies. In years past Coché has screened videos from Slowinski's *Better Sex* series (in which sex educators talk about various positions and methods, while "real couple" actors demonstrate). Then Sunday the group will be together again, for the second day of a weekend that perhaps should be rechristened "Hide-and-Seek: Finding the Erotic Pot."

For now, though, the couples go their separate ways; the two who live relatively near Coché's beach office return home, the other three check in to hotels. Clem and Marie did not come in together that morning. She took the car because she had an early obligation at church, and he rode his bike. The whole day was cloudy and dull, and by the time Clem mounts his bike to go home, the skies have opened up. He is a physical guy: He loves to swim, bodysurf, work out at the gym. It felt good, Clem will tell us tomorrow, to pedal home in the rain.

CHAPTER 3

―――――――――

Spouses Are Made, Not Born

T hey fuck you up, your mum and dad." By the time the weekend-long group is over, the poet Philip Larkin's immortal words will play in my head like a dirge. Larkin's point is the universality, and banality, of the parental stain: "They may not mean to, but they do/ They fill you with faults they had/And add some extra, just for you." But even accounting for that, a substantial swath of the group seemed to have suffered more than is usual at their parents' hands.

The group will learn that when Rachael's parents decided her first husband-to-be was wrong for her, they drove three hours to Melbourne, where she was living and working, showed up on her doorstep at 11 P.M., and insisted she return to the family farm with them. "My job, I can't," Rachael, then twenty-one, pleaded. She went—it did not occur to her to disobey, she will say. Her parents said not a word the entire ride home, and the next morning awoke her, only to begin describing her fiancé as a pompous and untrustworthy roué. He was, in fact, the wonkish son of a judge, as intelligent as he was socially awkward. A few days later, Rachael's mother, persuaded that her daughter should return to work, accompanied her back to the city and moved in with her. After several weeks of having her mother shadow her every move, Rachael still refused to cancel her engagement. At that, her father announced that the family would have nothing further to do with her. Rachael's wedding was five months later; neither her parents nor her two brothers attended.

We'll learn that Sue Ellen gets so agitated when she imagines her childhood home, teeming with siblings and presided over by parents who "wouldn't speak to each other for months at a time," that she gets sick to her stomach. So nauseated that she'll barely be able to speak. "When I first started working with Sue Ellen I thought maybe she wasn't very bright, she was so halting in describing what was going on," Coché will say. The group will learn that Leigh's beloved mother died when she was thirteen, leaving her to care for her reclusive and critical father and her anxiety-ridden younger brother. And so on.

I'll decide to move my chair closer to the group this day, position myself just a touch outside of the circle. I don't want to have to crane my neck to see people's expressions—it makes my observer status glaringly obvious. I'm feeling a little less like an observer, anyway, more caught up in the drama of what's going on around me.

"Drama" is an appropriate word to describe today's group. The members get a glimpse of each other's families because Coché has planned an exercise to examine the origins of their sexual attitudes and feelings. Using guided imagery, she induces everybody to retrieve from memory a snapshot that captures the emotional and sexual tenor of their parents' marriage. Then each person is to become the director of the scene from his or her past, choosing a trio of fellow members to perform the parts of mother, father, and a younger version of themselves. The group is putting on a show—call it "How, *Precisely*, Mum and Dad Fucked Me Up."

First, though, Coché takes the stage for a monologue—more a sales pitch—about various how-to sex videos available through a catalog of erotica called "Good Vibrations." It's an extension of yesterday, the group session itself and the evening's entertainment. As the members shuffled in this morning, there was less chitchat than usual; they saw each other just twelve hours before, at the movies. Not these people again—that thought must have flickered across one or another of their minds. If Coché notices the lack of eagerness, she ignores it. Her husband tells her that she wakes up every morning and "goes chirp."

"*Ecstasy Outlaw,* exhibitionism for the shy," Coché begins. "That might be something that interests you?" Coché smiles winningly at Sue Ellen, like a woman who's just cooed to her husband, "Darling, I know how much you adore washing the dishes—could you?" Sue Ellen manages not to move a facial muscle in response. With her nimbus of frizzy, graying brown hair, she is a Mona Lisa, her eyes issuing less an ambiguous come-hither than an ambiguous don't-you-dare. By contrast, Coché is big and blustering, all arms and legs. "It's about how to take your blouse off," she says to the impassive face across from her, "and *like* it.

"It might be a little early in the morning for this," the therapist says—ah, she read the group's mind. But there is to be no reprieve. "Then there is the screaming orgasm series, which shows you how to use vibrators, how to do dirty talk, and how to have fun. And there's something on ejaculation and the G-spot. Do you know Debra Stendal?" she asks her sidekick Slowinski, referring to one of his fellow instructional-video hosts.

"No," he says.

"I don't either," Coché hurries on, all businessy, "but they say she's the mistress of this topic"—that would be female ejaculation and the G-spot. "And, Rachael, in regard to your question yesterday, here is Violet Blue—she did the ultimate guide to fellatio and cunnilingus, so you might do a review of that for us."

"Sure," Rachael says. She and Michael were late for movie night the previous evening because they'd fallen asleep at their hotel, after having sex. (I only know this because I joked about it when they rushed in, and Rachael nodded, smiling.)

"So Rachael is going to do fellatio. Does anybody want to do cunnilingus?"

"Baby, baby, hmm," Rachael teases Michael.

"Ha ha ha," Michael's choppy laugh startles, though it is not insincere. "I've been volunteered."

"Okay, great." Coché keeps going, briskly ticking off movies people might want to review for the next group.

"We're not going to be here next time," Leigh says.

"You're not going to be here next time," Coché repeats, irritation in her voice. Her intent was to push the more sexually reticent members of the group past their "comfort level," and so far the only couple who has offered to review a movie is, arguably, the one who needs it least. Intentionally or not, Leigh has changed the subject. Coché lets her, though later she will tell the group, "If I say something is a good idea, like movie reviews, it's probably a good idea." When they're so inclined, the group can be impressively withholding.

Last night, for the movies, they'd gathered in the smaller room of the Stone Harbor office, squeezed themselves onto two couches and a few chairs. Everyone was shoulder to shoulder with his or her spouse, except for Marie and Clem. Marie chose the floor in front of the wide-screen TV. She lay on her side, her waist-length hair for the first time loose, and entangled with the black fur of Coché's large dog, whom she never stopped languidly petting. At times, she seemed to be dozing, but that was unlikely. She, like the other women, had applied some lipstick, dressed up a bit for group night out. For Bella, that meant designer jeans and a filmy top; for Marie, dangly gold earrings and a voluminous floral dress that nearly reached her ankles.

First up were scenes from . . . *March of the Penguins,* the nature documentary about how the birds mate and nurture their young in the harsh conditions of the Antarctic. It seemed like a lame start for sex-movie night, yet there was something weirdly intimate in sitting with the group and watching the long slow shots of the coal-eyed penguins stroking each other with their wings, holding a mate's beak in their gaping mouths. Was this what Coché meant when she later commented that movie night was a "bonding" opportunity for the group?

The penguins gave way to the last part of *The Full Monty,* with its conga line of working-class British men, who coyly, then brazenly, and, ultimately, joyously strip for a hooting audience of their wives and girlfriends. "So you don't need to tell us," Coché said, hitting the pause button and plunging the room into quiet, "but how many of you had that much fun together in the last month?" Leigh, Aaron, Marie, Clem, Mark, Sue Ellen—nobody betrayed their answer, but the question was exposing, nonetheless. *You* knew how rote and lifeless things had been, even if no one else did—is this all there is? Your partner knew, too, of course, and suddenly the weight of the arm against yours, initially so comfortingly familiar on this bizarre night, was invasive. Now you wished you were sitting next to a stranger.

Coché's final offering was the most explicit, a sex—and love—scene from the 1989 Mickey Rourke movie *Wild Orchid,* credited for ushering in the NC-17 rating. There would be no educational videos of the Slowinski variety, it turned out, no ordinary people demonstrating sexual maneuvers, fortunately. For the group, sex seems to be more about the stories people tell themselves than the positions they assume.

In *Wild Orchid,* the thin plot centers on the seductively greasy Rourke and a beautiful young woman who has come to Rio de Janeiro to do business with him. After psychologically and sexually toying with her for the first nine-tenths of the movie, Rourke's character drops the games and makes himself vulnerable to her. The two have passionate, acrobatic sex, before literally riding off together into the sunset, on a motorbike. In those who can suspend disbelief, the scene can inspire longing or jealousy—*I want that, why can't I have that, did I ever?* Which is where Coché shamelessly took the discussion: "How many of you have had this happen, where this level of passion occurs?" she asked. The lights were back up. "When it does, it's a happening, an event for people."

One of her principal tasks, Coché has told me outside of the group, is "titrating anxiety," challenging people enough so they'll feel the pressure to change but not so much as to send them spinning off in alarm. With this question perhaps, she is twisting the dial a notch higher for those who are avoiding attending to the hollowness, or perfunctory quality, of their marriages. Only Marie and Clem seem in high dudgeon, after all. Coché pricks the organism with a pin—does it feel pain? Where is the dejection or distrust or foreboding that brought them here in the first place?

"Okay, I'm going to pick the players first," Michael says. Michael is the sixth member to stage a snapshot from his childhood, and the casting so far has been fairly uniform: People who need a cold, cutting mother tend to go with Marie, which she accepts with surprising good humor and plays with nasty flair. And Mark, based on the story he told in the first group about nearly strangling his son, gets the part of the apoplectic father. The child's role is passed around among the men (and women). Boyishness is a salient characteristic of every male member of the group except for Mark, though even he, when he wears a baseball cap to the group and tugs on it at charged moments, reminds me of a boy.

"Um," Michael says, considering where to put people. Mark and Marie, his parents, are to sit in chairs in the middle of the room; Joe, whom Michael chose to play himself as a seventeen-year-old, is to stand by the door. Michael sighs. "Um, this is about a—um, my auto accident," he says. "My first car was a 1969 Volkswagen square back. Um, it was my father's first car, he bought it brand-new, um, and uh, as time went by he didn't use it anymore, he stored it in the backyard, and it kind of fell apart. He, graciously, let me buy it from him"—sarcasm slips into Michael's voice—"and I restored the car, okay." Michael is speaking fast, like he's trying to outpace his feelings.

"You bought it for a dollar?" Joe says as much as asks. Michael couldn't have had to pay real money for his dad's old beater, could he?

"I paid street value, book value," Michael replies. The group laughs at his father's boot-strapper ethic—or is it the old man's cheap audacity that amuses? "So it was not in the best of shape. I mean, the paint was becoming all powdery and dry, and the springs were coming out of the seats, but it was mine."

"Wait, can I say something? Do this without your remarkably wonderful sense of humor as much as you can," Coché coaches Michael.

"Well, okay, I just want to set the scene." Michael sighs again. "So I, um, get the engine working again, put new tires on it; I had just had the brakes redone with an uncle. And, uh, this particular evening I was down playing video games with my friends, at an arcade, and, um, on the way back my best friend said, 'Can I drive?' Okay, no problem, so we're driving back, and he goofed around, and he was inexperienced and"—Michael clears his throat—"he, um, as you know, Volkswagens, the weight is in the back of the car, so the car started to move, and he jammed the brakes, because instinctively you want to slow down, and the car started to fishtail, and it hit the curb, and rolled over, and we were all okay, but the car was destroyed." Michael stops. He pushes a shank of hair from his face. He looks exhausted, but it's not over yet. Mark, Marie, and Joe still have to play out how Michael's parents reacted when he broke the news. It was around midnight, he says, when he was dropped off at home by a police officer. His parents were in their darkened living room watching TV.

"Uh, yeah, Mom, Dad," Joe says, coming through the door. Joe sighs, raking his hand through his hair. (Coché has mentioned that Joe has done some amateur acting, and it shows.) "Something happened."

"What happened?" Mark demands.

"There's been an accident." Joe is hanging his head, but glances up quickly, to sneak a peek at his parents' reactions. Marie looks stern, but she's staying out of it, as directed.

"Is the car okay?" Mark asks.

"Uh, in a manner of speaking."

"Car's not okay, is it?" Mark taunts.

"No, it's not," Joe whispers.

"What did you do to . . . the . . . car?" Mark discharges the bullets through gritted teeth.

"I was with my friends, we jerked the steering wheel the wrong way, and we rolled."

"Actually, you have to be much more angry," Michael interrupts, addressing Mark, "like stand up and say—"

"What did you do to the car?" Mark roars, rising up from his chair before Michael can get the instructions out.

"Freeze it," Coché says. Mark is towering menacingly over Joe.

"Wow," Slowinski says. There are nervous titters, a low whistle. It's acting, yes, but Mark's height combined with his decibel level makes you shrink in actual fear.

"That's why Michael is worried about what other people think," Coché says softly. Michael's relationship with Rachael has not been under much scrutiny yet in the group; rather, the focus has been on his dread at having to speak to his boss on his own behalf. And his job itself doesn't seem right, Coché has intimated. Why has a man of Michael's quick intelligence and curiosity spent his entire working life as a line manager at a middlebrow retailer?

"What would it feel like to grow up like this?" Coché asks the group. "How worried about other people's judgments might you be?"

"I can tell you," Michael says, "it was frightening, just frightening." He is trembling. "And also I felt like I was nobody. Because his first reaction isn't 'Are you okay?' It's all about the car, and it isn't even *his* anymore."

Aaron, Leigh, and Bella second Michael's bruised amazement at the treatment he received. "And the other side of it is my mother," Michael says, "who didn't say anything."

"It's like being abandoned," Coché says.

"Yeah, it is." This outburst from his father wasn't an isolated incident, just a sharp distillation of his blistering attacks on his children, Michael says. "I'm the oldest son, too—but I can't even stand up for myself." He sounds ashamed. "Thankfully, there wasn't physical abuse, but I was terrified."

Coché bids Michael to talk back to his father (Mark) now, and he does, telling the man he has "no right" to yell at him like that. "Don't you care about me?" he asks. Mark says little in response, and while the exchange is stilted, it's not without impact on both men. It has unsettled Mark to play the bullying father time after time; he's wiping at the corners of his eyes. Coché asks if he's okay. "I think the pain I feel is how bad I feel about doing this to my own children," he says slowly. "It really hurts, having done that and—" He breaks off.

In one of my first substantive comments in the group, I say that I relate to Mark, that I, too, blow up at my own two daughters, and feel horribly guilty about it. My voice cracks nervously, both because of what I'm confessing and because I don't want to overstep my bounds with the group. But I feel compelled to speak: From what I can tell so far, Mark is the only member whose anger ever gets out of hand, and he deserves some company. The group expresses surprise that a skinny blond writer like me can go on a rampage, but I assure them that I'm not exaggerating—and I'm not. Sitting next to me, Mark nods in appreciation, and Coché says she's glad I acknowledged the similarity between us: "Who ever thinks of extremely competent people as having trouble with anger?"

As for Michael, his quavering is beginning to subside. "I must say, I'm angry with my mother, too," he says. "She didn't stand up for me. She's equal."

"Well," Coché says, glancing around the group, her gaze landing briefly on Marie, "it's easier to feel victimized and noble."

The group feels for Michael, it's clear, though the meaning of his father's fury and mother's acquiescence is enticingly, but probably falsely, simple. That, out of fear, Michael has been sentenced to passivity in relationships—is that what we're to conclude? Introducing the exercise, Coché told the group that reenacting childhood memories would not be an end in itself, nor would it yield instant change. "If we're successful, the experience will creep under your cognitive awareness; it becomes part of your future and should be more powerful in six or eight months than it is today." In other words, the "family sculpting," the name psychologists have given to this form of role play, is not a way for members to wallow in past injuries—or cathartically relieve them—but to begin to grasp some of the automatic impulses that shape their behavior.

But my oh my, when Clem lays out his scene, it's impossible not to think, Now, this, *this* explains everything. The setting, he says, is the dinner table, and his parents have just come back from some social function. Fueled by martinis, his mother starts in on his father, indiscriminately insulting him. And his father, "he just took it good-heartedly," Clem says tremulously. "My dad touched a lot of people. When he passed away people said they never saw a bigger crowd at a funeral. But, uh, my mom never had any respect, or didn't have any interest in him."

"What was it about your dad that touched so many people?" Coché coaxes.

"He is very caring, loving." Who is Clem referring to in the present tense, his long-deceased dad? "He helped a lot of people, in his spare time. He was a machinist, and he would show me how to work on things and fix things. When my wagon broke, he'd machine a new part. It was like a tank when it was done."

"Awww," Bella says warmly, amid the sympathetic laughter of the others. They're helping Clem pay tribute to his father. It's in moments like these that someone suspicious of the whole group therapy enterprise, of the idea of admitting to others what you can barely admit to yourself, might think it's worth the potential shame or embarrassment. Maybe.

His sister participated in the donkey treatment of his father, Clem continues. "She and my mom would be like, 'We need some milk,' or

'We need some sweet cream—go down and get some,' and he'd do it, he just took it." In fact, if Clem does things for his two daughters, "they call me Pa Sweeney," his dad's nickname, Clem says. "They say that I'm just, uh, doing everything to please."

"That's painful," Coché says. "Tell us."

"I think my dad deserved better."

"Absolutely," says trusty Leigh.

"And part of it is the pain of realizing what your father went through year after year, and is part of it that same feeling for yourself?" Coché asks.

"A lot of the same things have occurred in my marriage, in a different way, but similar, I guess," Clem says, finally.

To say that Clem chose a woman just like his mother is too easy, of course. One of the most durable concepts in marital therapy is something called "projective identification," which dictates that Clem should be more properly considered not to have chosen his mother in Marie but to have *created* her in the older woman's image. The term was coined by British Freudian Melanie Klein to describe how infants project destructive parts of themselves onto parental figures as a defense against reckoning with their own violent impulses. (It's frightening to want to annihilate the woman who feeds you, the reasoning goes. Likewise, it's frightening to believe that the woman who feeds you wants to annihilate *you,* which is why the next step in Klein's theory is that once the infant projects its violent impulses onto the mother, he or she psychically splits the woman into two: the "good breast" and the "bad breast," as Klein famously put it.)

Back to the grown-ups, the idea of projective identification is that Clem, unable to bear his own anger and aggression, stokes it in Marie. Then he can live out his threatening aspect voyeuristically while simultaneously distancing himself from it and disdaining it. Clem's aversion to displaying aggression is striking. Later, when Mark declines to play Joe's ferocious, drunken father—he's had enough—Clem is given the role instead. It's a huge stretch for him. He only manages to screech out his fury, and then only with prodding. "I—I'm not very good at being assertive and authoritative," Clem says during the denouement of the scene. "It was tough, it was tough. It was very hard."

Clem practically prances through the projective-identification door, but if all of it seems too clever by half, it is. Is there nothing fundamental about the person Marie is? Does she not have some inborn temperament? Did Clem, for example, "make" her depressed? (Well, actually, external circumstances *can* nudge someone in that direction, therapists, and just about everybody, believe, but only if the so-called biological tendency already exists.) Projective identification both overexplains and underexplains, but limits aside, an awareness of the process might usefully get a couple puzzling over the constraints they've imposed on each other, as well as themselves. "The most distressing parts of your partner provide a starting point for considering your own needs and fantasies," writes psychoanalyst Peter Kramer, the author, most famously, of *Listening to Prozac.* So if Marie and Clem are engaged in *mutual* projective identification, which is the sorry state of many distressed marriages, Marie might ask herself why she has to leave all the submission and indecisiveness to Clem. To put it crudely, things are not as simple as Clem's a wimp and Marie's a bitch.

What we hear most about these days is the biological study of the brain, and, interestingly, that research tells a related story about how spouses call each other into being. According to brain network theory, every thought or feeling is accompanied by the firing of specific neurons, which are laid down as neural pathways. Those that become especially ingrained are known as "attractors," and they collect and shape all future incoming sensory data. Which is why, writes the psychiatrist Thomas Lewis, in *A General Theory of Love,* "We are disposed to see more of what we have already seen, hear anew what we have heard most often, think just what we have always thought." Lewis and his fellow MD coauthors give tangible examples of how tightly yoked our brain is to the past. Read the following:

T⊢E C⊢T

Even though the middle letter of both words is identically shaped, the vast majority of people read the first as an *h* and the second as an *a;* in fact, they find it nearly impossible *not* to do so.

Attractors explain why Clem, or any husband, tends to read his wife like his mother—no matter the supposed "reality." But how could he go further and trigger Marie to act, or react, like his mom? That's where a second brain operation comes in. To enhance survival, mammals have evolved what is called "limbic resonance," such that they can sense other mammals' emotional states and adjust accordingly, causing adjustments in the other, and so on, in an endless, unspoken feedback loop. "So familiar and expected is the neural attunement of limbic resonance that people find its absence disturbing," Lewis writes. "Scrutinize the eyes of a [nonmammalian] shark or sunbathing salamander and you get back no answering echo, no flicker of recognition, nothing."

Since "limbic states leap between minds," Lewis goes on, "we all embody an emotional force field that acts on people we love, evoking the relationship attributes we know best." So while neurobiologists tend to dismiss Klein as a fabulist (along with the rest of the floridly unscientific Freudians), she was describing this emotional force field a half century ago—only the *why* is different.

When Marie designs her scene, she puts herself as a girl sitting cozily on the couch with her mother and youngest brother. Her father comes in and gives her mom a punch on the shoulder. "It's Saturday night, the night before church," Marie tells the group, "and he wants to be intimate with his family, so he hits my mom."

"Oh my God," Leigh exclaims.

"Now," Marie says to Rachael, who's playing her mother, "that hurt, so you need to tell him."

"Ow," Rachael says, "that hurt."

"No, it didn't," Michael (her father) replies, at Marie's direction.

"This is how you teach people to be crazy," Coché remarks. "Tell them, 'Your reality isn't correct, *my* reality is correct.'" (Marie's vignette is reminiscent of a case history reported by psychiatrist R. D. Laing. Laing tells of treating a paranoid schizophrenic woman, who believed that random conversations going on around her were *about* her. When Laing meets her parents, he notices that they sit in front of their girl exchanging titters and whispered comments about her looniness. When the patient asks her parents what they're saying, they say, "What do you mean? We didn't say anything. We weren't talking about you.")

"But was [your father's punch] like a love tap?" Michael asks Marie. The dissonance of the interaction is confusing.

"Yeah," Leigh says. "Was it a love tap, or did it hurt?"

"Clem has seen it," Coché says.

He nods. "Marie's dad will be walking by her mother," Clem says, "and he'll just push her. He'll say, 'Hey,' and give her a shove."

"So it was a way of communicating?" Aaron asks, still perplexed.

"Yes," Marie says.

Clem adds the detail that makes the thing comprehensible: "Her dad grew up on a farm where they had many children, and they were just treated as farm animals; they were hit a lot. He went into the air force as soon as he could get away." The picture that comes to mind is similar to the one Larkin evokes in the second stanza of his poem, where he's sympathetic to the "mum and dad" who hobble their children: "But they were fucked up in their turn/By fools in old-style hats and coats,/Who half the time were soppy-stern/And half at one another's throats."

A persistent frustration with Marie in the group is that she can sound duplicitous, like she's hiding something from them (if not herself). She'll go on and on about whether her "interpretation" of something is "correct" while I'm thinking, Enough already. You know what I'm thinking or feeling, just say it! Many times, Marie probably *does* know more than she's willing to reveal to the group—her recondite caginess can be a kind of power play—but then . . .

"I'd say I was mad," Marie says, giving the group another example of how her family operated, "and they'd say, 'No, you aren't. You aren't mad.'" It helps to remember her stories.

The group members who seem no more than ordinarily fettered by their childhoods are Mark, Bella, and perhaps Leigh (owing to the mother who nurtured the woman until she died when Leigh was an adolescent?). It's a dicey proposition, to judge one person's upbringing as better than another's. We can't help but assess not just the stories that someone plucks from the past but the person who presents him- or herself to us in the present. If we detect an ugly scar, we look for the weapon that was used to make it. But this sort of reasoning backward ignores the strength of an individual's inborn weave, the flak jacket he or she is born with. Perhaps Leigh's experience on the whole was as abominable as anyone's, but she happens to be innately resilient (and she's had ten years of therapy to work out her kinks, Coché would say).

The clue that Mark's childhood was relatively decent? He struggled to come up with a single mental snapshot that captured the aura between his parents (which was Coché's original instruction, though most people end up bringing to life a memory of how their parents related not to each other but to them as children). Yes, the scene Mark produces gets him choked up. It's of his father using a table saw and accidentally slicing in half a portrait of his sister his mother painted, then asking nine-year-old Mark to share the blame, in hopes of avoiding one of his wife's fits of anger. But while there was a regrettable level of tension in the family—and Mark absorbed that "normal wasn't good enough," he had to be "perfect" not to set his mother off—he says he called up a collage of images (some good, some bad) when he imagined his parents together. "Around our dining-room table, for example, those were probably some of the best times we had," he says. He's drawing a contrast with Aaron, who has already done his boyhood one-act. The script was of his mother harping on him during meals, for slouching, for endless minutiae, and then goading his father into banishing him to the kitchen to finish dinner. "That's why I ate alone a lot," Aaron said.

For Mark, "every meal was fun, laughter, there were a lot of good times." Later in the year he will have cause to mention, with a smile on his face, how as a boy he overheard more than once the primal scene between his parents. Not only did the noise fail to persuade him that his father was murdering his mother, but the experience actually seems to have been heartening. The enthusiasm issuing from his parents' bedroom stirred in him optimism about the possibilities of marriage.

What stands out about Bella, an Ivy League MBA, is that her parents were invested in her and her younger brother. Though their marriage itself had considerable strife—they divorced when Bella was in her late teens and remarried each other later—they had the wherewithal to nurture her talents, to ask her what she wanted to be when she grew up and to listen to the answer. She, like Mark, has a zest, a confidence in herself that does not seem misplaced.

Before the group ends, Coché returns to yesterday's crime: Clem's vasectomy. When he mentions that the evening before he'd been so angry that he could barely concentrate on the movies, Coché asks him to say more.

"I was, uh, just, angry that, uh, we had, uh," Clem begins, inauspiciously. "I was angry about all the things that brought me to get a vasectomy. We had a one-year-old and a three-year-old, and our marriage wasn't going that good. I didn't want to bring another child into it, and I looked around the group, and I felt everybody was looking at me like a monster."

"Did it feel like *everybody* was looking at you like a monster?" Coché asks, the implication being that perhaps it was just the therapist whom Clem perceived as his Javert.

"Most of the people, I guess," Clem answers. "I just felt that everybody was—"

"Ganging up on you?" Coché asks. When Leigh starts to say she hadn't thought as poorly of Clem as he imagined, Coché interrupts. What Clem felt made complete sense, she says, taking him in with her eyes. "Yesterday I was concentrating on how angry Marie was, because I wanted her to feel heard. You *would've* felt ganged up against, like your dad in your house."

Now, extending the same listening courtesy to Clem as Marie previously was granted, Coché and the group let Clem expand (again) on how financially desperate he felt when he got the operation, how messed up his marriage was. Then Coché urges the couple to linger on her own mistake: Marie and Clem had an appointment with her specifically to discuss whether or not to proceed with the vasectomy, and Coché didn't suggest they stop it.

"I remember you recommended that I had to mourn the loss of the next child," Marie says, "and you suggested that I take some of the girls' stuff that I adored and save it in the attic."

"What did that feel like to you?" Coché asks.

"I wasn't heard at all."

"So how angry are you with me?"

"Oh, on a continuum, well," Marie says, seemingly referring to the endless others who've failed to hear her. "Mostly I feel like I have to question whatever you say."

"And it's been that way ever since? How is it that we're only speaking about it now?"

"Because Clem and I were in really bad financial shape, and I just had to bite the bullet and go on." In other words, Marie doesn't blame Coché, or not totally.

"Is there a way I could have heard you better?" Coché keeps on.

"At the time I was very depressed, so I'm not sure."

"I admire Clem for keeping his cool yesterday," says Slowinski, who's spoken very little this day, "and letting Marie give her side."

"Well," Coché adds, "Clem's goal was to set the stage for intimacy, by understanding where Marie was coming from. He really showed that he was able to do that." It's doubtful that Clem had been so strategic, but there is no harm in feeding his sense of agency.

"You have been wonderful just letting me tell you how I feel with some situations," Marie volunteers. "You don't argue or put it down. You just let me tell you, and that has really helped a lot. It really has."

"Well, thank you," Clem says. "I try."

"So it wasn't that Clem sneaked off and had a vasectomy," Coché concludes. "Clem and Marie and I talked about it in my office; there was a decision reached. Marie just felt misunderstood and has felt misunderstood . . . her whole life. So I just became the next in line."

"Mm-hmm, yeah," Marie says, "just next in line."

When the group is over, Coché offers to drive me to Philadelphia to catch a plane. Zipping along on the country roads in her Volvo convertible, top down, is a relief. The air is warm, and moving. Coché looks sporty, with a black baseball cap pulled down over her unruly hair. Talking loudly enough to be heard over the wind and the engine, she says that the group is still in the tentative "joining stage": They're relying on her to be highly directive and are as yet too timid to confront her. "Nobody got angry at me about forgetting about the vasectomy," she offers (unless you count Marie's barbs).

Even so, new groups may build mass that pulls away from the leader. The family role-plays were supposed to pivot on sex, Coché points out, but without anyone's acknowledging it, the group, one by one, resisted her efforts to stick to that. "They took it where it needed to be," she says, too patly for my tastes.

It was probably premature for such a specific topic as sex, she concedes, but it was the only time of the year that fit into Slowinski's schedule. She wanted him there for the men. And she figured the veteran couples might profit from it. The typical line from Sue Ellen and Mark is that their sex life is just fine, just fine, but then you listen, Coché says, and it's "only if Sue Ellen's in her nightclothes, and never during daylight. The question was whether I could shake things up a bit." (The answer was no, or at least there were no detectable tremors in the couple during the group.)

"With Clem and Marie, I thought the subject would be interesting to him, and she would be terrified by it. But Marie is tenacious. I thought she'd hang in." Coché sees progress there, she says. Last year during movie night, "Marie was curled up on the floor practically in a fetal position. At least this year she was stretched out." I'm surprised to hear last evening's performance was an improvement for Marie. She'd seemed to alternate between disengagement and disgruntlement, except one time, come to think of it, when she propped her feet up on an ottoman from her prone position on the floor, and her Laura Ashley dress fell away to reveal her legs. It had occurred to me that she looked rather Lolita-like.

Back to Coché: No matter what Marie throws at her, she says, "I won't treat her like her family did." She looks over at me briefly, then returns her eyes to the road.

CHAPTER 4

———

A Couple Never Lay on

Freud's Couch

A dirty little secret in the therapy world," writes University of Minnesota couples therapist William Doherty, "is that couples therapy may be the hardest form of therapy, and most therapists aren't good at it." This wouldn't be a "public health problem," continues Doherty, who delights in jovially tweaking his profession—which includes Ph.D. psychologists, social workers, state-licensed counselors, and a smattering of psychoanalysts—"if most therapists stayed away from couples work, but they don't." Surveys suggest that up to 80 percent of therapists see couples, yet only 12 percent of all practitioners are certified in marriage and family therapy—the sole branch of the field that always requires couples training. To be sure, there are other ways to learn about marital therapy, through supervision by a senior colleague, for instance. But people curious about a potential therapist's credentials usually just have to come out and ask.

The challenges of marriage therapy are perhaps obvious: the risk of taking sides or appearing to do so, the fact that a fair portion of your clientele has no intention of improving their relationship—they merely want permission to divorce. But perhaps most intimidating is the ragged emotion, husbands and wives bring to the hushed confines of the therapist's office. "In individual therapy, you can always say, 'Tell me

more about that,' and take a few minutes to figure out what to do next,"
Doherty writes. By contrast, "Couples sessions can be scenes of rapid
escalation. . . . Lose control over the process for fifteen seconds, and you
can have spouses screaming at each other and wondering why they are
paying you to watch them mix it up." Once, Doherty says, he watched a
tape of a therapist who "announced that the sessions did not seem 'safe
enough' for the angry spouses." Such an intervention might be necessary for a marriage marked by physical violence or extreme emotional
cruelty, Doherty writes, but there was no evidence of that. "The real
issue was that the therapist did not feel safe."

Doherty's own realization that he had to "structure" couples sessions
more tightly—or, less euphemistically, rein in the madness—came when
a badgering husband I'll call Ethan ignored the therapist's repeated
entreaties to stop interrupting his wife. "Ethan, I'd like to reinforce the
ground rule that neither of you interrupts the other," Doherty would
implore, in classic therapist-speak. "Is that something you can commit
to?" The husband would always agree but go right back to cutting off
his wife midsentence, until Doherty bluntly ordered, "Ethan, stop interrupting your wife. Let her finish." After that, when Ethan started to
butt in, Doherty says he'd keep his eyes peeled on the wife while waving
his arm in Ethan's direction, "shooing his comments away."

Given that marriage therapy is so full of pitfalls, it raises the question of whether it works, and as an empirical matter, the answer isn't
straightforward. Dozens upon dozens of studies have been conducted,
but most are hampered by design flaws. They may lack control groups,
such as couples in a similarly disturbed state who went without therapy.
Or subjects "self-select," meaning that those who get treatment often
chose it, potentially biasing the results. It could be that people who opt
for therapy are more motivated to improve and thus more likely to do
so. Conversely, those who submit to spilling their guts to a shrink could
be worse off than their peers—who else would agree to do that?

Most studies that are relatively well controlled test various cognitive-
behavioral therapies. That's because CBT, as it's called, is characterized
by discrete, brief interventions that are amenable to academic investiga-
tion. So in behavioral marital therapy, the therapist might guide spouses
in contracting for what they do and don't want from each other (hus-

band: greet me warmly when we meet after work; wife: don't leave the bathroom a mess) and then at two months, the pair would be surveyed as to whether they'd abided by their partner's wishes. If they did—and were generally pleased with the results—voilà, a "proven" therapy is born.

This points up another limitation of the more scientifically rigorous studies: short follow-up times, often six months, rarely more than two years. The upshot is that the really big question—does couples therapy prevent divorce?—has not been answered. The most that can be said, according to Northwestern University psychologist Jay Lebow, who specializes in interpreting data about the efficacy of therapy, is that about 70 percent of couples report being more satisfied with their marriages post-therapy, citing lower levels of conflict, for example, and better communication skills. Importantly, that figure holds no matter what type of therapy is tested.

A 70 percent success rate is more than respectable. Less encouraging, however, is Lebow's conclusion that the improvement often doesn't catapult couples into the realm of the genuinely happily married, as judged by standard written instruments, such as the Marital Dyadic Adjustment Scale, which assess spouses' agreement on hot-button topics like money and sex and query them on everything from how frequently they quarrel to how frequently they laugh. Perhaps most nettlesome of all, method-specific evaluations of therapy are removed from the real world, because the vast majority of clinicians, like Coché, mix and match. A seven-hundred-page text in the field, the *Clinical Handbook of Couple Therapy,* has chapters on twelve separate models, each written by a devoted practitioner of the model in question. Yet reading the book, it's clear that even the purists borrow heavily from their competitors. To put a finer point on it, two of the twelve purportedly distinct therapies fall under the heading of "Integrated Approaches"—these authors openly embrace (or cherry-pick from) the chaos.

There *are* major lines of thinking in marriage therapy, many of which evolved in isolation, or opposition, to each other. In the beginning, there was nothing: A husband and wife never lay side by side on Freud's couch. (The bearded genius did once counsel a patient to divorce his dull wife and marry a wealthy woman whom both men knew—Freud hoped the replacement spouse would donate some of her fortune to the psychoanalytic cause. The unethical conduct is a favorite bit of lore among Freud detractors: His patient became depressed and psychotic, the second marriage ended in divorce, and the man ended up in an institution.)

It wasn't until the 1960s that a handful of brave, iconoclastic analysts in America and England began to see husbands and wives together. These early forays into so-called conjoint therapy were inspired in part by psychiatrist Harry Stack Sullivan, the one who argued that life is a series of "security operations" to fend off anxiety. Individuals learn about anxiety in the first place, or learn what to be anxious about, through early maternal interactions, Sullivan contended, which leads to his grand theory: that no one can be understood outside of his or her relationships. "The personality or self is not something that resides 'inside' the individual, but rather something that appears in interaction with others," write Stephen Mitchell and Margaret Black, explaining Sullivan's interpersonal analytic school in *Freud and Beyond: A History of Modern Psychoanalytic Thought.* It's hard to appreciate how heretical Sullivan's view of human development was sixty or seventy years ago (and in the closed analytic world, for most of the twentieth century, in fact). Like Melanie Klein—she of projective identification and the baby who pushes hated aspects of himself onto the mother—Sullivan was arguing that the infant is primarily driven by a need to connect with others. That marked a fundamental break from Freud, who saw infantile drives as entirely internal efforts to reduce tension. Mothers were merely the objects upon which sexual and aggressive impulses might be discharged.

To get at how the different emphases of Freud and Sullivan manifest in the consulting room, Mitchell and Black examined a case that Sullivan himself had written up: that of a young man distressed because his "life had been centered around a series of 'grand passions'" that always fizzled out. For the strict Freudian, all the crucial action would be seen to take place "inside" the patient, Mitchell and Black write. "The ill-fated romances are likely to be entangled with oedipal dynamics, conflictual wishes to win the mother." To test the hypothesis, this therapist would probe the patient's fantasies about his girlfriends and his mother, eventually offering interpretations about how the dead-end affairs "both expressed and preserved the patient's tie to the oedipal parent."

Sullivan, in contrast, wanted to know the ins and outs of the man's present-day relationships in great, gory detail. With intensive questioning—forget the mute analyst who occasionally issues an interpretation—Sullivan figured out that what happened was that the guy "invested" each of his loves with precisely the qualities she lacked and then lavishly praised her for them. So that "if she is quite domineering, then he will find in her an extraordinary consideration for other people's feelings," Sullivan wrote, and after a while, she "cannot overlook the fact that she is not the person he is in love with." Only after Sullivan had ferreted out this unconscious rejection strategy did he delve into the patient's childhood, his past relationships and his fantasies. In Mitchell's and Black's words, "How did [the man] learn to destroy love in this fashion? Was he loved in this fashion? Were significant others in his early life reachable only in this way?"

In addition to psychoanalysis, other therapeutic schools began to be repurposed for work with couples: The early behaviorists, applying Skinnerian principles of operant conditioning, conceptualized a satisfying relationship as one in which spouses exchanged more positive behaviors than negative. To improve the ratio, the therapist would ask the husband and wife to list what they wanted from each other, and then when one partner delivered, the other rewarded him or her with a token. This morphed into simple contracting between spouses—too many "Honey, whad'ya do with the tokens?" moments, perhaps—and it didn't take long for the C (cognitive) to be added to the BT. Practitioners saw, and research demonstrated, that not only could two people interpret the same behavior in unrecognizable ways but those "cognitions" could interfere with couples' best efforts to change.

If behaviorism and Sullivan's interpersonal psychoanalysis were the mortar for building a new field called couples therapy, family, or "systems," therapy provided the bricks. Extrapolating from anthropological studies about the intricacies of social patterns, family therapists focused exclusively on what happened among—or between—intimates. This doesn't sound so far off from Sullivan's conjecturing (though, again, nobody was cross-pollinating then; each new therapeutic innovator was too busy killing the oedipal dad), but unlike Sullivan and *like* the behaviorists, systems therapists ignored the unconscious. It's not that they didn't believe in motivations outside awareness—they did—but they didn't think people changed by unearthing them. The therapist's role instead was to scan the web of interaction for the undesirable patterns and endeavor to interrupt them, thereby ushering in a healthier system.

Jay Haley, known for his fiendish "paradoxical directives" to disturb spousal systems, approached therapy like a chess player. Husbands and wives were the pieces he moved around, for their own good, of course. A favorite technique was to explicitly command couples to stay with a behavior that they presented as troublesome. In a path-breaking 1963 article in the *Archives of General Psychiatry,* Haley offered the case of a couple in which the wife suffered "anxiety feelings and a terrible pain in the eyes" whenever she left the house unaccompanied. Haley instructed the husband to tell his wife to stay home each morning before he left for work—he could say it firmly or jokingly, it didn't matter. The third day the man did this, "the wife went out to the store alone for the first time in eight years." In the next session, however, the guy spent the whole time fretting about what might happen to his wife out on her own, "where she might go, whom she might meet, and would she even get a job and become so independent that she would leave him."

To Haley, the magic of such dictates was that they shifted the distribution of power in marriage—and "who is to tell whom what to do under what circumstances" was at the crux of all major conflicts for him. In this instance, "Although the wife had been behaving like the helpless one, *she was in charge* of being the helpless one by insisting on staying home," Haley wrote. "When her husband directed her to stay at home, the question of *who* was laying down the rules for their relationship was called into question."

Other kinds of systems therapies weren't quite as top-down as Haley's, which evoked the omniscient analyst (ironically enough, since as one of his colleagues later observed: "I got the impression that Haley wanted to make sure that psychoanalytic thinking [was] prevented from ruining the newly emerging field of family therapy"). The central wisdom of the leading systems developers was the same, however: Behaviors aren't the product of internal forces but of people acting on, and reacting to, each other. Causality is circular.

If none of the above sounds like what you think when you think "therapist," that's because running alongside them was the gentle, bespectacled giant of American therapy, Carl Rogers. Coming of professional age in the 1950s and '60s, he, more than any other figure, is the stereotypical touchy-feely therapist. To Rogers, people weren't driven by bestial impulses but by the desire to "self-actualize," or live the best life they could. It was a premise well suited to a prosperous postwar world, and particularly to a nation whose founders included the "pursuit of happiness" as a basic right.

What left the biggest mark on the field were Rogers's notions about how therapists should interact with "clients," never "patients." A gifted clinician by all accounts, Rogers argued that therapists must be empathic and display unconditional positive regard. They should mildly guide people toward arriving at their own insights; interpretations from on high encourage dependence. And it was Rogers who first advocated active listening, though he called it "reflection." The whole package eventually came together under the label "humanism"—as distinct from Freudianism or behaviorism, which paid scant attention to people's values or conscious intentions to improve their condition.

Coché's existentialist psychology falls under the humanist umbrella, with its emphasis on the power of the individual to make meaning out of meaninglessness. As a certified marriage and family therapist, she is also explicitly trained in systems theory. (A teaching videotape Coché made focused on a couple in which the husband was flamboyantly enmeshed with his mother—the old woman lived with them and the patient got "physically sick" imagining having dinner without her. Taking a page from Haley, Coché instructs the man to have a single dinner alone with his wife in the following week, but he must not "enjoy it.") From there, however, Coché dips into a theraputic grab bag. She employs a fair number of cognitive behavioral techniques, makes some observations that are analytically tinged, and others that resonate with currently in-vogue attachment theory. She can draw from such areas in part because she's acquainted with them, and in part because, jargon notwithstanding, the once dueling orientations are looking more and more alike. Not to mention that, as analyst Peter Kramer observes, concepts like projective identification, once confined to insular professional forums, have become so widely disseminated that they're "today's common sense." Who *couldn't* listen to Marie and Clem group after group without starting to ponder how each conjured the other into being?

Since evaluating therapeutic models can seem rather futile in a world where eclecticism prevails—and in which, recall, no model has yet outshone any other—a small cadre of investigators has taken another route. Instead of comparing therapies, they've decided to compare *therapists.* What happens in treatments where clients leave reporting change for the better versus those where they shuffle away untouched? Efforts to define high-quality interactions have generally turned up several common factors: The patient and therapist agree on goals and on means to achieve them (Coché is big on the couples' setting goals for themselves, by the way); and they share what's termed a "positive therapeutic alliance," one in which the client rates a therapist as empathic, respectful, authentic, supportive, and so on.

The latter sounds clear cut. We think we know what it means to be authentic and supportive—Carl Rogers did—but what do such salutary qualities really look like behind the closed door? Would the empathic therapist give love, or tough love? Or both, at different times? Would she brainstorm solutions for her patients, or nod her head and imperceptibly lead them to their "own" answers? Or again, would she do both, depending on the circumstances?

Some of the most interesting current thinking on how therapists should envisage their role comes from psychiatrist and author Mark Epstein. At the forefront of merging Eastern thought and Western psychology, he talks not about what therapists should say but how they should "be." Among other things, his formulation draws on the Buddhist practice of mindfulness and the British pediatrician-analyst D. W. Winnicott's famous notion of the "good enough mother." To be mindful for Buddhists is to observe external stimuli *and* inner sensations curiously, openly, without automatically reacting. Likewise, Winnicott's good enough mother makes herself "available" to the child, emotionally and otherwise, without unduly intruding on him. She lets him be, onto-logically speaking, which may or may *not* require letting him be in the moment. What this means for therapists isn't that they're supposed to regress patients into thumb-sucking babies (wasn't that a seventies fad?). Rather, it refers to a kind of ideal therapeutic presence: nondemanding yet alive, simultaneously tuning in to the person in the chair and to glimmerings from one's own unconscious, the willingness to be affected by a client, not just affect him or her.

Epstein's preferred stance also contains strong echoes of what neu-robiological and videotaped research has revealed about mother-infant attachment, about preverbal, limbic bonding between the two, and the back-and-forth nature of the relationship. Which is closer to how Coché thinks about her job, fan that she is of books like *Scientist in the Crib: What Early Learning Tells Us About the Mind.* "I use the emotional part of my brain as a feeder for my intellect," she tells me at one point. And in general, she says she goes into each session of the group with only a sketchy idea of how she wants it to go. Mostly, she follows her "gut," which, by the way, biologists call the "second brain": the place where premammalian life-forms registered external stimuli. One of Coché's professional heroes, Virginia Satir (the sole female among the first gen-eration of family therapists), spoke of her work in literally embodied terms. "I felt a warmth from within that told me the son was open for some contact," she'd reportedly say.

Watching Coché interact with the group, my mind often returns to other admirable traits of Winnicott's good enough mother, including his to-nonanalytic-ears-shocking discussion of how the mother "hat[es] appropriately." In a paper that Winnicott wrote explicitly comparing mothers to therapists, he tells of his experience with a nine-year-old boy who was sent to a foster home in the English countryside during World War II—he'd been running away from his mother and various institu-tions since the age of six. Winnicott met the child in the foster home, but after he disappeared and had to be retrieved from the police station, the boy came to live with the therapist and his wife. At first they gave the boy complete freedom and a shilling every time he went out (a para-doxical directive, if ever there was one). Eventually, "the truancy symptom turned round," Winnicott writes in "Hate in the Countertransfer-ence," "and the boy started dramatizing . . . his own inner world, which was full of persecutors." He became a nightmare to live with, and—to the point of the paper—forced Winnicott to reckon with his own hate.

> At crises I would take him by bodily strength, without anger or blame, and put him outside the door, whatever the weather or the time of day or night. There was a special bell he could ring, and he knew that if he rang it he would be readmitted and no word said about the past. He used the bell as soon as he recovered from his maniacal attack.
>
> The important thing is that each time, just as I put him out-side the door, I told him something: I said that what had happened had made me hate him. This was easy because it was so true.

Put in everyday parenting vernacular, what Winnicott is getting at is that children test their parents' love by misbehaving, and if the adults fail to react in some proportionate manner, children doubt the sturdi-ness of parental affection and/or their own lovability. Similarly, Win-nicott writes, "If the *patient* seeks objective or justified hate he must be able to reach it, else he cannot feel he can reach objective love" (empha-sis mine).

In case you wondered, Winnicott isn't suggesting that therapists unload on clients every time they register a twinge of dislike. What he is saying is that therapists need to use their countertransferences to consider if and when the patient might benefit from a judicious shar-ing. Winnicott's riff on hate is at bottom an example of the responsive-ness he believed therapists must cultivate—and that's what I notice in Coché. She is not a smiling sphinx, phobic about betraying irritation or impatience. At times she becomes stern or skeptical. ("Do I get angry? Yes, I get angry," Coché says. "Do I tell people I'm angry? Yes, if I think there is some clinical function to it.") Other times, she conveys real love. She laughs, hard.

There are moments when I think, Oh no, here she goes again, when Coché is doing one of her repeat-after-me numbers or name-dropping about her contact with this "renowned expert" or that. But somehow

Coché usually manages to pull it out, or pull it off without seeming false, or even overly ridiculous. This isn't to say that she is not sometimes acting to an extent. Coché—who fondly remembers her days singing in an elite college chorus and who's sent me old newspaper clippings about her daughter Juliette's turn as Maria in the Philadelphia Ballet's *Nutcracker*—welcomes the performative aspects of her job.

Which evokes yet another quality of the good enough therapist (and mother) as portrayed by Winnicott. She must "seem to want to give what is really only given because of the patient's needs." It's a skill, or deportment, that Winnicott also described as "acting naturally." "Acting naturally" is the kind of oxymoronic phrase he loved, and, like all oxymorons, it makes you think, and think again. Filtering the words myself, what they capture is the bedrock authenticity that emanates from the best therapists—whether they're giving a husband strict instructions on what to tell his agoraphobic wife, or reflecting back a client's words, "What I hear you saying is . . ."

There is one last way in which I like to conceive of Coché's talent, and it comes from someone who works a few miles from her office in Philadelphia. Jay Efran, a psychologist and professor emeritus at Temple University, specializes in constructivism, which basically means that he believes we don't discover reality, but invent it. Constructivists, for instance, wouldn't say Freud's or Winnicott's ideas were wrong per se, only that both men were mistaken to believe that they'd found truths about human nature that transcended themselves or their culture.

This isn't an unusual perspective these days, whether people consider themselves constructivists or postmodernists or merely twenty-first-century citizens of the world. What's intriguing about Efran is how he's used the idea to explain why no matter how many well-designed outcome studies are generated, they'll always seem somewhat beside the point. The problem is one of frame of reference, he says. Therapy doesn't fit the medical model into which it's been forced, starting with Freud and ending with managed care. "The profession has gotten itself into a bind," Efran tells me, "because it wants to be seen as a science, and it wants to collect money. It has made this category mistake of thinking it provides treatments for diseases and not just conversation or community or human contact, or offering new slants on life."

Therapy boils down to a talent for conversation, Efran believes, which is something Coché has in abundance. While I sometimes zone out when she's expounding on big-picture theories of "coupling," Coché is nimble in the moment, when she's talking *with* someone. She thrives on interceding in or interpreting the to-and-fro between a husband and wife, or among the couples. At the same time she's like a pattern-seeking satellite. From her elevated perch on her black leather chair, she'll quickly pull back to note a common, though not necessarily obvious, theme in the stories whirling around below her.

Defining therapy as good conversation may strip it of some of its mystique, but Efran's argument is not anti-intellectual, or antieducation and training. At a minimum, one would want a marriage therapist to have been immersed in theories of human development and change, to have grappled with philosophies of what makes for a meaningful and satisfying life, to have a subtle understanding of how people influence each other—all of which Coché has. But none of this prescribes *how,* or how skillfully, a therapist will wield her knowledge. In graduate programs for would-be clinicians, Efran says, the assumption is that anyone who meets admitting standards can be taught to perform decent therapy. Yet "almost immediately there are some students who seem to intuitively have the right impulses, and there are others with whom we can spend hours and hours and hours, and they'll never be any good . . . [W]e accept that there are inspiring teachers, crackerjack lawyers. Why are we less willing to acknowledge that some therapists are better than others, and that there are 'super-therapists' whose sterling results can't be explained by current research?"

In a journal for clinicians, Efran wrote about a tactic he's used only once in his forty years of practice. He was working with a couple in which the husband was having an affair that he couldn't bring himself to stop, though he kept promising to do so. Meanwhile, the wife wanted to stay in the marriage but was becoming increasingly frustrated at her husband's waffling. "As I met the couple," Efran wrote, "a single question kept popping into my head: 'Given their circumstances, what options are they unable to contemplate.'" He decided to suggest as an "experiment" that the couple separate for three months, during which the man had free rein to see his mistress. The end of the story is that when his paramour was no longer "forbidden fruit," the husband lost interest and he and his wife happily reunited.

Of course, we have to take Efran's word on this. His radical (Haleyesque?) maneuver wasn't tested in a randomly controlled study. Which is precisely his point: "Advise husband to temporarily bunk with mistress" will never be systematically researched, or included in a therapy manual. That doesn't mean Efran was wrong to try it. "It was tailormade for this couple, taking into account their background, and their level of sophistication," he says. "We may have to get used to the fact that the [therapeutic] process, like all conversations, has improvisational elements."

The couples group—with its members riffing off each other and inevitably making unpredictable music—fits Efran's metaphor well. So instead of the orchestra conductor that Coché imagines herself, maybe she's the leader of a jazz band, giving the players enough freedom to create while also tethering them to a melody she wants them to hear.

CHAPTER 5

The Impossibility of Pleasing in an

Unhappy Marriage

Everyone notices it, but it will not be until three-quarters of the way through the year that anyone acknowledges it. Just before lunch during the eighth group, Coché will say, "I have one more question for you, just before we stop, because we don't talk about this very often in this room, and it's important. Do any of you have a sense when you sit with Mark and Sue Ellen that they share a great love? Does anybody feel it?"

"Absolutely," Joe will say.

"Yes, yes," Clem will add. And the rest of the group, including me and excluding perhaps only Leigh, will nod their heads.

"Are you aware that people feel it, that it's palpable?" Coché will ask Mark and Sue Ellen.

"No," Mark will say. Sue Ellen will be strenuously quiet. Later, both tell me that they *did* have some idea about what Coché was talking about: They feel different from the other couples—more "connected" is the only way Sue Ellen knows to describe it. They're not sure why they didn't acknowledge this to the group. They didn't know what more they could add, for one thing. My guess is that Sue Ellen in particular felt embarrassed—for herself *and* the other couples—to be singled out as special. The woman who was hidden away in closets as a girl recoils from being the center of attention.

By the bare facts, there is nothing extraordinary about Mark and Sue Ellen—if anything, their existence seems parochial. Their nearly three decades of married life mostly have been lived in the same beach town, on the same bit of land where Mark grew up. His family ran the motel that his wife now manages, and he and Sue Ellen live in a modest home a few hundred feet from it.

Every morning from April to October Sue Ellen walks over at 8 A.M. to open the motel office. She attended a vocational high school for photography and design, and has worked off and on in that field while raising her children, but now the motel is her full-time job. Meanwhile, five days a week, Mark, the primary breadwinner, makes the two-hour drive to the consulting firm where he's worked for the last two decades. A college-educated oceanographer, he's moved up the ranks and holds a position of considerable authority.

It's a Sunday when we meet to talk, so Mark is off work, but Sue Ellen is pretty much always on duty in the summer. We take a seat in the dining room just off the motel's reception area so she can handle the trickle of guests checking out. The office is part of a small, prefab-looking ranch house that was Mark's boyhood home, and hanging everywhere are landscapes and still lifes and portraits painted by his mother. Not to be missed is the early, rather crudely rendered painting of his blond, blue-eyed sister, the one his father accidentally slashed. You can't tell at all. Mark's father managed to repair it without leaving a mark.

What does distinguish Mark and Sue Ellen is their story of meeting and deciding to marry, which they tell me over a breakfast of strawberries and Irish soda bread. "Did Sue Ellen tell you she baked it?" asks Mark, who is forever pushing his wife forward.

The couple's story is one of romance and inevitability, set against a backdrop of late 1970s beer-soaked, beach-town bacchanalia and the Dickensian tragedy of Sue Ellen's childhood. From the time she was a baby, Sue Ellen and her nine brothers and sisters spent summers in the town where Mark lived full-time. They stayed in one of their great-aunt's homes; she owned two gingerbread-trimmed two-stories, side by side. The family was there at the old woman's sufferance more than invitation. In addition to her own large brood, Sue Ellen's mother, Ann, cared for a wheelchair-bound sister who had multiple sclerosis. It was the invalid upon whom the great-aunt showered her beneficence, and if she was to come take the sun in the summers, well, then Ann and her mob would have to come, too.

The lack of welcome did nothing to dampen Sue Ellen's ardor for the place, which was teeming with not only her own siblings but her cousins. "Mother's other sisters would also be there, with their children," she says. "You got to go to the beach every day. You went to bed in your bathing suit, got up in it, it was—" She breaks off. "You were able to be free . . . of the concerns." The "concerns" were the drunkenness of her father, the acid tongue of her mother. "He was violent, toward my mother. And then, in turn, we would catch it from her," Sue Ellen says in her characteristic broken cadence. But in the summer, "Daddy was not there. He would stay home and work and come down on the weekends. I *loved* it. It felt like home." In the glow of her fond memories, the words fairly rush from Sue Ellen.

The summer after she graduated from high school, Sue Ellen says she kept seeing this cute boy, tall with curly dark brown hair, around town. A girlfriend from that time has told Sue Ellen that she remembers standing with her on the beach, when Mark sauntered by. "Do you know him?" Sue Ellen asked her friend. No, the girlfriend said, she'd never met the guy. "I'm gonna marry him," Sue Ellen replied.

While Sue Ellen doesn't recall this incident, she doesn't doubt it happened. She and Mark first spoke outside of a bar called the Ugly Mug, she says. "One night I was standing out front, waiting to meet somebody, and he and three of his friends were off to the left of me, and I could hear them, and they were talking about going to a party that started at eleven o'clock." In that single sentence, she's given more scenic detail than she usually does over the course of an entire six-hour group.

"My *girlfriend's* party," Mark interjects, with an arch of his expressive eyebrows.

"The guys turned around," Sue Ellen says, "and asked me what time it was, and I said, 'Oh, you have just a few minutes.'" Mark and his friends laughed at her cleverness, that she'd been listening in on their conversation. Then they went on their way.

"We go to the party," Mark says, "and all I could think about was Sue—at my girlfriend's party! So I decided I was gonna hunt her down.

I was just very attracted to her. She was beautiful. She was funny. She was outgoing."

"So the next night," Sue Ellen says, "wasn't it at—"

"Gloria's," Mark says.

Another bar? I ask.

"It wasn't just another bar, this was *the* bar," Mark says.

"Where everybody danced," Sue Ellen elaborates, "and it was local bands that played. It was a lot of fun. And it was, uh, did I go up to you? I think I went up to you and introduced myself. I introduced myself as Sue Ellen. And he says, 'Oh, Sue.' He ignored me saying 'Sue Ellen.'" She thought it was presumptuous but never corrected him (and he calls her Sue, exclusively, to this day). His brash self-confidence was one of his charms.

The next day, Mark visited Sue Ellen at her job, spinning glass at a shop on the mall. They talked, he asked her out, and within six months he asked her to marry him in the front seat of his van. She was nineteen, he was twenty-one. "We never thought we were young, we never thought it was risky," Mark says. "We never thought anything but that it was the right thing to do."

Another time, Mark describes his feelings for Sue Ellen this way: "I always wondered what it was like to be in love, but it wasn't until I started dating Sue that I ever felt the way I felt when I dated her." He has bumbled into a tautology, but one that makes his point. "It was so overwhelming that I never wanted to lose the feeling," Mark says. "It was one of the most powerful things that ever happened to me."

Coché's observation to the group about the couple's great love is not an idle one. Some of the other members are floundering, she believes, because their marriages aren't built on such singular passion, and they don't know what to do with that knowledge. "If you didn't have that experience—it's an event, a happening; sort of like a tsunami, it sweeps you up—what do you do?" the therapist will ask quietly. "How can you move forward? Can you make it more of a tsunami than it was in the beginning, or not? There has to be a way to acknowledge what is, and work with what is." Coché will bow her head, lips pressed together. "There are many, many models of marriage that are viable. Companionship, for example, turns out to be extremely important."

In contrast to Mark and Sue Ellen, most of the rest of the group married in a modern (or is it old-fashioned?) way. There was a balancing of pros and cons, a pondering of a potential partner's stability, financial and otherwise. There was a consideration of alternatives, of who else might be available in the marriage market. For two couples, there was breaking up and getting back together. Nobody in the group fails to mention love and admiration as part of the mix that led them to marry, but as Bella puts it, her love for Joe was a "factor" among many. A factor does not, by definition, overwhelm.

Such sober deliberation is what you're supposed to do, of course. As Coché says, "Sometimes the person you fall madly in love with turns out to be an extremely lousy life partner." But wait—we're also not supposed to "settle," to marry someone just because he or she is merely kind or responsible or otherwise unobjectionable. How calculating, how boring, how un-American.

For most of recorded history, we know, practical considerations held sway over the choice of a spouse. Marriage was an economic bargain struck between families—for the upper classes, its purpose was to magnify wealth and power; for the lower, to choose someone who could contribute sweat or material goods to the small business that was each household. Love was an afterthought, if a thought at all. (Because the idea of love within marriage was so "radical," in fact, Chinese intellectuals in the 1920s actually invented a new word for it, writes historian Stephanie Coontz in her book *Marriage: A History.*)

That began to change in the West with the spread of wage labor. Increasingly through the eighteenth and nineteenth centuries, men struck out on their own rather than stick around home to inherit land or wealth that may have dwindled across the generations, anyway. Simultaneous to these economic shifts (or *because* of them), Enlightenment thinkers were agitating for individual rights, including the right to choose a spouse rather than have one thrust upon you. Relationships between men and women were to be "based on reason and justice rather than force," Coontz writes, ushering in a romantic model of marriage.

Jane Austen neatly captures the conundrum as it existed two centuries ago—and in some form still today. The exaltation of the "love match" was at its peak during the novelist's lifetime, but financial exigencies could be ignored only at a couple's peril. So on the one hand, Austen declares, in a letter to her niece, that "nothing can be compared to the misery of being bound *without* love." On the other, in *Pride and Prejudice,* she has the pragmatic Charlotte calling marriage "the only honourable provision for well-educated women of small fortune, however uncertain of giving happiness." Perhaps Austen settled the dilemma for herself, albeit conditionally, nine years before she died, at age forty-two. "I consider everybody as having the right to marry *once* in their Lives for Love, if they can," she wrote her sister Cassandra.

This being the twenty-first century, social scientists have conducted hundreds of studies examining the risk factors for marital unhappiness and divorce. Nobody, however, has ascertained the importance of marrying someone who has at some point intoxicated you versus someone who never quite did, according to prolific University of Denver couples researcher Scott Stanley. Such a project may not be possible or worth it, he tells me, because what's likely to carry the day is the *interaction* between "big love" (as Stanley dubs strong romantic attraction) and compatibility. Researchers have demonstrated decisively that compatibility—similarity in attitudes, leisure activities, religion, and education—contributes to marital harmony. And couples whose interests and backgrounds meld are apt to share some "big love," he says. Conversely, however, romantic rapture can be deleterious, wiping out obvious clashes in values and worldviews. "No amount of big love," Stanley dutifully informs, "will overcome strong deficits in compatibility in the long term."

So obvious, yet so dispiritingly fuzzy. Big love matters, and it doesn't. "In our culture at this time it would be a pretty bad sign if a couple were not feeling the head-over-heels thing *sometime* early on," Stanley continues. "The pressure to feel that way—and doubt yourself if you don't—is too great." But then, "People with more realistic expectations seem likely to do best in marriage, and it's *not* realistic to expect the crazy levels of love, infatuation, and happiness that people currently do."

No matter how much we wish for certainty, this question may not yield to science or logic mainly because what it means to be "in love" is itself an unknown quantity. As literary critic Phyllis Rose writes in the classic *Parallel Lives: Five Victorian Marriages,* "Worldly wisdom says you will know it when it happens, but worldly wisdom is often wrong." She offers the fascinating example of Jane Welsh, who, after fending off Thomas Carlyle's proposals for five years, finally agreed to marry him. Welsh's letters suggest that she had no more than a sisterly affection for him, but confused and under pressure, she decided to test whether she felt enough for Carlyle by monitoring her behavior. Since "passionate love was the kind of love that would move [one] to ignore the demands of duty and expediency," if she made sacrifices on Carlyle's behalf, she reasoned, she must be in love with him.

"Her formulation is sensible," Rose writes, "because it is easier to . . . say what you did for a man than what you felt for him. Her formulation is dangerous, because, if a person can bring herself to behave in the way defined, then she can *deduce* the feeling that inspired it. Perhaps more of 'being in love' is of this kind—deduced—than we care to admit."

It's another gray day in Stone Harbor when the group convenes for the third time, on a Sunday in mid-July. Leigh and Aaron are missing, as they'd announced in the last session. Sue Ellen and Mark look mellow as they take chairs next to each other. They've had a month to recover from the unruly emotions prompted by the family excavations—his shame at his threatening anger, her nausea at her girlhood trauma. Sue Ellen's greenish gray eyes are luminous and a little curious, her guardedness slightly fallen, while Mark, in khaki shorts and an olive-green polo, looks like he's ready to flip some burgers on the grill.

The topic for the day is "Skillful Loving," Coché says once people settle into their usual places. She has a couple of exercises the group can do, she adds, but depending on the collective will, the day can be freeform. "Last year the feedback you gave me is that you just wanted time to work," Coché says. "This is one of those times when you just have me, and you don't have a guest."

"What does 'skillful loving' actually mean?" asks Rachael, twirling one of her curls with her finger. Good question. She has a bold naïveté, a frank girlishness, that serves the group well.

"Skillful loving? I made it up. I've not heard anybody use those words before," Coché begins, though such a generic phrase hardly seems worth claiming credit for. Luckily, Coché's idea is somewhat richer than its label. It means, she says, loving someone the way he or she wants to be loved, rather than the way *you* (or your ideal partner, which some would argue *is* you) want to be loved. Coché tells the story of a man who gave his wife silky nightgowns for her birthday eight years running and never noticed, or cared, that they hung in her closet in a neat row, unworn. Even when there is not power at issue between partners, or hostility—you will like silk because you *should*—there is creeping insensibility.

Coché's standard practice is to begin the group with some introductory blandishments and an overview of the day's agenda—the therapeutic version of softening up the crowd for the main act—then circle the room asking people how they feel about being there. Today, Rachael goes first.

"It feels like hard work," she says.

"You're looking forward to hard work—how does that feel?" Coché asks.

"No, I'm *not* looking forward to hard work," Rachael says. She laughs. "Usually I feel like being here, but today I don't."

"And is there something special about today, or is it about other stuff going on in your life?"

"We're going on vacation after we leave here," Rachael says, now quiet. She is always respectful of Coché, though never pandering. "And I just want to go on vacation."

"Are you feeling the same way?" Coché asks Michael, who's slumping on the couch next to his wife.

"Oh, I'm in total agreement," he says, flippant. "I just came off a long string of days at the store, and being here is like one last day of work."

Coché looks away from Michael. "Who else is feeling like this is a lot of work?" They all agree that it does indeed seem like work, though their reactions to that vary.

Like Michael's, Joe's family scene from last time was a tale of men and their car fetishes. New-driver Joe was in the driveway, at the wheel of the family car, when he accidentally lurched forward and plowed into the back of his father's Corvette. In response, his father, in a drunken rage, grabbed a two-by-four and "beat the crap" out of his own beloved automobile, Joe had informed the group, while his mother screamed at her paralyzed son to get in the house.

The memory shook Joe, and he says today that he's approaching the group as if it's a "roller coaster." Once he's "strapped in," he thinks he'll be fine, but imagining being here scared him. Clem, too, is ambivalent. He just realized a few days before that this was the group weekend, and he says he's "ready to do some work"—would he dare say anything different?—but he's disappointed because he loves his summer weekends. Sue Ellen echoes him. While the topic "interests" her, "part of me—" She hesitates. "I have one day off a week from the motel, and this is it."

The last three members give three very different versions of "glad to be here." Marie, in the manner of a straight-A student who feeds on being unlike the shallow popular kids, says something she will say many times: She *wants* the group to be a lot of work, "Or else, why would I be here?"

Bella is also a straight-A student but one who was class president and a cheerleader, too—Tracy Flick to Marie's Goth girl. She's wearing soft navy capri sweatpants, a red tissue T-shirt, and Michael Kors wedge heels. She's "excited" to be in group, she says. "It's, like, something to do for me." Bella is the only member who is still young enough *and* suburban-affluent enough to slip into Valley-girl speak. She's got another reason to be excited: "We're having a baby," she says, to congratulations.

"It felt weird until I told you," Bella says, with Joe beaming proudly on. The pregnancy is brand-new. "I think we're like six weeks," she says, "something like that."

Last up is Mark, who says that he's looking forward to the day. He speaks slowly but without fussiness. High school metaphors don't work for him—he's like a cowboy preparing to reclaim his dusty town from a gang of outlaws. If a man's gotta fight, a man's gotta fight. "I always feel," Mark drawls, "like I get the most out of sessions we have turmoil in." He pauses. "So I don't mind."

The turmoil this time comes from a new quarter. In Bella and Joe's debut in the group, the talk was of multiple orgasms and marital beatitude.

But either the events of the ensuing month brought them low for the first time, or marketing exec Bella had been doing a sales job—for the group or herself?—with Joe her loyal assistant. (Remember the couple's response to Coché's question about how many days of their marriage had been happy? "There's like two days that haven't been blissful," Bella said. "That was actually my answer," Joe added.) Throughout the year, Coché will regularly suggest that the challenge for Bella is to "join" the group rather than lead it—"We know you have masterful leadership skills"—to which Bella will respond with an earnest nod or assurances that she understands. Then she'll change the subject.

Bella is what Marie might have been had she been well loved as a girl, her precociousness encouraged and nurtured. She went to a selective college, then to an Ivy League business school, and, until recently, had been climbing the ladder of corporate America. Bella is warm, articulate, laughs easily, and looks you in the eye when she speaks. Joe's outlines are less crisp. He, too, has a professional degree, in law, but he is not as one with his career, as Bella is. Behind his small, rectangular-shaped glasses, his eyes are squinty and can almost seem to disappear—are his lenses smudged, or is there no *there* there? One thing is clear: He has it bad for Bella. He often refers to her as "my wife" instead of by name, as in "my wife" said this, or "my wife" did that. It's as if Joe is deeply pleased and proud to call Bella his own.

Bella and Joe recently moved from one East Coast city to another. The move was brought on by Bella's decision to leave her company to go into business with a friend and fellow MBA, a woman named Tara. Tara has started a venture that involves buying and selling real estate, as well as running a restaurant acquired in a deal. At first, Joe didn't relocate with Bella—he stayed at his law firm and visited her on the weekends. But it didn't take long for him to miss his new wife, and he resigned from his job to join her.

He also agreed to manage the restaurant, and the place is turning out to be a disaster—this is the problem Joe is bringing to the group, in a frenzied oration. "I have a very short temper; I can't deal with so many things going wrong. I feel like I'm a kindergarten teacher, 'cuz I have nothing but five-year-olds saying, 'Joe, this doesn't work, Joe, this doesn't work.'" In the past week, a liquor order failed to show, the air conditioner went on the fritz, two freezers and two walk-in coolers broke down, and some spoiled food ended up being served. He doesn't have the budget to buy the food necessary to prepare the full menu, and "we're on discontinuance notices with everybody—the gas company, the electric company, the phone company, water." If that wasn't bad enough, he and Bella "have very few dollars in the bank, and we do not have the capacity to absorb something going wrong," like the flood they just had in their apartment, after they'd laid a new rug. "It's like I'm treading water, except I'm underneath the water. So I'm staying in one place, but it's not a position where I can survive."

As much as cursing his circumstances, Joe is heaping opprobrium on himself. It's "selfish" to feel testy and overwhelmed with the demands of the job, he says; after all, he agreed to take it. He's never been able to delegate, he says, when retailer Michael suggests that that might lighten his load. Mark, the closest thing the group has to a father figure, pulls Joe into an exchange about how perceived helplessness can lead to anxiety and, in turn, anger. That was his own experience with his sons, Mark says. Yeah, that's exactly how it feels, Joe agrees. He is putting me in mind of a type of client that Irving Yalom describes in his group therapy text: "Obsequious and carefully avoiding any sign of aggressivity, they are often masochistic, rushing into self-flagellation before anyone else can pummel them."

Because Coché has indicated that it's Joe's turn to vent, Bella is silent as her husband tells the group he never wanted to be a lawyer—it was his parents' idea. "I'm Forrest Gumping my way through life," he says, with a grimace of self-disgust. Bella remains quiet when Coché has a dialogue with Joe about how maybe if he were less self-critical, he'd free up energy to run the restaurant. And Bella does not interrupt when her husband theatrically declaims, "I need all the kids back in college, and I need them in college *now*." (When the university near the restaurant is back in session, presumably they'll have more customers.)

By the time Bella speaks, her dark eyes are blazing. "When Joe gets negative, you feel very sympathetic," she says. "But it's so extreme, how he thinks." She shakes her head. "Because my partner and I"—that would be her business partner, Tara—"are around him saying, 'You're at the restaurant every minute—you're gonna have to sleep so you're not like a zombie. What can we do? What money do you need? How can we support you?'"

"And none of that [support] ever materializes," Joe mutters between clenched teeth.

"Okay," Bella says, clipped.

"Bella," Coché says, "how are you feeling?"

"I think he has a negative view of life. If Tara were here, we'd say the same thing. We tell him something positive, and then it will turn into something negative. And we're like, where did that come from? I think if you're negative, then life turns out negative for you."

"So this really worries you," Coché says, bringing her back to the question she actually asked, which was how Bella was feeling.

"Yeah," Bella says, her voice high.

"And it frustrates you."

"I'm very frustrated. I don't know, I just feel like there's a negative pattern that's not success building." Joe didn't have to quit his job, she goes on, but he said he wanted to leave the law, to do something entre-preneurial, so she and Tara urged him to join them. Now he's moaning about the restaurant, but when Bella's father tells Joe he's "insane" not to snap up a well-paying legal job that he was offered in his new home-town, Joe's like, I'm happy to be running something for a change. So which is it? Bella turns to Joe, seated next to her. "You have to say like, what are you going to be happy with? When are you going to find your own happiness? How are you going to define success? How are you going *to be* a success?"

The group is quiet, a little stunned by the rat-a-tat-tat ferocity of Bella's achievement ethic, and confused about the couple's conflicting stories.

It's a shame, Coché says, changing the subject, that the pair did not "sit down calmly as a couple" in the first instance and talk about whether it was wise for Bella to join Tara's business. *What?* Bella quit her job, moved to another city, and sank her (their?) money into a start-up company but never discussed it with Joe? Nobody asks for clarifica-tion—and Bella and Joe don't volunteer any.

It's getting time for the next couple to take the floor, and the oth-ers, intentionally or not, are trying to give Joe and Bella a gentle send-off. Marie says she's happy that they're hashing out this matter early in the marriage, so resentment won't build up as it has between her and Clem.

"Is the baby kind of like a very bright light, amongst all this other stuff that's going on?" Rachael asks. (Oh, that's right, Bella is pregnant.)

"Perhaps wishful thinking on your part?" Coché says to Rachael, before Bella or Joe has a chance to respond. Rachael's pale cheeks redden.

"All I can say, Joe, is I feel for you," Clem says. "I had trouble making a change of careers. I can see you're doing a good job and want things too perfect and you're stressing yourself out."

"You can remember being in this place, with your baby on the way?" Coché says to Clem.

"I got laid off, and I couldn't make ends meet."

"That's the other thing right now," Joe says. "The restaurant has to work. It's our only source of income. She's got some deals in the pipeline, but until they close . . ."

"Yeah, that's a lot of stress," Coché says.

Bella rolls her eyes.

"Bella, do you see that differently?" Coché asks.

"I do, that's fine."

"Okay," Coché says, "but you—"

"I can't live, I can't live—"

"When your eyes look upward, then it's clear that you're feeling contemptuous."

"Okay, got that." Bella laughs.

"You were saying—"

"I just don't live in that kind of world." Now the disdain is in Bella's tone.

Sue Ellen quietly interjects that she's worried about leaving Bella and Joe in such churning antipathy.

"We won't have a huge argument. We'll just talk it through," Bella says. They will, because she says they will. Bella is finished showing the raw spots in her marriage. "I mean," she says, "my biggest concern about being married to Joe is like having to be the motivation, having to carry that all the time. And I'm really proud that he's here, and sharing, because I think he needs to build skills—"

"Who are you proud of?" Coché asks, cutting her off.

"I'm proud of Joe." Bella pauses for a split second—does she hear how condescending she sounds? Apparently not. "Yeah, I'm proud of Joe for the work that he's doing."

"Guess what," Coché says, trying to push Bella off her high horse, "maybe what you feel is relieved."

"Relieved about what?" Bella asks.

"Relieved that Joe is here working."

"Oh," Bella says airily, "I don't necessarily experience that."

"You don't feel relieved?" Coché says skeptically. "How important is it to *you* that you carry less weight, because you're describing yourself as carrying a lot?"

"I'll make it either way," Bella pronounces, and you almost expect her to break out in song, "I Will Survive." She's Gloria Gaynor crossed with Ayn Rand, or maybe it's success guru Stephen *Seven Habits* Covey. "Because I have a totally different view of life. My money will kick in at the end of August, September, and then I'll be successful at this new career, and then we won't have to worry ever again for the rest of our lives."

Could she be right? The particulars of her business are vague, and she sounds grandiose, but who knows? Maybe Bella is a tycoon in the making—she has the prestigious MBA. Outside the group, Michael has said he's rather in awe of Bella and Joe. "They're motivated, educated—they're real go-getters," he says. Back in the group, it's Joe's turn to keep mum.

When I sat with Sue Ellen and Mark, talked with them about how they met and married, I was a little envious of how simple and sweet their courtship was. In the snapshots of their wedding, Mark in particular looks very young, a tall boy in a black tuxedo. His hair is tousled curls, his cheeks are rosy, his grin a puckish overbite. Sue Ellen, in a picture taken just as the couple starts their first dance, looks straight into the camera, her smile reaching her eyes. She's wearing a white Victorian dress, with a high neck, a sheer panel that scoops partway down her chest and back, and tight sleeves that turn flouncy at the wrists, emphasizing her small hand against Mark's back. Lightly tanned, she looks pretty, happy. And I see a straight line—a golden thread—between the couple's early days and the "palpable connection" that the group notices almost three decades later.

Just as I interviewed Sue Ellen and Mark outside of the group about how they got together, I speak with the other couples, and I'm struck by how Leigh and Aaron's story, and Bella and Joe's, reverberate with their current troubles.

The first thought that occurs to Leigh when I ask what she remembers about meeting Aaron is: "I remember he was extremely anxious, even more so than he was later, actually." Their first date was in a café; Leigh responded to an ad Aaron placed in a local magazine. "He'd just come from the dentist, and he said he was petrified of all that." In the next sentence, she discloses that she also was charmed by the affection he expressed for his three children, and the lengths to which he went to share custody with his ex-wife in an era when that wasn't common. The anxiety came first, however.

For their second date, Aaron asked her to go to a New Year's Eve party at a friend's home in an exclusive suburb. Leigh wasn't sure how she wanted to spend the holiday. She knew she didn't want to stay home—it had been two years since her first husband's death—but she couldn't decide among three invitations: a gathering at a relative's house, a singles event, or the party with Aaron. "I thought, Well, I'll go to the party. How bad can it be? Nice house, interesting people to talk to. So, it didn't really have that much to do with Aaron."

Although I speak with him separately, Aaron offers an almost identical rendition of their early days. First he mentions his jittery reaction to the dentist, though not as a harbinger of his deeper anxieties, then recalls how pleased Leigh was at his devotion to his children. Finally, he says he'd been one of three New Year's options for Leigh, as a point of pride, however. "She had three choices, and she chose me." That's all Aaron has to say, before he launches into the present "challenges" between them.

As for Bella and Joe, they were set up by a mutual friend, and Bella had to cancel and reschedule a couple of times before their first date, which actually was useful, she tells me. "I have this really crazy schedule. So I was just, like, this is what my life is like, so if you can't deal with it . . ." When the date night finally arrived, Bella was coming from work to meet Joe. "I changed the time, like, I was being so anal," she says, laughing at herself. "Like I said, okay, nine o'clock; no, I'm sorry, nine-fifteen, and then, okay, it's gonna take me ten minutes to get there in the cab. Maybe I should say like nine twenty-five. Joe goes: 'How about nine-thirty?' He was probably thinking, What a psycho . . ."

Actually, he was scurrying around changing separate dinner reservations he'd made. This was a tactic Joe had used before for first dates. He'd make multiple reservations and then ask his date, impromptu, what kind of food she preferred. She'd pick, and then they'd just glide into some fancy boîte and instantly be seated. It would look like Joe was a big shot—he could get a table anywhere.

So from the beginning there was an element of facade in Joe's presentation of himself, and from the beginning Bella was blaring that she was committed to her work and living at a breakneck pace.

Couples researchers, interestingly, use a more formal version of the interviews I conducted not to predict the substance of future conflicts but to get a bead on the current state of marital affairs, almost like a diagnostic test. Videotaped "oral history interviews," as they're called, were developed in the Seattle "love lab" of psychologist John Gottman, a University of Washington professor emeritus who's far and away the most celebrated marital researcher in the country.

"In happy marriages, couples tend to look back on their early days with fondness," writes Janice Diver, once a student of Gottman's, who summarized his two decades of work for an academic book called *Normal Family Processes*. "In a distressed marriage, the wife is more likely to recall that her husband was 30 minutes late to the ceremony. He, in a similar way, may focus on all the time she spent talking to his best man and may even speculate that she was flirting with him."

Unhappy couples' descriptions also "lack appropriate detail," the videotapes show, and spouses don't interrupt each other to fill in or embellish the picture—in contrast, for example, to the easy banter that characterized Mark and Sue Ellen's recounting of the beginning of their romance. (By the way, the determination that a couple is "unhappy" is made by standard instruments like the Marital Dyadic Adjustment

Scale. Since the oral history interview is also a diagnostic test, the enterprise definitely has circular aspects.)

The oral history interview is rooted in cognitive theory suggesting that people under duress exhibit an unwitting "perceptual bias." So unhappy couples would be expected to rewrite their marital stories, to selectively attend to the discord and disappointments, and effectively forget the happier moments. Which is precisely what the investigators have discovered.

Another compelling example of perceptual bias comes from a study in which researchers went into people's homes and recorded their interactions, then asked the spouses to say what happened while the tape was running. The unhappy couples underreported the number of pleasurable moments between them, as rated by neutral coders, by as much as 50 percent. Further, in one of Gottman's "apartment lab" studies, where couples are periodically videotaped over twenty-four hours in a homey environment, distressed wives interpreted their husbands' humor and affection, as well as anger, more negatively than their relatively content counterparts.

Valerie Manusov, another University of Washington relationship researcher, in the department of communication, explains how the mind of the miserably married man, or woman, might work, faced with a kind deed or word from a spouse: "What's up—why is she doing all these nice things all of a sudden? She probably just had a good day at work, and tomorrow she'll be back to nonstop complaining." Or, worse, "She's *never* this generous—what is she trying to hide?" In the language of cognitive attribution theory, the unhappily married tend not to ascribe positive behavior to their partners' innate goodness but to fleetingly specific circumstances, factors that are "external" to them. (The opposite holds for the decoding of negative behaviors: He acted like such a jerk because he *is* a jerk, was always a jerk, and will never stop being a jerk—the jerkiness is "global, stable, and internal" to the man she married.)

Compounding the problem is that spouses are more likely to *reciprocate* each other's negative moods or behaviors—to respond to a frustrated groan with a smirk, for instance—than they are to reciprocate positive ones—to respond to a kind hello with a smile. It seems to be part of human nature to gloss over small positive interchanges, to take them for granted, Manusov says, which might be an example of healthy entitlement if it weren't so self-defeating. The implications of such patterns are daunting. Positive spirals are as hard to start as negative cycles are to break, which means that in a tainted setting, there exists a certain impossibility of doing good. Or, at the least, rising out of the marital trough once you're in it is not for the fainthearted.

CHAPTER 6

──────────────

The No-Cry Rule

(and How Sex Is Like Croutons)

During the family role-play weekend, Michael opened a tantalizing window into his childhood, judging from the anguish that welled up in him. Here was someone who'd remained petrified of his father well into his teenage years, whose memory suggested he felt demeaned if not abandoned by the man—less important to him than a rusted hunk of metal. In the month following, however, it was as if the scene had never happened. While Joe and Bella gave a glimpse of why they'd signed up for couples therapy, unspooling starkly opposed portrayals of the restaurant and their finances, Michael and Rachael, sharing their customary spot on the couch, said little. They had that vacation to get to, and while she seemed slightly preoccupied, he looked positively bored, when he wasn't sneaking catnaps.

"Michael, I'm wondering how you're doing?" Coché asked at one point.

"Oh, I'm fine, fine."

"Because sometimes people are sleepy because they're tired, and sometimes they're sleepy because they're upset."

"This is strictly tired. It's okay." He laughed, his short, habitual laugh.

The only real interchange between Michael and Rachael came near the end, after all the other couples had spoken. They had to contribute *something*. Rather sheepishly, Rachael told Michael she'd like him to do some "work" with the stamp his family had left on him. The immediate reason for her request was that she believed Michael's past had something do with his inability to see a way out of his deadening retail job. His career dissatisfaction was the main problem the couple had presented so far. Rachael was especially interested in pursuing the topic because Michael recently had done some psychological testing at Coché's urging. He'd discovered he was quite intelligent (which no one but him had doubted) but also that he was virtually unwilling, in test parlance, to "modify his environment," a product perhaps of something else that turned up on the personality inventory: a dearth of confidence.

Michael turned instantly peevish when Rachael mentioned his parents. "I think it's strange that Rachael's concerned about it, because my family doesn't really come up between us, whereas she's concerned about hers a lot. It feels like it would be more useful talking about *your* family." (Rachael had already talked about her parents that day, actually—about how desperate she'd been for her father's affection, how as a result she "ran straight into the arms of the first man who was nice" to her, her first husband.)

"I'm"—Rachael paused, as if searching for a delicate way to continue—"very aware that you are good at avoiding, and I'd like to see you—"

"But that's more about me than my family," Michael protested.

Coché seemed to think Rachael was onto something, but she was indisposed to pursue it without acquiescence from Michael. She kept asking his permission to proceed, and saying that she preferred not to do therapy "without a contract" with her client. He acceded to continuing while simultaneously sputtering about the futility of revisiting the past. Coché nodded, lips pursed, venturing only, "I'm wondering if there's some piece of you that doesn't know how to look deeply into yourself."

Although Coché is an instigator, she rarely flies straight at anyone's so-called resistance. "It's respecting people's sense of timing," she says, "their sense of their own movement." More abstractly, she tries to keep in mind that efforts to hold on to what's known, on to some sense of stability of self, is part (though certainly not all) of what defines mental health. In an academic article on resistance Coché wrote in the early 1990s, she quoted this passage from existentialist psychologist James Bugental: "Perceptions of the psychotherapy client's 'resistance' as being . . . neurotic or as being something which must be overcome, analyzed away, or circumvented—such perceptions themselves are countertherapeutic . . . Our lives, our well-being require that we maintain a measure of continuity in our way of living."

The fourth group is held on a Sunday in mid-August. It is finally hot on the Jersey shore, and the air conditioner is whirring. Behind the sealed windows, the seagulls' cries are faint, the accompaniment to somebody else's summer day. There is another coleader today, a local "life coach" whose height, sturdy frame, and broad-planed face make her look like Coché, the blond version. Like sex therapist Slowinski before her, however, this woman will not end up contributing much. To keep the group affordable for people like Marie and Clem, who soon will be paying college tuition for both their daughters, Coché did not hire a full-time coleader this year. The occasional guests aren't clicking, however. There *are* therapists who can make powerful cameo appearances—at conferences through the years, I've seen terrific live demonstrations from some of the profession's leaders (supertherapists?)—but Coché's partners aren't those people. They seem more like foils that reflect her own luster, platitudinous Ed McMahons to her incisive Johnny.

August's theme is "Pirates of the Self," or how people sabotage their own efforts to get what they want, which is really an invitation for the group to talk about whatever, and they do. Today will be Michael and Rachael's unveiling. The group knows little about them so far other than that they both had dubious childhoods and prior divorces, that they're physical ballasts for each other—the couch seats three, and they're the couple who always claims it—and that Michael is professionally frustrated.

Michael starts. For the better part of a year, he and Rachael discussed his buying a motorcycle. Despite her fear for his safety,

Rachael had eventually signed off on it, provided he make various concessions such as getting a less powerful bike than he'd planned. Then, the day Michael was to actually purchase the coveted machine, Rachael started fretting about the money. "And I just withdrew, just like my [psychological tests] predicted I'd do," Michael tells the group. "To keep the peace, I decided, you know what, it's just not that important."

He knew it wasn't really about money, Michael says, because he and Rachael had a similar conflict before: He "loves" to ride roller coasters, they scare the wits out of her, and so he'd had to drag her on them during a vacation at Disney World. As for the motorcycle, "She had plenty of examples of her brothers coming off bikes, of my friends coming off bikes, but no one had been killed or seriously hurt. Just the fact that it could happen was enough. It can be physical risk, financial risk, emotional risk." (Michael is the big risk taker? The guy who's stayed in the same job for the last fifteen years?)

"It hurts when you talk about it like that," Rachael says to her husband.

"Anybody understand why Rachael is hurt hearing Michael talk about it 'like that'?" Coché asks. "Because this is something that Michael is not doing on purpose, but it's important."

"I can tell you," Rachael says. "He talks about it like it's no big deal, like get over it, but there are real feelings here, and, I don't know, you talk about it so . . . nonchalantly."

" 'Clinically' is the word I would use," Michael corrects. The group shudders—who is this prig?

Rachael doesn't react; she is noncombative by temperament, and she also seems vaguely under Michael's thumb, which is odd. Michael, so overtly pliable he almost seems rubber-limbed, doesn't seem the controlling type.

Coché suggests that the couple is falling into old patterns: Rachael is chastising herself for being too emotional and "overreacting," echoing her parents' criticism of her; Michael is abruptly dropping his motorcycle dreams, capitulating rather than facing his wife's disapproval and distress—echoing precisely what from his childhood Coché either does not know or does not say.

How do you feel about Rachael's hesitancy over your riding a motorcycle? Coché asks.

Michael seems confused. He already forswore the bike, he says.

But how do you *feel* about that? Coché asks.

"Hmm-mmm," Michael says. "I'm kind of grudgingly saying, 'All right, if you feel that way, then I will not do this,' but I'm not happy about it."

"So how you're *not* feeling is happy," Coché says. Touché. Combing through Michael's utterances for a feeling is turning out to be sweaty work.

"How I'm *not* feeling is happy," Michael repeats, with a bray of a laugh. He pushes the hair from his face. He has no idea how he can change Rachael's mind, and he won't do anything she doesn't want him to do.

"Can you ask a different question?" Coché says. "Can you ask yourself how you can handle your resentment in a way that might move you both forward?"

"I don't know how to handle my—" Michael will not say he has resentment: He will not, he will not, he will not. "Because it seems very unfair that I have to limit myself over someone else's feelings, when this is pretty low-scale stuff. This is not bungee jumping or jumping out of planes." (Motorcycles are safer than bungee jumping and skydiving? As any decent couples therapist will tell you, it doesn't pay to factually parse most marital disputes—listen for the music, the atonal patterns.) "She doesn't want me to ride a bike, so I just won't think about it anymore, because it'll drive me crazy. But I can't go through my life voiding out things that are not met with approval."

"Say that last sentence again," Coché instructs.

He does, dutifully.

"So will you do some thinking on the times in your life that you have voided out experiences because they weren't met with approval?" Coché asks.

Michael nods. "Sometimes I think it would've been better if my early upbringing was more unstable, because it would have made me bolder. I'm just being my mother: Things aren't good, but just cope with it."

"How stable is that, Michael?" Coché asks, laughing raspily. "Stable is giving you the freedom to figure out who you are and make the most of yourself."

"If my childhood weren't so static," Michael tries.

"Stable is giving you wings," Coché continues.

"If it wasn't so static, never changing. It was always the same."

"That sounds more like 'limiting' than stable."

"Okay, okay," Michael says, irked. "If it wasn't so *limiting*."

"Then maybe you wouldn't be so angry when your wife limited you."

Sounds like a wrap—they've been on this for close to an hour—but no, Rachael has something else. "Irrespective of all that you're saying, at some point I expect Michael to just go and do what he wants."

"What you don't know," he says, not without compassion, "is that I won't."

"So you're accustomed to not having anybody care what you think, not taking you seriously," Coché says to Rachael, who starts to quietly cry.

"I mean, I was angry at her about the whole motorcycle thing," Michael says, apropos of nothing, "and then she brought up the money, and I kinda threw it back in her face, 'cuz she told me with her ex, there was this six-thousand-dollar chessboard that she purchased. And I'm like, I'd get a lot more utility out of a motorcycle. Are you riding around on the chessboard today?" Michael is prattling.

"Can I just stop you for a moment?" Tears are streaming from Rachael's eyes, and Coché wearily rubs her own face, as if trying to massage a thought into being. "If one of you were weeping with the knowledge that people had not taken you seriously in the past," she says to the group, "and weeping because here was a person who was actually taking you seriously, and you were just overwhelmed with the emotion of it, how would you want your partner to handle it?"

"I'd want them to understand, and, uh," Clem says, after a pause.

"And to relate to my emotions right now," Leigh says.

"Put their hand on my knee?" I blurt. Rachael looks utterly forlorn, while Michael is making no motion to comfort her—it's wrenching to watch. Pliability, apparently, should not be confused with empathy. ("I have seen couples in therapy who create a regime of terror through the use of saintliness, rationality . . ." begins one of my favorite sentences, in one of my favorite books about marriage, the aforementioned *Intimate Terrorism,* by therapist Michael Miller.)

"Do you know what's going on next to you, Michael?" Leigh demands. She is the only member of the group who could be described as quick-tempered. Marie exudes rage, yes, but hers is of the oceanic, icily controlled variety. (As for me, I hold myself back in the group owing to my role, which is probably good isomorphic practice for my marriage. My combative side is, if anything, overdeveloped.)

"Do I kn—" Michael begins.

"There's a small flood going on," Rachael says, smiling wanly at Michael. She is reflexively trying to save him: from Leigh, from the group, from his frozen-eyed, Gumby self.

Michael laughs. For now, he's beyond rescue. "You told me many times to ignore your crying," he says, looking into Rachael's pink-rimmed eyes.

"I know, because you just can't deal with it."

"I hate to see her—"

"Whoa," Coché says. "Where does it say in the map of Michael that he does not have the capacity to deal with his wife's crying? When did we give him this permanent disability?"

"'Cuz he told me he couldn't," Rachael says in a small voice.

"That's accurate," Michael says. "I told her whenever she starts to cry, I can't reason anymore."

"Maybe that's okay," Coché says.

"Okay not to reason?" It's like Coché told him it was okay not to breathe.

"Maybe a lot of people get upset when their partners start to cry, and they're not able to reason."

"That's usually my signal, though, to . . . just to stop where I am."

"And do what?" Coché asks.

"Just let it drop."

"And I don't—I don't like that," Rachael says.

"It's hurtful to me to see you cry," Michael bleats.

"Is that the best you can *do?*" Leigh says. The group bursts into laughter—Leigh is old enough to be Michael's mother, and she's letting him have it.

"I really don't think this is funny," Leigh says. "I'm very, it's very upset—" I'm guessing Michael is reminding Leigh of Aaron, how when she cries he seems to go deaf.

"It's not funny, Leigh," Coché says placatingly. "It's the straightforward way you're handling it. That's why everybody was giggling."

"Take Rachael around, please," Leigh orders. She wants Michael to put his arm around his wife.

"All right," Michael says, "for you, Leigh." He smirks.

"For *me*. Oh my God," Leigh says.

"Well," Michael retorts, "I think Rachael and I actually sit close to each other all of the time. I mean, we're usually touching, compared to . . . others." He notices, too.

"You're angry at what Leigh just said?" Coché asks.

"No, I'm not angry," Michael says. What calamity does he think will befall him if he admits a negative feeling? (In the third session, Coché said to Michael: "While you're here, if you have a difference of opinion with me, could you get into a big argument with me about it?" "It'd be difficult for me to do," Michael replied.) "I just think Leigh is misunderstanding that when we're having a serious discussion, we aren't . . . touchy-feely, you know. You want me to comfort her, but I don't think it's appropriate."

"Well, in some way I want you to show that you're relating to how upset she is," Leigh pleads, "because I haven't really sensed it or seen it."

"What I do sometimes is say something ridiculous, change the subject to make it funny," Michael says.

"Because?" Coché asks. Leigh's face has taken on its judgmental pout—what more can she say to the guy?

"Because it's painful," Michael says.

"Painful to?"

"Me," Michael replies.

"Yes, I know to you," Coché says, "but painful to *do* what?" Coché answers her own question: It's painful, she tells Michael, to stay in the moment when Rachael is suffering.

"Yeah, it's painful," he says.

We're about a third of the way through the year, and most of the meetings, I've come to see, star one or two couples, although at the beginning of each session there is usually a plan to divide up the time equally. The couples who are "off" for the day don't recede altogether. They give updates or offer an easily contained disagreement, like film shorts before the feature. Bella and Joe are on for a quickie today, and the story line is: All is well for them, once again.

"I'll go first," Bella says, when Coché asks for people to check in. "You guys weren't here last time," she says to Leigh and Aaron, "but Joe and I were kinda fighting, to be honest. Joe had gotten to a dark place." They saw Coché for an individual session, however, and since then, she says, "Joe has been saying some positive affirmations every day to me, three things he's grateful about, and it's really helping. And he did some research for the baby, which I can let him share, because he was cracking me up."

"That's wonderful," Leigh says. She and Aaron had missed Bella's pregnancy announcement.

"You can't be absent here," Coché says as the group gives Bella and Joe another round of congratulations.

"Yeah," Bella says, smiling broadly, "and we're dealing with finances, and my first deal is closing Tuesday. And I have another one closing in a month, so, by September or October, it should be resolved. And I'm loving what I'm doing. I'm so happy, like I just helped this woman buy a new house for her daughter; I'm helping another couple retire. I'm just . . . in love with what I'm doing."

Joe concurs that he's a new man. He's realized that he doesn't need to be at the restaurant twenty-four hours a day, and that no mishap is truly an emergency, a perspective motel manager Sue Ellen had advised in the last group. He's taken to blasting tunes and dancing with his cooks and waitstaff in the morning, to loosen them up. Then there are his affirmations, "thanks to my wife," he says. And in the same notebook where he scrawls three things he appreciates each day, he lists three things he must get accomplished. "When I'm done with them, I cross 'em off," Joe says. "You start a new day, you move the stuff you didn't get done to the next day." A particular wifely hand definitely has been at work in molding Joe.

"Do you blame yourself when you don't get something done?" Coché asks.

"No, but I gotta look and say, 'Why didn't I get it done?'" says Joe, whose eyes even have taken on a new cast in this group compared to last, from squinty to flinty. He's Bella's Howard Roark.

"Can you do that without blaming yourself?" Coché asks again.

"I think we're working on that part," Bella intervenes.

"Yeah, we're working on that part," Joe repeats (so amiably that no one in the group questions Bella's cringey use of "we"). When he's in a "down cycle," Joe explains, it's hard not to start beating himself up. Coché gave Joe a basic depression inventory when she met the couple outside of the group, and he'd tested in the borderline bluesy realm, but not as clearly depressed. To make sure that she wasn't missing anything diagnostically, she asked Joe to visit a psychiatrist for an assessment, but he had yet to make an appointment.

Now Coché suggests that if he can't accomplish all three of his goals, he should pick the most important one and ignore the rest. "Because when you're even a little bit depressed, your energy level is less, and I'm worried you're going to do a number on yourself about what you can't get done."

"Okay," Joe says.

"Dynamite!" Coché responds.

Joe's conversion seems suspect—too much, too soon, too like he'd donned a Bella suit whose buttons eventually would pop. But Coché seems to be on board—"Dynamite, Joe!"—so what does the group know? Later, when I'm having a glass of wine with her on the office's balcony, she says she's just "rolling" with Joe and Bella for the time being, and learning from them. "Joe does what he does, and Bella does what she does. They're demonstrating to us the way they try to maneuver their lives."

It occurs to me, too, that even if Coché believed that resistance was what Bella and Joe were putting up, she still might exclaim, "Dynamite!" In her article on the subject, Coché discusses Milton Erickson, famous for his hypnotherapy as well as his interventions with fully sentient patients. Many of Erickson's techniques were rooted in his desire to avoid the "polarity response," which says that when given a direction, the unconscious mind retorts: *Why should I?* To prevent the patient from becoming preoccupied with proving he's right, the therapist should "encourage" resistance so the "subject is thereby caught in a situation where his attempt to resist is defined as cooperative behavior," wrote Jay Haley, in a book he authored about Erickson called *Uncommon Therapy*. (Haley's strategy of telling people like the agoraphobic woman to continue their usual behavior was an Ericksonian special.) Erickson used the analogy of a river to make his point: "If [the therapist] opposes the river by trying to block it, the river will merely go over and around him. But if he *accepts* the force of the river and diverts it," a new channel will be cut.

But then maybe I should take Coché at face value. Maybe she doesn't know for sure what's going on with Bella and Joe, like the rest of the group. Thirty years and counting of hearing people's woes, Coché still conveys a genuine sense of curiosity about the people sitting in front of her. Again, Erickson comes to mind, specifically a conversation between him and Haley that almost takes the form of a Buddhist koan. Erickson believed in probing the past only to the degree that it bore on the resources the client could marshal in the present, and Haley asked him how he applied that principle in treating a woman with a severe handwashing compulsion.

"I didn't go into the cause or the etiology," Erickson said. "The only searching question I asked was 'When you get in the shower to scrub yourself for hours, tell me, do you start at the top of your head, or the soles of your feet, or in the middle? Do you wash from the neck down, or do you start with your feet and wash up? Or do you start with your head and wash down?'"

"Why did you ask that?" Haley pressed.

"So that she knew I was really interested."

"So that you could 'join her' in this?"

"No," Erickson said, "so that she knew I was *really interested.*"

Out on the balcony, Coché tells me that she imagines that the common ground Bella and Joe found—or rather Joe's emphatic jump onto Bella's plot of earth—won't hold. But she may be wrong; the affirmations and to-do lists could work, she says. If so? "Great." Coché shrugs her broad shoulders. "Then we don't need to pay any more attention to the problem."

• • •

At this stage, Marie and Clem are also swinging from low to (sort of) high, group to group. In the last session, following the one in which Clem's vasectomy had been at issue, Marie was full of good humor. She called Clem "honey," praised Sue Ellen as "wise" and a "mentor" to her, and laughed heartily, and kindly, at Clem's deadpan bluntness. Marie had been comparing her and Clem's relationship to Bella and Joe's—both women are the uncontested captains of their marital ships—and expressing sympathy for Clem. She worried that he'd "forfeited a lot of things that were very meaningful" to him in deference to her.

"For you?" Clem said. "Really? I thought I stayed pretty much the same, just got colder and harder."

The whole group hooted with laughter, none more than Marie. Tears were dripping from her eyes, she was laughing so hard. Clem put his hands up in bafflement, like, "What's so funny, woman?" (He calls Marie "woman" sometimes, and coming from him, old-school macho sounds unaccountably sweet.) Then Clem smiled sheepishly; he'd caught on to his own joke.

"I've never heard you wail with such laughter," Rachael said to Marie.

"But he said it to me with a straight face," Marie gasped.

That was then. This is now. In the fourth session, Marie and Clem are swinging low.

"You ask me for intimacy," Marie says to her husband, "the same way you ask if I'd like croutons on my salad." She speaks slowly, deliberately, each word chipping out of her mouth like an ax striking wood. "I don't hear the difference in the question."

"I guess I've tried so many ways, and nothing seems to—to . . . It doesn't seem like you hear me no matter how I say it," Clem says.

"If you did hear a difference, would you respond differently?" Coché asks Marie.

"Oh yeah," Marie says brightly.

"You would?" Coché sounds skeptical.

"Oh, most certainly."

"I'm—I'm—I'm not sure how to ask that way," Clem stammers. "What frustrates me is that you don't even have the want or desire to . . . I mean, if I ask you one day a month and the answer's always no, it gets frustrating. It's—it's . . ."

"Clem," Coché says, "you're saying it almost doesn't matter how I ask. Isn't that what you're saying?"

"Yes. I mean, I don't feel like I should have to raise my voice, or shake ya, 'Hey, come on, take some time out with me tonight.' Why would I want to work that hard or be that assertive to—to have someone spend time with me. You're talking about wanting to go back to school now, and I just see the rest of our [lives], down to the end, you never have the time or interest to be with me."

"Nor do you make it clear to me," Marie says, swatting away Clem's aching recognition of his mortality, "when you've reached the, what they call, 'tipping point.'" What, does the guy have to be crawling the ground on his hands and knees, begging for water, for Marie to quench his thirst?

"You know, some of this," Marie continues, "is about getting to the point where we can compromise, because I have my position clearer."

"Uh-huh," Coché says, putting her chin in her hand, and planting her feet firmly on the ground—here we go again. Marie is always invoking transparent "negotiation" as the cure for what ails her marriage. She clings to this cramped and cold way of expressing herself, it seems, because her major complaint about Clem is that he obdurately sticks to pleasantries, leaving her wrapped in a lonely gauze, at best, and at worst bewildered by his sudden claims of injury at some wrong she hadn't known she perpetrated. Her fervent desire is for Clem to tell her exactly where he stands.

So as the couple again hashes out their differences about sexual frequency, it seems less about the substance of the matter for Marie—less about a wish that her husband seduce her rather than offer croutons—and more like a set piece for her to demonstrate to him that he never talks straight to her.

"Some of it is getting to the point where we can compromise," Marie says. "So if he'd say something like, 'Marie, right now I'm lonely and need your company,' it would give me the opportunity to put everything down and go with you, to show you how much you mean to me."

"Why do you need to hear him sound like he genuinely wants and desires you?" Coché asks, trying to nudge the conversation away from the realm of State Department diplomacy. She wants the couple to acknowledge that neither is adept at expressing tenderness.

"It lets me know his position, first of all," Marie says—so much for Coché's nudging. "And it's a reminder to me that this may not be the natural way to go, but because it's Clem asking, I need to go that way."

"Could it be because you love him?"

"Yes, and, um . . ." Marie says.

"It's important to say that part."

"Okay, because I would love you."

She *would* love him.

CHAPTER 7

―――――――――――――

The Science of Marital Satisfaction

M y goal is to be like the guy who invented Velcro," marriage
researcher John Gottman once told an interviewer. "Nobody
remembers his name, but everybody uses Velcro." Gottman may well be
on his way—does any of the following sound familiar? For a marriage
to survive, couples must make five positive comments to every negative
one, *during a fight* (in everyday interactions, the ratio is twenty to one).
It's not whether couples fight but *how* they fight that matters. Those
who display contempt are in real trouble; the other "horsemen" are also
dangerous: criticism, stonewalling, and defensiveness. Because conflict
sparks strong physiological reactions in men (increased heart rate, blood
pressure), women should raise problems gently, avoid "harsh start-ups."
For a marriage to last, the husband must be able to "accept influence"
from his wife.

These conclusions—generated from videotaping couples discussing a contentious topic and classifying their verbal and nonverbal communication, second by second, using a twenty-point coding system
(-3 = disgust, -1 = anger, +4 = affection, etc.)—first burst onto the scene
in 1998. That's when Gottman and three colleagues published an article
in the *Journal of Marriage and Family* announcing that they'd tracked
newlyweds for six years and could predict with 83 percent accuracy
who would divorce simply from watching fifteen-minute conflict interactions in Gottman's now famous "love lab."

His accuracy later climbed to 95 percent—observing couples for an hour to predict their marital status fifteen years later—and over the next decade, his narrow bald head, fringed by a neat gray beard and topped by a discreet yarmulke, was everywhere. He and his powers of scientific prognostication were touted on *20/20* and the *Today* show, in *The New York Times Magazine* and *The Atlantic,* and in newspapers across the country. In 2005, he reached perhaps the apogee of his fame when he became part of Malcolm Gladwell's publishing juggernaut: the subject of a chapter in the bestselling *Blink,* which was about the knowledge gleaned from rapid, often unconscious cognitions. In a 2007 survey in *Psychotherapy Networker* magazine asking readers to select the ten most influential members of their profession over the last century, Gottman was the only one of four to make the cut who wasn't deceased, and, in his late sixties, the youngest of the still-breathing group by at least a decade. "Many in the field now believe that most of what we know about marriage and divorce comes from his work," states an article accompanying the top-ten list.

Coché is definitely acquainted with the Gottman canon. She mentions him by name, and factoids from his research pop up semi-frequently in her comments. The contempt that Coché highlighted in Bella, when she rolled her eyes at Joe, is straight from Gottman. She tells the women in the group, Leigh in particular, to beware of angry outbursts; because of their physiological sensitivity, husbands will hear a sharper attack than their wives perhaps intend. In a list of "Tips for Successful Couples" Coché put together for the group, one item is "ratio of 5 to 1 pleasurable to negative experiences," another is "willingness for both partners to be influenced by what their partner thinks."

As Gottman's acclaim has grown, I've many times thought that if we were brave enough—all of us marrieds and, most important, would-be marrieds—we'd take a trip to the love lab. We'd sit facing each other, video running, pulse sensors attached to our fingertips, discuss a problem for an hour, and come away knowing the awful or joyful truth. We'd know whether to marry or—no matter how good the relationship seemed in the present—whether to pull away and save ourselves (and any children) the future heartbreak. I imagine a chain of love labs around the country, scanning couples' marital chances like mammograms screen for breast cancer. True, a love-lab on every corner might leave Coché scrounging for work, but she wouldn't mind sacrificing for the greater good. If *only* we could be this practical, I think, this rational.

Then, for the first time I looked deeply into Gottman's research, and bit by bit, saw that there were reasons other than the antiscientific to think twice before trusting his formula—or anyone else's—to predict the outcome of your marriage. Beyond that, I realized that there is a complicated story behind some of the variables Gottman has decreed are either decisive or irrelevant in determining marital success. Some of his "science" is at times closer to extrapolated theory that happens to jibe with gender stereotypes.

Undeniably, Gottman has made enormous contributions to the study of marriage. When he and a handful of other research teams began videotaping people in conflict in the 1970s, it was revolutionary. Instead of just asking people how they argued or resolved disputes, a notoriously limited means of gathering information, researchers could see and hear them in action. A math major at MIT before he switched to psychology, Gottman developed a coding system that tracked not only the content of speech but the emotional messages that spouses send, evidenced by minute changes in facial expression, vocal tone, and body language. As Gottman wrote in a 1982 paper, "We think we know what a smile is. Most investigators have specified simply that the lip corners are up in a smile and that the mouth is shaped somewhat like a U. That will not do." Using facial recognition systems, Gottman's code accounts for the fact that, for instance, in "coy, playful, or flirtatious interactions," the lips are often turned down. "It looks like the person is working hard *not* to smile," he writes. Conversely, "many 'smiles' involve upturned corners of the mouth but are often indices of negative affect." Such meticulous parsing allowed Gottman to coin the phrase "negative affect reciprocity," because he saw, frame by frame, the vicious emotional circles that characterize clashing spouses.

The advances Gottman helped bring to his field weren't just methodological; they were conceptual. The earliest academic explorers of marriage, most of them sociologists, focused on mate selection: the personality characteristics of who married who, and from there, which pairs flourished (or not). To study the notion that it was the *relationship* that mattered meant stepping out of a framework in which individual characteristics determined marital outcomes and into the flow, or muddle, of couples interaction. "Two neurotics can be happily married," as family therapy leader Nathan Ackerman memorably put it. Gottman helped pioneer a rigorous means to capture what happened in the so-called in-between.

Gottman wouldn't have become a psychotherapy star, however, without his storied powers for predicting divorce. "He's gotten so good at thin-slicing marriages," Gladwell enthuses in *Blink*, "that he says he can be at a restaurant and eavesdrop on the couple one table over and get a pretty good sense of whether they need to start thinking about hiring lawyers and dividing up custody of the children."

Throughout the 1980s and 1990s, when Gottman and a small cadre of couple watchers were beginning to publish their findings, most studies floated risk factors for divorce or discontent but steered clear of making predictions. Then, in 1998, came the Gottman blockbuster, "Predicting Marital Happiness and Stability from Newlywed Interactions," in the *Journal of Marriage and Family*. It was promoted by a publicist (the first time the journal had hired one to do so), and was followed the next year by the even more astounding "Predicting Divorce Among Newlyweds from the First Three Minutes of a Marital Conflict Discussion."

So what does it mean to *predict* divorce? For the 1998 study, which focused on videotapes of fifty-seven newlywed couples, I assumed that Gottman had, in the first instance, sorted them into three groups— will divorce, will be happy, will be unhappy but still married—based on the conflict variables he believed distinguished marriages that last from those that don't (contempt, little positive affect, etc.). Then, at six years, he'd checked to see how right, or wrong, his predictions had been. That isn't how it worked. He knew the marital status of his subjects at six years, and he fed that information into a computer along with the communication patterns that turned up on the videos. Then he told the computer, in effect: Create an equation that maximizes the ability of my chosen variables to distinguish among the divorced, happy, and unhappy.

So what Gottman did wasn't really a prediction of the future but a formula built *after* the couples' outcomes were already known. Which isn't to say that developing such formulas isn't a valuable—indeed, a critical—first step in being able to make a prediction. The next step, however, one required by the scientific method, is to apply your equation to a fresh sample to see if it actually works. That is especially necessary with small data slices (such as fifty-seven couples) because patterns that appear important are more likely to be mere flukes. Why Gottman has never tried to replicate his work using an existing formula is puzzling, considering his large cache of videotaped couples. Each paper he's published heralding so-called predictions is based on a new post hoc equation.*

To understand why this isn't a prediction, start with the old saw "Hindsight is 20/20." Then imagine hearing that someone could "predict" the outcome of future football games based on analyzing what happened in a single game. In this game, the opponent's quarterback was named Roger, and he completed twenty passes, while the team's own quarterback was intercepted twice. "Aha," the not-so-astute researcher deduces, "when my team plays opponents with quarterbacks whose names begin with *R,* who complete twenty passes, and our quarterback throws two interceptions, we lose!" The point of this analogy isn't that Gottman's variables are trivial (like the first letter of the quarterback's name)—in fact, they're probably fairly powerful—but he hasn't come close to *predicting* who will divorce based on after-the-fact calculations.

Further, even to talk in terms of an equation's having an 80 percent "accuracy" rate is misleading—typically scientists simply report false-positive and false-negative rates, not accuracy—and inflates the real-world strength of his findings. Why? Because it ignores the natural prevalence of the event at issue, in this case, divorce. Taking the U.S. divorce rate into account—and assuming false-positive and -negative rates of 20 percent—Gottman's predictions would be right

---

*When I contacted Gottman in late May 2009 for an interview, his assistant e-mailed me that he was not available until October. His office never replied to my follow-up e-mail stating that I would need to talk to him by mid-July to meet my book deadline.

43 percent, or less than half, of the time.* So much for the love-lab business.

Richard Heyman, a psychology research professor at the State University of New York who wrote a 2001 *Journal of Marriage and Family* article showing the lie of divorce prophesizing, uses an analogy from the stock market to explain why predicting the future of any individual couple is so tough. "It's not like Gottman is just trying to take particular variables and predict what's going to happen to the S&P 500. He is using variables to say he can predict the outcome of *each* individual stock, with over 90 percent accuracy." It's seductive, Heyman says, to think that there are a few discrete factors—namely, how you communicate during a fight—that are going to "trump everything else in your life that might influence whether you'll get divorced or not." That way, you'd know what to concentrate on—if I can just do *this,* we'll be fine. (Conversely, I'll never be able to do that, so we're finished. The predictive nuggets can be pernicious, too, squashing any hope for, or effort toward, betterment.) There are some spheres in which you can tell a lot by knowing just a little—for example, SAT scores and high school grades have been shown to predict success in college far better than more detailed analyses that take into account variables like teacher recommendations. But so far marital relations haven't succumbed to such delightfully efficient approaches, no matter how forcefully Gottman or Gladwell declaim to the contrary.

---

*Here's how the math would work: Take 1,000 couples in the general population married three to six years (as Gottman's couples were), a group for which the prevalence of divorce is 16 percent. In other words, among any 1,000 American couples entering their third year of marriage, 160 will be divorced and 840 will still be married six years after their wedding.

Then suppose to get an overall accuracy rate of 80 percent, Gottman set the false-positive and the false-negative rate to be equal at 20 percent (which is a reasonable estimate, though all we can do is suppose because Gottman doesn't provide those figures in the 1998 paper). False negatives are couples who are divorced but the formula misses, so with a 20 percent false-negative rate, Gottman would call 32 couples married who were actually divorced (160 x .20). False positives are people whom the formula classifies as divorced who really aren't, so with a 20 percent false-positive rate, Gottman would call 168 couples divorced who were still married (840 x .20).

Finally, to gauge the accuracy of the prediction, first calculate how many total couples Gottman pegged as divorced. That number is 168 plus 128 (the sum of the false positives and the couples who were divorced that the equation did not miss). So Gottman would categorize 296 couples as divorced, but only 128 of those actually would be, yielding an accuracy rate of 43 percent.

Beyond the soothsaying, there has been debate within the field of psychology about other conclusions Gottman draws from his data. Take his bête noire, contempt. Based on his longitudinal data sets, Gottman has repeatedly declared, in his academic papers and in his popular books on couples, that anger doesn't harm marriage. What threatens the edifice are the pounding hooves of the "four horsemen" (of the marital Apocalypse—to finish Gottman's metaphor): contempt, criticism, stonewalling, defensiveness. Later, he added a fifth, belligerence. But as his chief critics, University of Denver family researchers Scott Stanley and Howard Markman, write: "After the codes for defensiveness, belligerence, criticism, contempt, and stonewalling absorb their variance in the coding system, what is really left to label as anger? Is it not 'angry' to be critical, belligerent, and contemptuous simply because different labels are chosen for the behavior?"

So what *is* innocuous anger—can we know it when we see it, or dish it out ourselves? It's something like, "Bob, it really makes me mad when you leave me to pick up after you," she said with her tone only slightly raised. You can probably imagine saying that alone in your kitchen or sitting at your desk. But now imagine it when Bob is in the room, and he doesn't respond *just right,* in exactly the way you subconsciously hope. And then imagine maintaining the relatively neutral content and flat tone for five minutes or ten minutes or more. Imagine not saying, "Bob, you treat me like the *maid*"—criticism. Or, "Bob, you're useless!"—contempt. Or, slamming poor Bob's cup down on the table and yelling, "God, Bob, you piss me off"—belligerence.

Bland, nonaccusatory anger (is "anger" even the right word for it?) seems like something to strive for, if only because, intuitively, certain iterations of the emotion seem more destructive than others. But "safe" anger is likely hard to pull off in the heat of the moment, which brings up an internal contradiction in the advice Gottman has spun from his labwork. In the 1998 study, he got heaps of attention for proclaiming that therapists should "abandon" efforts to teach couples active listening. "Husbands, forget all that psychobabble about 'active listening' and 'validation,'" was how the *Los Angeles Times* summed it up. Gottman's rationale was that not one of the twenty couples in his happy subset paraphrased their partner ("Bob, it sounds like you feel burdened, too"), or used I-statements ("I feel overwhelmed when the kitchen is a mess"), or validated a spouse's feelings ("Bob, honey, I understand why you're feeling attacked").

The logical fallacy in this, which Gottman acknowledges, is that just because happy couples don't do something doesn't mean that unhappy couples wouldn't benefit from a dose of it. (You don't give aspirin to people without headaches, as Stanley and Markman said.) But Gottman quickly bats away his own caveat, contending that active listening requires "emotional gymnastics" that shouldn't be expected of couples in conflict. The argument has merit—especially when active listening is considered in its most rigid, easily mocked form—but is Gottman's proposed alternative any easier? Is it any less of an emotional stretch to express anger without jumping on the back of a horse?

This all may smack of internecine bickering, and to some extent it is: Markham was one of Gottman's graduate students in the 1970s, and now presides over his own family research institute with Stanley. At the University of Denver, the pair is known for studying (and promoting) premarital education, a main component of which is, you guessed it, active listening. Stanley and Markman are respected by their colleagues but despite having done their own videotaping, and building their own small mountain of research, they aren't close to becoming Velcro.

Another bit that stuck from the 1998 study was that the happiest marriages are ones in which husbands "accept influence" from their wives. As Gottman good-naturedly complains in his book *The Seven Principles for Making Marriage Work,* that finding was reduced to "Anything you say, dear" and "parodied on *Saturday Night Live,* pilloried by Rush Limbaugh, and picked on by Bill Maher, the host of *Politically Incorrect.*" But comics are expected to mangle the truth, and in this case they might be excused: The pattern Gottman found in his happy couples and the plain-English meaning of "accepting influence" are two very different things.

To explain, what Gottman codes as "accepting influence" is simply when a videotaped husband responds to one of his wife's utterances with the same amount of or less negativity than she displayed. So if Bob grunted "uh-huh, I hear you" to his wife's entreaties about picking up after himself, that would be "accepting influence." He didn't "escalate the negativity." Or if Bob said to his wife, no more edgily than she'd said to him, "But I never had to pick up after myself as a kid," that, too, would be considered "accepting influence."

Gottman et al. wrote that they were "quite confident" of calling nonescalation "accepting influence" because of a dissertation on power in violent couples that had recently come out of their laboratory. Perhaps a single dissertation, and one about violent couples, was all it took for this inference to take hold (though one would hope not). Its seeds probably also can be found in Gottman and his fellow researchers' notions about male-female power dynamics; after all, Gottman has counseled hundreds and hundreds of couples over the years. But then it wouldn't do for the scientist to proffer advice based on his wealth of clinical experience. That's not the brand. As Gottman says in the *Seven Principles,* "Before the breakthroughs my research provided, [opinion] was pretty much all that anyone trying to help couples had to go on . . . Because until now there really hasn't been any rigorous scientific data about why some marriages succeed and others flop."

Gottman's beliefs about the natural proclivities of men and women also seem to influence what might be considered his "hardest" evidence: the readouts of the various cardio monitors hooked to the couples. Again and again, he observes that men are more physiologically responsive to stress and anger than women, and take longer to recover. The source of the difference is our "evolutionary heritage," Gottman says. Because their role was to hunt and protect, males whose "adrenaline kicked in quite readily and who did not calm down so easily were more likely to survive and procreate"—while females awash in calming hormones, which spur milk production, won the natural-selection sweepstakes. This male hormonal surge is maladaptive for modern living and explains why in "85 percent of marriages, the stonewaller"—the one who shuts down or flees the fight—"is the husband."

Yet the vast preponderance of the data suggests that *wives* are more physiologically reactive than husbands and take longer to return to baseline. Jan Kiecolt-Glaser, a professor of psychiatry and psychology at Ohio State University, and her molecular virologist/immunologist husband Ronald Glaser, are perhaps the world's experts on physiology and relationships. "There is no evidence that men have maladaptive arousal during arguments, but there is good evidence that women do," Jan says matter-of-factly. "The pattern is very clear across measures." By this she means that whether researchers have looked at increases in blood pressure and heart rate, or stress hormones like adrenaline and cortisol, or declines in immune-system proteins like cytokines, wives are the ones whose bodies most dramatically register, and suffer from, arguments.

And, in fact, Kiecolt-Glaser says, as far as she knows, Gottman has never actually published any data comparing the physiology of husbands and wives during or after hostilities. The cardiovascular finding he cites in his 1998 study, for one, is far narrower than his commentary might suggest: It's that in happy, stable marriages, the husband's heart rate declines in those moments when either he or his partner moves to mute a conflict, when one of them jokes, for example, or says something affectionate. That's all.

Now, it could be that husbands are more *psychologically* undone by anger than their wives, meaning, despite relatively low levels of physical arousal, men freak out (the colloquialism seems perfect) and want to escape or explode when a fight gets going. But that's not Gottman's line. And Kiecolt-Glaser believes the psychological and physiological are tightly linked, anyway. Her reasoning is that since female identity is more dependent on close relationships than male identity, wives are the ones who are both more attuned to marital strife and more threatened by it. So maybe Gottman's advice should be turned on its head: Husbands, raise issues gently so as not to stress your physiologically impressionable wives. That recommendation would never take, though, would it? It's too countercultural. As Kiecolt-Glaser says, "Women are supposed to be the caregivers—no matter what."

The conceit of the prehistoric male, adapted to warring with beasts and left frothing at smaller, weaker humans, evokes an idée fixe of another marriage guru but one who is the antithesis of everything Gottman stands for. That is John Gray, the author of *Men Are from Mars, Women Are from Venus,* who is notorious for his *lack* of scientific cred. In sixteen books and counting, Gray opines that when men (or Martians) are stressed, they need to retreat to their caves—it's a biological impulse—and that Venusians must learn to "make peace" with that. (Husbands need to understand that frazzled women can't, well, shut up.) Gray also is one of the chief floggers of perhaps the most popular idea *ever* in the history of coupledom: Men are driven to fix problems, women to commiserate, to identify.

This takes us past Gottman—almost. Linda Roberts, a University of Wisconsin marital researcher who as a graduate student coded tapes for Professor Gottman, has investigated the husbands-are-fixers/wives-are-empathizers dichotomy herself, in her own observational lab, and she's also reviewed the work of her colleagues who've done the same. There is little if any proof for it, she says. Now, *that's* a shocker.

At least at first. When you pause—clear your befogged head of the Martians and Venusians, push aside pop linguist Deborah Tannen and her aggrieved spouses who "just don't understand"—different shapes and forms appear. In the group, granted, Clem in the first session said fixing was more comfortable for him than listening, and Michael used the fixer conceit to excuse his intolerance for Rachael's crying: "You know, it's just how men are." (Coché, noticeably, did not second his biological determinism.) But Mark and Joe—and Clem and Aaron, to some degree—regularly sympathize with their wives. Not with elaborate verbiage, maybe, but with a few caring words, or a look of concern. Their wives do no more. And do Bella, Marie, and Leigh sound any less eager to solve their husbands' problems than the men do theirs? I myself tell the group that once when my husband was in a funk, I suddenly became aware of what a monumental effort it was for me merely to put my arm around his shoulder and murmur sympathetically. We were sitting on a park bench, and I was pretty sure that reassurance and affection were all he wanted, but as one, then two minutes passed, the words kept rising up in me: "Here, Tim, do this. Everything will be better if you just do x, y, and z." (Thankfully, however, I kept quiet.)

The informal observation of me and five couples does not a study make, but it's interesting how easy it is to forget, or ignore, the images that do not conform to our stereotypes. Because our partners' ills make us anxious, Coché believes that men and women alike share a "fix-it" reflex, she tells the group. "Fix-it" usually translates into "eliminate it," she says. "We just want our husband or wife's problems to"—Coché swats the air with the back of her hand—"go away." Just like I wanted to slap a Band-Aid on my husband's woes, pat his butt, and send him off to keep conquering the world.

The studies in which Linda Roberts has examined this matter fit into the next generation of couples observational research. Gottman trained his scientific eye only on quarreling husbands and wives, she says in an interview, which was "wonderful" but limited. "We only had one paradigm for assessing natural interaction between partners: the conflict paradigm," Roberts says. "So we learned a lot about how happy versus unhappy couples fight, and what some of the repair mechanisms are, but not how they do much else. There was a period where research-ers were actually saying, 'Well, we know intimacy doesn't really matter. It's about how you resolve conflict.'"

What Roberts has tried to develop is an experiment to elicit "affectional feelings in the lab," as she writes in one paper. It hasn't been easy: "Our first attempt piloting the task involved instructing partners to think about, and then discuss, 'why I love my partner.' However, we found it necessary to broaden the instructions." Some people, particularly those who scored as distressed on a marital adjustment test, couldn't answer the why-I-love-him (or her) ques-tion, and became unnerved. Think of Marie. (Could it be that one reason you want to have sex with Clem is that you love him? Coché asked her. "Yes, and um . . ." Marie replied. "It's important to say that part," Coché said. "Okay," Marie said, "because I would love you.")

So Roberts simply asked couples to talk about "positive feelings" for one another. She also devised a second task, in which spouses were asked to share vulnerabilities, "things that we feel insecure about, things we don't like about ourselves . . ."

Roberts can't yet make grand pronouncements about the differences between how happily and unhappily married people intimately relate— she had to develop a brand-new code to rate the love and vulnerability interactions, for one thing. But both her women and men were just as likely to display vulnerability, show care, try to interpret their spouses' utterances, practice active understanding (a broader version of active listening), and give guidance (positive or neutral fix-it behavior) or intrusive advice (domineering or presumptuous fix-it behavior). The only intimacy category in which women scored higher than men was in directly complimenting their spouses.

There are similarities, Roberts says, in the misapprehensions about men's physiological sensitivity and the fixer/empathizer myth. Studies outside of romantic relationships show that men *are* more physiologically reactive than women to many stressors—to loud street sounds, for example. Likewise, in studies of men and women gabbing with people who *aren't* their spouses, women open up more than men and share vulnerabilities. It is only the data focused on couples, itself not vast, that has run contrary to that: "No significant differences in emotional disclosure," Roberts writes.

To come full circle, Roberts turned up "active understanding"— encompassing the simple paraphrasing and restatements that character- ize active listening as well as words or gestures that convey emotional availability and a "deeper understanding of partners' feelings"—in a full 93 percent of the interactions. So though Gottman found none of it in his squabbling subjects, she found a whole lot of it in men and women who were trying to connect, which makes some sense.

While Gottman's call to banish active listening may have been a bit of a publicity stunt, Roberts acknowledges the method can be ill used: "What we don't want is to teach impression-management, to teach couples to give the *impression* that they're listening." This reminds me of how Aaron seems merely to mouth the active-listening script, though he doesn't seem to be intentionally manipulating Leigh, just protecting himself.

"Active listening," "active understanding," they're pallid, uninspir- ing phrases—their importance made most poignant by their absence, which group member Michael would dramatically demonstrate later in the year in what I came to consider his Dukakis moment. (Interviewer, to presidential hopeful Michael Dukakis, in a 1988 debate: "If [your wife] were raped and murdered, would you favor an irrevocable death penalty for the killer?" Dukakis, coolly: "No, and I think you know that I've opposed the death penalty during all of my life . . ." Not a word of suffering or outrage on behalf of poor Kitty.)

Having to field a "gotcha" hypothetical with the whole country watching, Dukakis may be forgiven for his omission. From her video library of couples spilling their guts, Roberts pulls out a situation that is more typical, and all the more tragic for its infernal everydayness, its lack of apparent maliciousness. It features a mute husband, and a wife who strikes out like a wounded animal when her spouse doesn't empathize with her vulnerability.

> **WIFE:** Mine is my weight, you know that. I'm very insecure . . . Every time I walk into a room I know they're talking about me. I know those people are talking about me because I'm fat.
> **HUSBAND:** (No response, twelve seconds, but looks at her kindly) So . . .
> **WIFE:** I wonder, you know, if the people really like me, personally.
> **HUSBAND:** Are you talking about your friends?
> **WIFE:** So-called.
> **HUSBAND:** (No response, for ten seconds)
> **WIFE:** (Challengingly, flicking a pencil at him) Even *you.*

In a couples group this husband and wife, ideally, would get busted for this gnarly exchange. (Or, in less pugnacious terms, they'd be made aware of its destructive dynamics.) So far, however, the ten members in Coché's group have been rather cautious with each other. Leigh's roughing up of Michael in the last group—her order for him to put his arm around his teary wife—stands out for her unconcealed exasperation.

Coché isn't surprised by the group's general politeness; it's part of most newish groups, she says. In the book she wrote with her first husband, she posits five stages for a closed-ended group like hers (though most couples reenlist for another year or two), the first being "joining." "Joining" is what it sounds like: People get to know each other and establish trust, gradually shedding their fear of "washing their dirty laundry in public."

Until the members get acclimated, the leader does most of the heavy lifting while occasionally commenting on what she's doing, to tip off the group that eventually they'll have to depend more on one another.

After joining comes the "beginning working phase," which is marked by members' ability "to adhere to a group norm of openness even when honesty feels disloyal to the partner." (This isn't just confession for confession's sake; it assumes that the secrets being kept bear on the sore spots in the marriage.) Before this switch, spouses often "minimize" the problem that brought them to the group in the first place, "leave out important aspects, or deny large chunks of the trouble."

Tentativeness toward the other members aside, by the end of the fourth session, in August, all five couples have stepped, or sidled, into the beginning working phase. They've each, at different intervals, gone beyond superficial chitchat. Clem has revealed his sexual frustration and Marie her bitter discontent—and revealed it and revealed it. To what end, who knows? The sources of Marie's anger seem everywhere and nowhere: Is it Clem's slippery agreeability, their incompatibility (her tendency to live in the mind, his in the body), her rotten family—or is her churlishness an expression of a constitutional anhedonia that will persist indefinitely, like a low-grade fever? In short, the group wonders whether it's in Marie's power to change. As for Clem, his story seems thin, somehow: He's just a guy who wants to take walks with his wife and get laid (and it often seems like the former is code for the latter), but haven't these twenty arid years shaped him somehow, changed who he is or what he wants?

Bella and Joe have let the group see the power imbalance between them, if only by accident. They don't act like it's much of a problem, and the group isn't sure: Maybe the arrangement works for them. Most disconcerting are the diametrically opposed versions of reality the couple throws up. The restaurant is humming along, and they'll be in the money by the fall; the restaurant is flatlining, and they're virtually penniless, with no relief in sight. True, in the August group, Joe, like Bella, was ac-cen-tchu-a-ting the positive, but the group had its doubts about that. (And this exchange in the September group, when Rachael will ask the couple about their finances, does nothing to dispel them: "We're a mess, the restaurant's a mess," Joe replied. "It's not a mess," Bella said. "The restaurant has some things that need to be addressed," Joe corrected himself.) With Bella and Joe, it seems less a question of ordinary subjectivity than: Is one of these two delusional?

Michael and Rachael still seem like a good physical fit, companionable *and* sexual, but his aversion to her sadness, which arose last time, seems extreme, especially for a man who presented himself as someone who worried about sacrificing himself to his wife. As with Bella and Joe, something seems to be missing from the picture they paint for the group, a "chunk" of the trouble they haven't yet disclosed, or admitted to themselves.

The quality of Leigh and Aaron's sexual relationship is their most pressing concern, but much of what happens between them seems to go on offstage, away from the group. As Aaron won't let anyone forget, this is their last year, and the two aren't about to pick at a scab that might require them to stay for an eleventh go-round. Even if it's just Aaron who feels like that, Leigh isn't interrupting his dash for the finish line.

For Mark and Sue Ellen, the worst is in the past. Mark isn't blowing up at his sons anymore, and the couple says they're communicating better, and working together as parents. Their biggest marital problem seems to be Mark's demanding job and grueling commute—they estimate they spend about eight waking hours a week in each other's company. Mark keeps saying he really wants to cut back, wants to be with Sue Ellen, but in August he finally admitted what seemed obvious: how hard it would be for him to give up the power and prestige of his job, even if he and Sue Ellen could afford it. Nonetheless, this couple is the group's yardstick, the one the others measure their own marriages against. Their "palpable connection," as Coché will call it, is either inspiration or reproach, depending on how you look at it.

Coché calls the third stage of the group the "crisis," and I'll come to think of the September group as the calm before the crisis. At this juncture, one couple may suddenly threaten to drop out because, for example, the group is "bullshitting," Coché writes, or someone "suddenly loses his/her temper and noisily attacks the leaders or another member." Such a dramatic happening isn't inevitable, according to Coché, but she's seen it often, and it usually moves the group into a deeper working stage. On the most tangible level, the couples may realize, "Hey, if that person is willing to go there, or act like that, why not talk about my crazy self, or our wack marriage—I'm/we're not *that* bad." More subtly, marriages are rife with crises, large and small; and citing the principle of isomorphism—encounters in one social system spread to others—Coché says that if the group can handle a crisis in its ranks, the individual couples may bring the lesson home.

But in September, a crisis hardly seems imminent. There are unexpected reports of progress, and the mood is light. It's a perfect early fall day, warm but not too warm, the sky cloudless, the green reeds of the marsh surrounding Stone Harbor tipped with gold. The windows in the office are wide open, and the pressure in the group seems to have lifted along with the heavy, moist summer air.

The spot next to Rachael on the couch is empty, and she starts off explaining that Michael couldn't come today because he has a bad cold. She doesn't mention the motorcycle, or the couple's no-cry pact. As Coché would put it, Rachael is dwelling in the "comfortable part of her life" this day. She's excited—she got the job she wanted, with a company that will train her to be a hearing-aid specialist. "Well, congratulations," says Mark, in his fatherly baritone. "That's fabulous, that's wonderful," Leigh says. And Clem puts in a compliment, too.

Rachael, dressed in a bright pink T-shirt and jeans, accepts the praise with her customary grace. Her rosy lips are blooming against her porcelain complexion, and I notice the dimple on her right cheek.

"I'll go next," Marie says. In the last group it was sex and croutons, Clem's cry to be wanted, Marie's wish to be engaged with rather than placated and thereby dismissed. ("It's possible in a relationship to be dominant by becoming submissive," Coché had observed.) Now Marie sounds practically eager, and I remember the couple's pattern so far: one group up, next down. In the third session, I thought she and Clem were getting somewhere; in the fourth, it was same old, same old—but then, that's what marriage often feels like. Just when you think it's getting better . . .

"A couple of things have happened since we last met," Marie begins. She's sitting forward in her deep chair, her arms resting loosely on its sides, hands dangling. "I started an online course [in molecular genetics], and I love it. And Clem has been wonderful just picking up everything around the house when I'm working on the course." Her second piece of good news is that she was chosen for a project that sets up health clinics in underserved regions of the world. "So I'll be going over to Africa for them."

"Wow, wow," Leigh says over the rest of the group's exclamations.

Marie says she's only agreed to two-week stints abroad, as opposed to six-month or yearlong. "But I did tell them I'm willing to go to a remote location."

Bella laughs appreciatively at her daring. Marie sounds so proud of herself. Graciously, she turns to Clem and asks if he wants to "share" what happened with him the day before.

"Um, my sister gave me a call," he says. "I haven't heard from her in four years or so." Clem's sister and his mother, he has intimated, ganged up against him as an adult, and he cut off contact with his sister when their mother died. The call was "cordial," he says, "but it upset me the rest of the day. I tried to just switch the channel and think about something else, but it was just tough, but, uh . . .

"Anyway I swam a mile in the bay last night and felt better and met up with a couple of my friends and we took a boat to a restaurant and had a few beers, and I feel better—"

"The oldest form of psychotherapy," Coché says, over the group's laughter,

"And according to my book," Leigh says to Clem and Marie, "you two have an anniversary coming up." (At the beginning of the year, Coché appointed "sunshine director" Leigh to keep a "book" of the group members' anniversaries, birthdays, and such.) "So what has happened for you together?"

"Well, what's really lovely is because our time is so short," Marie begins—she could be sent to Africa at any time—"we're making, like, dates, and we're really enjoying them." It's Bella, not Marie, who typically uses the youthful "like." "And, um, my back hurt and Clem gave me a massage." The couples' efforts to connect can be so plaintive and childlike.

"And it's beautiful to see you smile," Coché cuts in.

"Thank you," Marie says, simply and, it occurs to me, maturely. The woman with the long ponytail does not sound one bit petulant.

"You have a beautiful smile," Coché continues.

"Yes, you do," Leigh adds. They're milking Marie's surge of sanguinity for all it's worth. Marie nods, dips her chin slightly. She doesn't ruin the moment.

"What about you, Clem?" Leigh asks.

"It was nice to, uh, let Marie, uh, give a massage," he says. "It was nice. I liked it. So it's nice that she, uh, I think her back started, and I said, 'Should we give massages?' and she said okay, so it was nice." Talk about a cold shower. Perhaps Clem is understandably wary about making too much of a single massage; maybe it wasn't as lovely for him as it was for Marie; or maybe he doesn't know what to do with his wife once he has her. Clem has been a long time in the sexual wilderness, a long time without a guide.

Coché doesn't comment on the incongruity between them, on Marie's dart forward, and Clem's tepid acknowledgment. Sunshine is dappling the walls, flitting across people's laps, and Coché is pulling toward the light, with her group. She recalls a scene between Marie and Clem from last year, during a session in which a massage therapist spent part of the day with the group. "One of the most poignant moments I've had in this practice recently was watching Marie follow [the massage therapist's] directives on giving Clem a shoulder massage with tears streaming down her face and dripping onto his forehead." Clem was lying on his back at Marie's knees, apparently. "Watching her so valiantly try to make it all work." Coché's large brown eyes are hooded with sadness, then, snap, she's back to the progress, back to the massages Marie and Clem recently gave each other. "So this is a big shift," she announces, nodding slowly, like a proud parent.

"Okay," begins Aaron. He's holding his own gem, and he's winding up to show it around, glimmering in the palm of his hand. "Since the group last met, Leigh and I had two very gratifying weeks up in New Hampshire, relaxing. We've been going to New Hampshire for ten years, and initially it was very challenging because of the sexuality and intimacy issues which I primarily had, and now ten years later it was very gratifying."

"Can I talk about how gratifying it was?" Leigh asks. She grabs his large hand, grinning. She's better at show-and-tell.

"Yeah," he says. "You may interrupt me and tell me." Everybody laughs, and Aaron smiles. He has perspective on *this* pattern in his marriage.

"You said the most wonderful thing—"

"Right, right," Aaron says.

"—one of the days—"

"Right."

"—I don't remember which day it was—"

"Right—"

"—and it just helped me. It made me so happy inside."

"Right."

Leigh doesn't break pace despite Aaron's patter of "rights." It's a tic. He does it when he doesn't know what to expect, when he's nervous. At the moment he's not overly apprehensive about what his wife is going to say, so the "rights" sound merely like comprehension checks, as in "I get it, I get it—so far, I get it." Other times, the "rights" burst forth like machine-gun fire, "Stop, stop, stop, I can't take any more."

"Do you know what I'm going to say?" Leigh asks cheerfully.

"Uh, I don't remember what I said to you."

"He said to me, 'I want to first climb the mountain with you, and then I want to be with you.'"

"Right."

"It made me so happy that I wrote it down, and I looked at it every single day."

"Oh dear," Rachael says, moved.

"Do you want to talk about what the context of it is?" Leigh asks Aaron.

"No, go ahead, go on."

Yes, please, do go on, the group thinks, because while Leigh is over the moon about Aaron's kind words, we're not quite sure what they mean. The sexual euphemisms are getting too thick. Was "be with you" the sex part or was it "climbing the mountain"? They were vacationing in New Hampshire, after all, and I imagine peaks out their kitchen window. I think of them hiking craggy hills.

"Well, I would say the first six years of our therapy was about dealing with you not being so intent on climbing the mountain—"

"Right, right, that's right . . ."

"—and just—"

"Right."

"—being blinded—"

"Right."

"—to anything else, me included." So is Aaron some kind of fanatical outdoorsman who insists on spending his days clambering up and down mountainsides before he'll commune with his wife? Though he's nearing sixty-five, he looks the part. He's tall and trim, with broad shoulders and long, muscled legs.

"Climbing the mountain in terms of performance and so on," Leigh continues. Ah, finally. "It didn't matter whether I was there or not."

Coché hacks further through the brush. "When they started the group—this was like a hundred years ago—Aaron, in his inimitable fashion, said something like: 'I will climb the mountain toward orgasm.' And [sex therapist and former coleader] Julian and I looked at each other, and we met shortly afterward for a break. We came back and I said, 'Aaron, can we make it like a flowing river instead of a mountain you have to climb?' So that was the context."

What thrills Leigh is that Aaron expressed both a desire to have sex with her and then to just be with her. And, apparently, he lived up to his word. Leigh felt seen, fleetingly known perhaps—an especially good kind of good sex, you might say.

Finally, Bella and Joe are relatively buoyant this September day, which is saying something, because they reveal that she had a miscarriage a few days after the last group. Granted, Bella sounds abstracted when she talks about the loss. "We have an announcement," she says. "We lost a baby a couple of weeks ago." *A baby?* Later, when Rachael tries to coax Bella to talk more about the miscarriage by revealing that she, too, had one with her first husband, and it left bigger emotional scars than she would've imagined, Bella responds nonresponsively: "One of the things I've been telling people is that I think with the word 'miscarriage' there's a physical part 'cuz you don't carry the baby to full term, obviously, but you also miss the 'carrying' of the baby [once born]. So I've been trying to honor the missing." And then there's this: "I feel very healthy about not worrying about not being sad. Does that make sense?" Uh, sorta.

Still, there is no "right" reaction to a miscarriage. Just because Bella and Joe aren't blubbering doesn't mean they're hiding something. Then again, maybe they aren't contributing to the goodwill in the group this day as much as allowing themselves to be swept along by it. Coché asks if any of the women have had miscarriages, and I, for one, tell Bella not to worry. I had one and later conceived on my first try, and then immediately again! Women trading fertility stories can be like men comparing penis size: the bragging and one-upping one another. That may be especially true for women (like me and Bella) whose adult identities weren't forged on the anvil of motherhood. When we decide to have children, some of us are veined with uncertainty about our fitness, emotional as much as anything. To have a body that pumps out babies— that proves something, doesn't it?

Later, Bella will tell me that as she listened to me enthuse about my ease at getting pregnant she was thinking, So what? It's easy to be confident once you've got your kids, but who knows what's in store for me. *I'm* scared.

CHAPTER 8

―――――――――

"Marie Shrinks from Physicality, So We Prescribe It."

As a person who's known you for six months, it's brutal listening to you," Bella is tearily telling Marie and Clem. The October group, which will meet for two days, is not even an hour old and already Marie and Clem are into another of their repetitive dialogues about sex. This one is especially convoluted, however, because Marie's purpose, the group only slowly deduces, is to force Clem to raise the issue rather than "sit back" and let her do the dirty work. To this end, Marie informed Clem on the car ride to Philadelphia that morning—the meetings are back at Coché's office in the city—that she didn't have anything to bring up in the group, but of course, that is not quite true. What she has to bring up is her long-held conviction that Clem isn't taking his share of the responsibility for the couple's problems, that it's only "gimpy" Marie who needs to be fixed. "I see [sex] as an area *you* want to change," Marie tells Clem, "so therefore I want *you* to be the impetus for creating the change you want."

Inadvertently or not, her presentation is doubly wounding to Clem, because it underlines what is rarely stated outright: Marie, it seems, could not care less about having sex with him. And he responds with a new level of specificity and honesty. "It really feels belittling, I don't feel attractive, I don't feel wanted, and then I just start thinking about our whole marriage, and it's just been the whole way, it gets, uh—it's hard to stay positive."

Marie does have a point, however. Although Clem occasionally pays lip service to the contrary, his stance toward his marriage is essentially reactive: If Marie shapes up, I'll be happy as a clam. It's also hard not to notice the eloquence of his complaints versus the flat, broken way he acknowledged in the last group that he'd enjoyed the couple's interlude of closeness: "It was nice to, uh, let Marie, uh, give a massage," and, uh, so on.

In any event, for the first time someone in the group is plainly criticizing what goes on between Clem and Marie. Bella is saying that the tension between them reminds her of her childhood. "My parents are still married, so it's not that it can't work out—"

"*Re*married," Coché corrects. The group knows that she first saw Bella when her parents were divorcing, about fifteen years ago.

"*Re*married," Bella says, throwing an annoyed glance in Coché's direction, "but now they're like actually happy and able to talk things out and joke about their differences. But it's hard. You have to just know the love is more important than any *position*."

"But today, I actually feel in a really good position," Marie counters, ignoring the jab at her fondness for "positions," just as she ignored Coché on it two months earlier. "I didn't give in in the areas that would hurt me, and therefore create anger and perpetuate the problem. I actually let you own the problem, because it's *your*—I'm not saying it's your problem." She's speaking across the room to Clem. "I'm saying that *part* of it is yours, and I need you to bring it to the table so we can sort it out."

"But there's another dimension," Coché says, "which Bella is bringing in." Coché's dog, Whitby, has left his bed on the floor to stand by the uncharacteristically disheveled-looking Bella. Her eyes are still filled with tears, and she smiles wanly at the dog, absently ruffling the fur on his head.

"Bella is resonating with what it feels like to grow up in a cold-war zone," Coché continues. "For parents who are as diligent and who treasure your children as much as you and Clem do, that has to be painful to hear."

"It's not a war zone," Marie retorts. She is proud to have raised her daughters in an environment more hospitable than her own childhood home, and she will not hear that she may have even unintentionally caused the girls pain.

"Bella is just giving you her experience," Coché cautions.

"The tension or anxiety in the dynamic, you pick up on," Bella tries again.

"I think it's actually eased, because it's not under the surface," Marie says.

"Oh, I think it's probably better than it was," Coché replies.

"And it's good to see you passionate," Bella says, giving up on Marie and turning to Clem, who's next to her, "and fighting for something." Bella is regularly solicitous toward Clem, I've begun to notice—showing him what she can't show her own husband?

"But, it's—it sounds like you want me to initiate sex," Clem begins anew. *That* is how he interpreted Marie's saying she wants him to share responsibility for their predicament: that he's supposed to initiate sex? The deep sexually deprived groove in his brain collects all incoming data. "But it's just hard to—to—to—because the answer's always no, or I get 'okay,' and that just doesn't turn me on. It just, it takes the wind out of my sails, to know that you're only saying yes to appease me."

Marie follows him into the rut: "When did you ask me to have sex? Go through it with the couples," she says, gesturing around the room. "Was it last night?"

"Last night—and then several times last week."

"Okay." Marie pounces. "Now what was going on last night when you asked me that?"

"You were doing a lot of study." Clem is a deer caught in headlights.

"No, I was not doing a lot of study. It's different, different."

"Can I stop you both?" Marie and Clem both train their eyes on Coché. "I want the group to give you a little feedback. Let's clue into the noncontent way you're communicating."

"It feels like seething," Bella says. "You're pissed," she says to Clem, "so you're kinda like back in your chair—you're not moving toward her to get something resolved. She's trying to communicate, but she's putting a pillow between you, and—"

"I think Marie must be exhausted trying to maneuver everything," Sue Ellen says. "Just what you said about driving up here: You wouldn't do this, so he would do that."

"It's like a chessboard, isn't it?" Coché says.

"Right," Sue Ellen says. "And, um, is there ever a time where you can just be yourselves with each other, without—this may sound harsh—hidden agendas? I just get lost listening to it." She looks evenly at Marie, who appears to be taking in what she's saying.

"Michael and Rachael," Coché says, looking across at them on the black leather love seat, "you guys haven't said anything."

"Um, I guess it just kind of brings back memories of my first marriage," Rachael says in her soft, melodic voice. Her eyes are almost as pure a blue as Clem's. Then she goes further, where no one has dared go before: "The key thing on my mind is: Do either of you really see a big future together?"

Clem's gaze flits around the room, while Marie keeps her eyes glued to her lap. She's wearing her ponytail on the side today, and it blends in with the furry pillow she's stroking, so that her hair almost seems to grow out of it.

Michael breaks the silence. He's been having flashbacks of his first marriage, too, of having to "beg to go to the bedroom," of his ex not so much as saying hello to him when she was studying. "And I agree with Rachael. Should you [two] just say, 'You know what, we should move on'?"

When Coché earlier in the year mentioned to me that Clem told Marie he wanted a divorce near the end of the previous year's group, I asked her why he changed his mind. "Marie told him she didn't want to get divorced," she replied, chuckling, "so he said okay." That perfectly captures the dynamic between them in the group, but when Coché raises the divorce threat now, and asks Clem to say why he backed off, I'm still taken aback at how baldly he states it: "Marie was upset, and she wanted to stay together, and I guess I thought if she wants to stay together, I'll—I'll, uh, I'll give it a go."

Now comes what qualifies, in my mind, as exactly the wrong advice (thus illustrating the perils of advice giving in the first place). This afternoon, Coché has scheduled a dancer and Pilates instructor named

Karen Carlson to take the group to her nearby studio for movement exercises, and she's here this morning, sitting in. Carlson is in her late fifties but looks younger, with her short, spiky hair, stylish glasses, and lean, swingy body. At Coché's behest, she gave a lengthy introduction of herself: describing her years playing ice hockey, returning to college in her late twenties to become a dancer and choreographer (after tiring of jewelry making), performing professionally, becoming a master Pilates instructor, and her suffering when her husband died from cancer when he was forty-eight (a bit of biography she shares with Coché and Leigh). She wrapped up by telling the group how she was eventually set up with a man who's become her life partner: "And now I wake up and look into a pair of loving eyes every morning. It doesn't get much better than that. So life is good."

Because of her talent, circumstances, or sheer luck, Karen has lived a wide and creatively satisfying life, or so it seems. Her outlook and expectations couldn't be more different from Marie's and Clem's. She also doesn't really know the couple or the group. So when, on the heels of the group's for the first time broaching the possibility of divorce to Marie and Clem, Carlson says, "You know, I heard the same complaints from my husband: You're never around, you're always studying. And so what I had to do was step back and ask what can I do to recapture some of the spark? So I made a rule there for a while that every Friday night I walked through the door with a bottle of champagne," I want to groan.

But I don't, and nobody else does either. The circle of faces remains benignly inscrutable—Carlson is a guest and she means well, the group knows. The first person to speak is Clem, who, like a pitcher of water floating surrealistically over a desiccated landscape, kindly smiles. "Thank you for your input," he says to Carlson, holding his hands in his lap. He, alone, may have taken her suggestion at face value, may have believed Carlson had a good idea. His wish that his life could be like that, with a wife who brings him champagne, is that strong.

Coché doesn't blanch, either. She rolls with it. "Sometimes going through the motions starts you in a good direction," she says. "If we take Karen's lesson, what she's saying is she figured out what she needed to do and she started doing it. It probably didn't feel completely joyous at first but got better."

"But—but I am figuring out what to do," Marie cries. Her voice has risen to a frustrated whine. "I mean, I really am. Like Thursday, I asked Clem if he'd like to take a walk, and we walked on the boardwalk. I mean, there's intimacy—"

"Which never would have happened before," Coché acknowledges.

"And when you're asking me to have sex last night, it wasn't that I was studying, Clem. I was in the middle of a *midterm*. So I feel like many times you set me up to fail. And then you can turn around and go, 'She's not giving me what I want.' Why is it only for you: When it's time to go bodysurfing, you go bodysurfing, even though I might have some minutes then?" Marie's tone is angry but blessedly free of manipulative flourishes. She isn't going to stop taking science courses, or give up on Africa, she says, because she'll "die inside." "This is who I am going to be, and this is who attracted you in the first place, somebody who was enthusiastic, energetic, enjoying life, looking at the marvelous things going on and wanting to share them with you. So I am going to be busy with my own projects, but then I want to share them with you."

The group looks on, impressed. "You're good when you're mad," Coché notes. "You're clear, you're crisp, you're respectful. When you get teachy, it's hard."

"Oh, see," Marie says, "I thought that was the nicer way to go about it."

"It's condescending," I say. I've been dying to say this for months—and maybe I should've done it sooner. By now I've realized that Marie seems to credit my comments, maybe because she respects that I haven't let marriage stop me from pursuing my professional ambitions.

"Really?" Marie says to me, sounding genuinely surprised.

"A lot," Joe says. The group bursts into laughter—how could it be that she didn't recognize this?

"Really?" she repeats, smiling.

"Are you surprised?" Coché asks.

"Yes, I am. Thank you," she says, to me.

Just when the group is losing hope for her, and for Clem, she's pulled it out. Marie and Clem remind me of a line from Mark Epstein, the Buddhist-influenced therapist: "We do not get lots of realizations in our lives as much as we get the same ones over and over."

Now Clem has his own small epiphany. "What I heard Marie say, it made some sense. Things have been going pretty well this past month, but it was just getting longer and longer," he says, referring to the length of time since they'd last had sex, "and I just was getting more frustrated, and it just sort of came to a head."

Clem is exhibiting the stickiness of the negative emotional and behavioral loops marital researchers have observed. Or, in the words of therapist Michael Miller, who's never seen the inside of a lab: "Much of the unchanging character of disturbed, anxiety-ridden intimacy comes from the reduced perceptions each person has of the other. At the beginning, these projections, as psychologists call them, tend to result in overly idealized images of each other; later, intimate partners are likely to take a paranoid reading of the other's motives and dwell on the worst episodes in their history together, which exacerbates their freezing each other into negative snapshots."

Over the years, Coché has referred clients to Pilates instructor Carlson for help with exercise, weight loss, or relief from somatic pain. For the couples group she asked Carlson to design a workshop based on the theory that much of the communication in marriage is nonverbal. "A solid foundation of nonsexual touching, of physical ease with each other, of, literally, arms to come home to" gives people a buffer against the inevitable bouts of conflict and estrangement, Coché tells me outside of the group. Not to mention that it might prime the pump for sex.

The two younger, recently married couples—Bella and Joe and Michael and Rachael—think they don't need help in this area, Coché assumes, but before the group walks the three blocks to Carlson's studio, she urges them to reconsider. "This is not about whether you can have orgasms," she says, swiveling her neck to take in the circle of faces. "This is not about whether you have sex once, twice, or three times a week. This is about living in the deepest internal part of yourself in the presence of another person."

As for Leigh and Aaron, anxious physical inhibition *is* their problem (or his), and Sue Ellen, on the sex weekend four months ago, specifically mentioned wanting to let go of some of her shyness about her body.

Finally, there is Marie. "She shrinks from physicality, so we prescribe it," Coché says briskly, "and help her with the reaction when it occurs."

Carlson's studio is in an area of central Philadelphia that is just edging over into seediness. Cities are like that: One moment you're walking alongside an impeccably restored brownstone or slick office tower, the next you're staring into a black-windowed strip club. The group walks over in a crooked line, like kids on a field trip. Carlson's studio is on the second floor, and it's large, about two thousand square feet, with wall-to-wall carpeting and mirrors running alongside the walls.

The couples seem a little nervous, and so does Carlson. She's used to working with people who seek her out, and this has the feel of court-ordered movement therapy, initially at least. During the walk here, I commented to Coché that most married people wouldn't be caught dead prancing around with a bunch of other couples, and she turned my comment on its head in a way that applied beyond the day's activity: "The power in the group gives people permission, at the same time as it holds them back." In other words, in the regular sessions a member might feel pressure to speak honestly because she hears someone else do it—positive peer pressure—or she might clam up for fear of being judged. "The trick to helping people change is to get the right amount of anxiety," Coché said, not for the first time, enough so they'll try something new but not so much that they'll head for the exits.

For a warm-up, Carlson directs the couples to stand in a rough line with their backs to the mirror. They're going to do a rhythmic "shaking-out" exercise. "Start with any body part," she says. "It could be your tail, could be any part you want."

The group members are resolutely themselves. Marie sticks to waving her hands—forget about her "tail." Clem is a little, but only a little, more adventurous: He jiggles his ankles and legs. Aaron's "shaking" reads more like a series of thrusts; he's jerking his shoulders up to his ears in a cartoony motion. Leigh is earnestly counting out the beats to herself as she loosens various parts (she's done Pilates with Carlson). Mark and Sue Ellen are doing some full-body shimmying, and laughing lightly between themselves, their own pod. Joe and Bella are following instructions, but they both are tight-lipped, and he looks as exhausted as she does. Michael and Rachael? They don't stand out in one way or another. Michael often seems blurry, it occurs to me. Coché plops down on an exercise ball, her long legs spread, ready to follow the action.

Carlson has planned a series of "movement choruses" that require cooperation and collaboration among the group as a whole, then just between the couples themselves. She has everyone stand in a line and deflate one after another, and then rise up again in the same domino fashion: "What you have to do is sense the person beside you, what they're doing," Carlson says.

"So if I don't choose to deflate?" Marie teases slyly.

"Even if the person beside you is out of sync," Carlson responds, ignoring the provocation, "keep your internal rhythm going."

Then she tells each person to improvise his or her own movement in the line, still going one by one. This is more complicated. "It's more uncomfortable," Carlson says, "but the unpredictability makes it a little more exciting." The metaphors are flying fast.

Next, they're weaving about the room, bouncing off one another like pinballs that don't touch. They're not allowed to talk. "You're adapting," she says. "You're finding by consensus a flow, a way of existing in the same place at the same time without catastrophe . . .

"How are you feeling?" Carlson calls out.

"Good," Sue Ellen says loud and clear, louder and more clearly than she's ever said anything in Coché's office. No one else responds.

The group pairs off for something Carlson calls a "walkabout": The women are to promenade slowly around their men, and then stop, standing motionless in their field of vision with no direct eye contact. Next, the men are to do the same. "There is electricity in the space between," Carlson says. Indeed, observing the couples circumvent each other, in broad loops, then dip in closer, then stop without a sound—it's like an erotic dance.

The first exercise in which the couples are to actually touch is called "melding." They're to lean into each other shoulder to shoulder, then flank to flank, then hip to hip, "negotiating counterbalance," Carlson says. "You must be able to carry your own weight, and at the same time have the willingness to offer support."

Then it happens. Marie's "reaction" occurs. Sometime during the hip-to-hip melding, she disappears. Not everyone notices immediately. Mark and Sue Ellen are sinking into each other, eyes closed, and Rachael and Michael are clowning around. After a few minutes, Coché leaves the room to check on Marie. When she returns, she waits for a natural break in the proceedings before gathering the group together. Clem stands. He's been sitting on a workout bench by himself, elbows on his knees, head in hands. It's really too bad, because this morning he and Marie seemed to have gotten somewhere, to have spoken forthrightly with each other.

"Marie can't continue," Coché says, "because she feels Clem broke a contract. She asked that he not tease her, and she cannot continue, she's really upset. Upset in a way Clem couldn't have dreamed of." While Marie has told Coché she wants to be alone, the therapist sends Sue Ellen after her, anyway. The two have been in a women's group Coché runs, and Marie seems to respect Sue Ellen.

What breach Clem has committed isn't clear, but people glance sympathetically at him, and Bella sighs, as in, "What a drama queen!"

"How are you all doing?" Coché asks the group.

"It's a little slow," Bella says.

A stern cloud passes over Coché's face. "Your level of investment determines your level of involvement. Fight moving faster, Bella, and see what happens with that."

Sue Ellen's attempt to talk to Marie evidently was rebuffed; after a few minutes, Sue Ellen returns to the group, alone. Marie can be heard blowing her nose outside the room. *What* is going on with that woman?

Carlson picks up where she left off, and what is most remarkable is the soulful contact between Mark and Sue Ellen. Verbally, Sue Ellen is stiff, choosing her words with the care of a police officer defusing an explosive. And while Mark is slightly more garrulous, there is a barrelchested complacency in his bearing that doesn't suggest he'd be willing to stretch and dance and otherwise cavort with his wife in public. Yet the pair move together with unself-conscious grace.

For the "Celtic knot," in which one person is supposed to strike a pose while the other "finds an opening, fills the negative space," Sue Ellen sits on the floor with her legs up in a pike position. That prompts Mark to drop down and lay his head in her lap. Next, she slowly, steadily rises into headstand. (Sue Ellen takes yoga, Mark will later inform the group.) Mark regards his wife admiringly, then rests his head on the soles of her feet while she's doing the headstand, content as a sleeping baby.

Carlson's final plan for the couples, she says, is for them to close their eyes and assume their partners' "shape, posture, stance." Then they're to open their eyes and contemplate the pose their spouse struck: How does he or she perceive them physically? Carlson knows that some people may find this intimidating, so she tells the couples to discuss between themselves whether they want to participate. Everyone gives it a try, but soon Rachael and Michael and Bella and Joe sit down on a pile of exercise mats. The two older couples stay on the floor. Leigh does Aaron walking, arms jabbing forward. He does her with his hands on his hips, a challenging expression on his face. They both nod knowingly when they see what the other's done.

Sue Ellen becomes Mark by puffing out her chest, holding her chin up, head high. She looks exactly like him. He does her with his arms wrapped around his body, head cocked quizzically to one side. It's sad to be reminded of her self-protective reflex when only minutes before she'd risked drawing attention to herself: She did the headstand with such aplomb.

Clem is still sitting on the workout bench, still with chin in hand, glumly watching the other couples frolic.

The session with Carlson ends just after four o'clock. When the group goes through her waiting room on the way out to the street, Marie is nowhere to be found. They traipse the two blocks back to Coché's office, then up the elevator to the fourth floor. It's a relief to be back here. It's a calm, predictable place to decompress, a suitable "holding environment," to quote Winnicott again, for the bedlam of feeling. That Coché's office seems so private and containing is a testament to what goes on here more than to its design: An entire wall is taken up by a floor-to-ceiling window facing an internal courtyard. It's therapy in a fishbowl, but it doesn't feel that way. The landscaped courtyard is usually empty, and even when it isn't, the few people smoking or chatting just outside seem as distant as the boaters on Stone Harbor's bay.

The mood is subdued, with a dash of anticipation. The group knows they're going to talk about Marie, and she can be like a car wreck. You stare with horror and embarrassed exhilaration (before the tedium of the traffic jam makes you want to pound your fist on the dashboard).

Coché starts generally, asking the couples to discuss what they learned about themselves during the workshop, what, if anything, was upsetting. And, yes, she says, they'll eventually need to work with Clem on how he feels about what happened. "So let's just open it up," she says.

Michael's first out of the box, and he goes straight for Marie. He doesn't understand why she fled, he says.

"We were doing the exercise where we were pushing our butts together on the side," Clem replies. "I was getting bored, and I guess I was just thinking of the dance the bump, and I gave Marie like an extra bump, and, uh, and—and, she, uh, she was really angry at me that I would tease her."

"You intended it to be playful?" Coché asks.

Yes, he says. "And then, she was really infuriated and said, 'Don't ever do that again.' And I said, 'That's fine. Let's just end the day, then.' And, uh—"

"Do you think her reaction was a little overboard?" Michael asks, obviously stating his own view.

"Show us what you did," Leigh says.

Clem stands up and swings one hip to the side: the bump, just like he said.

"It may seem small—it's just there have been times in the past, I guess with Marie's childhood and being teased, it's like setting off a bomb," Clem says. He's defending her; he knows her better than anyone else in the group, after all. And he may like her more than anyone else does, I sometimes think. "It brought back memories of other times I've teased her."

"Why did you decide to end the day instead of trying to work it out or apologizing?" Sue Ellen asks, reminding the torch-carrying mob that it was, in fact, Clem who said, "Let's end it." Marie merely took him up on it.

"It was just a knee-jerk reaction," Clem practically wails. "She looked at me with those eyes, and the way she said it. As soon as I said it, I knew

I shouldn't have, but it came out." He explains that in last year's session with the massage therapist, he'd agreed never to tease her during such exercises, the "contract" to which Marie referred.

Perhaps because they want to prop up Clem, perhaps because they're fed up with his wife's hogging the group, several people, myself included, convey to Clem that he doesn't have anything to apologize for. *She's* the one who's the "eggshell plaintiff," I charge. Eh, too clever by half (and, in case you're wondering, "eggshell plaintiff" is a tort law phrase referring to someone who has a preexisting vulnerability to being hurt). Sometimes I'm appalled at what pops out of my mouth.

"One second," Coché says, "before we get into whose fault this is, it's totally unimportant. If these people want to be married to *other* people, then they can decide whose fault it is. But if they want to be married to each other, then you've got a highly charged situation." Marie was "stretched beyond her comfort level" just standing in a line with Carlson, she says. "But it's not poor Marie, she was abused, everybody has to be careful." (Marie has been careful to say that while her father may have punched her arm to show affection, or smothered her in hugs until she cried and begged to be let go, no one in her family sexually abused her. She knew her sensitivity to touch aroused that suspicion.)

Coché goes on: "If you want to forge an intimate relationship with someone where there's damage—and we all have damage of one sort or another—how do we remember the boundaries, and what do we do when we cross them? Because you either figure out what to do with this, or you need to move on."

This is the third time Coché has echoed Michael and Rachael's mention of divorce for Marie and Clem. Outside of the group, the therapist has told me she doesn't see her job as either preventing divorce or encouraging it; in other words, if a couple decides to end their marriage, she doesn't assume she's failed them. "Most of the time when people get divorced," Coché says, "there's this sense of, man, this just *doesn't* work."

A few years back, there was a kerfuffle in the profession about whether therapists, by taking a neutral stance on divorce, were betraying their clients, who assumed that a marriage counselor's first goal was to keep people together. William Doherty, the Minnesota couples therapist who criticizes the inadequate training of his colleagues, led the charge with the creation of a Web site named the National Registry of Marriage Friendly Therapists. "I just got an e-mail from somebody today," Doherty tells me when I call him, "asking if there was a conflict of interest in a marriage therapist who also does divorce mediation, and who tells people he's not 'in the business of saving marriages.' It's sort of like your internist runs a mortuary."

This is perhaps an extreme example of agnosticism, and the fundamental issue seems to be not whether therapists treat the choice to divorce like choosing a paint color for the living room—blue or green, it doesn't matter—but whether because of poor skills, therapists give up on warring couples too easily: "I don't know what to do with you two nut jobs—maybe you should just hang it up."

The subtler argument Doherty makes is that marriage is best viewed not as a union between two individuals, each trying to maximize his or her own happiness, but as a commitment that once made should be broken only in the worst of circumstances. The latter smacks of oppressive religious sanctions for many, but whatever our attitude toward the priests and rabbis, most of us believe that reneging on our promises is wrong. Staying alive to that principle in marriage—the vows you took for better or worse—has a practical advantage, Doherty says. It increases the likelihood that a couple will apply themselves to improving their situation, if need be. He analogizes it with the parent-child relationship. "Even though this teenager no longer respects me and is going crazy, I got no choice here. We gotta work this out. I think that marriages do better—and there's indirect support for this in the literature—when people say to themselves, 'This is it.'"

Anyway, Doherty continues, the two values—personal fulfillment and honoring commitments—can actually line up. An important way people find meaning is by meeting their responsibilities, he points out, making good on their promises. It reminds me of Coché's existentialism, and of the swelling of purpose that comes from dwelling on one's marriage as an enterprise bigger than your self-interest, as something that must be tended to because you said you would. I know, I've experienced these pangs of dignity myself.

But then, I go back and forth on this, on both the utility and the morality of marital perseverance. So does *Intimate Terrorism* author Michael Miller, when I speak with him in his Manhattan office. "It is a form of heroism in this day and age to accept the challenge of marriage and deal with all the levels of meaning in it," he says, seconding Doherty. Then he stops, rewinds. His overriding goal, Miller says, is to guide clients away from living in a "trance," to shift them from compulsion toward freedom of choice. "Can we wake up?" the distressed couple must ask themselves, according to Miller. "Can we be together and *not* act this horrendously?"

If two people can't or won't be roused from their vile sleep, then, Miller says, "Divorce is a great act of liberation." And in those circumstances, isn't it also the moral thing, too? To be devoid of volition—isn't that quintessentially inhuman and thus, by definition, beyond morality's reach? Robots are only moral in *Star Wars* and children's stories.

These are the kind of high-flown thoughts I have (the baser imaginings involve muzzles) when I see Marie and Clem leave the exact same teethmarks on each other they have a dozen times before. I know Marie in particular takes keeping her marital vows very seriously. (She is punctilious about all her avowals, actually—maybe that's what happens when your father insists his punches are painless.) And like Michael and Rachael, I suspect, who spoke the id of the group when they suggested that maybe Marie and Clem should call it quits, I wonder if Marie's ethical conscience could use a pruning.

Although Coché professes to be impartial about divorce, she is not Doherty's cartoon therapist, the one who quickly cuts to: "I'm not in the business of saving marriages." When she floats divorce to Clem in the aftermath of his ill-timed bump, it seems like a tactic, a way to "pull for the despair" that Coché believes motivates people to change. In her article on resistance, she tells of upping the ante in this manner for one couple by asking, "How long have you been convinced that sex in this marriage is bankrupt?" And to another: "If you weren't too depressed to pull it off, what might you say to your wife?"

Now Coché says to Clem, "There's no wiggle room, and there won't be for some time. If you can negotiate this spot, then it's gonna open up freedom as time goes on, but it will never feel as it might in a different situation." (With a different woman, she means but does not have to say.) "So the decision you need to reach is the decision all of us reach, which is: Is it worth it? Do you love this person enough that you want to make it work? Is the rest of your life important enough that you want to make it work? Nobody can answer that question for you."

Coché goes on a bit, and the group bats about the notion of loving others the way they want to be loved, not the way you want to love them, which means accepting another's "eccentricities." Leigh and Aaron say they're proud that they hung in for the whole time with Carlson—and even enjoyed it—which they never would've been able to do when they started ten years ago. See, Clem, they're saying, there's hope.

Just the sound of words, the quiet, reasonable hum, comforts Clem perhaps, calms him for the long car ride home with Marie. This is a two-day session, but they didn't think they could afford a hotel in Philadelphia. There are those two girls' college tuitions to pay.

Joe gets a huge laugh when he says that when he assumed Bella's posture back in the Pilates studio, he immediately thought, "Hey, I feel like I'm about to get something done!" So the couples go back and forth, back and forth, but really the group is already over. "Is it worth it?" Coché asked, and the question will reverberate for more than just Marie and Clem. Is it?

CHAPTER 9

———————————

Crisis Weekend

I t's the second day of the two-day October meeting, and the group settles into their circle quietly, politely: *hello, excuse me, hello, no, you first*. They seem shell-shocked almost, yet they're not blank, not the walking dead. The opposite: Their emotions seem closer to the surface, like "don't touch," or "*please* do." The crisis has begun, and she's here. After yesterday's disappearance, Marie has returned. She's sitting in the corner of the room in her group dress, a long jean jumper with an embroidered smock, her eyes glassy slits. Whitby has taken up sentry at her side—dogs and their limbic attunement—and Marie hasn't stopped petting him since the group sat down.

She looks sickly, and so does Clem. In the waiting room, while people were pouring coffee and picking among muffins and minibagels, Coché took Marie aside to ask how she was doing. "Fine, thanks," Marie replied. Now, when Coché does her check-in with the group, Marie says, "I just sort of wanna go through the day." She barely looks up.

"Okay," Coché says, "and will you hang loose, Marie? Because if Leigh does a little work on anxiety, that oughta move you into your issues." (Leigh had just mentioned that yesterday she'd flinched when Aaron approached her during one of the excercises with Carlson. She'd welcomed her first husband's advances, but her comfort had eroded with Aaron, who himself once compared his early demeanor to that of a Hulk Hogan wrestler, the kind who might come at you from behind, hands pawing.)

"Right," Marie replies to Coché, but her tone says, *Wrong. You, Dr. Coché, couldn't be more horribly, pathetically, idiotically wrong.*

Coché doesn't take the bait. She just keeps talking. She talks a lot this morning, indulges in the discursive storytelling she's counseled the group against. (It's an avoidance technique, she has said.) Coché goes on about how she was trained by a famed eating disorder specialist, how she ran behavioral weight-control groups. She talks about how overeating is among the hardest "addictions" to treat because you can't give up food completely—and perhaps she can share some of this "knowledge" with the group? She seems to have grabbed this subject out of nowhere; the only reason I can fathom is that after yesterday's upheaval, weight seems safe—trivial perhaps, but safe.

The group gloms onto it eagerly. Bella hasn't lost her pregnancy weight since her miscarriage two months ago, and Joe says he feels "saggy," and Rachael is much heavier than before she married Michael but can't seem to diet, and Leigh has to watch her intake like a hawk, while Aaron (like Michael) can pretty much eat what he wants. But the most extra weight any of them is carrying is fifteen, twenty pounds. *Phew,* they all seem to be saying, *we don't have to deal with* her, Marie, who has her eyes closed, her head in her hands. Clem, next to her on the couch, looks like he's sitting on a pin cushion.

Sue Ellen changes the mood, if not the whole subject. "Um, well, I'd like to work on how I feel right now."

"Right this minute, right now," Coché says, sounding pleasantly surprised. She's the one who's usually telling the group to do that. "Perfect, okay."

"Judith," Bella says, in junior-therapist mode, "Sue Ellen is dealing with something with her skin, I don't know if you know that."

"Yeah, oh yeah," Coché says consolingly.

"We can see, yeah," Leigh adds.

Sue Ellen's eyes are puffy, like she's been crying all night, and there is a rashy swath across her chin. She's wearing the same white polo shirt and pale blue pants that she had on yesterday, when she stood confidently on her head.

"So when you see Marie looking down and sort of holding herself together," Coché says, addressing the group, "and you see Sue Ellen looking blotchy and really uncomfortable, how do you feel, and how can you communicate that? This becomes a model for the kind of interaction that you want to have with your partner." Her voice drops. "Let's start with Sue Ellen: What's really happening?"

Sue Ellen says that she's inflamed, she thinks, because she had wine last night, and her skin reacts to alcohol sometimes, as it does to dairy and excessive amounts of carbohydrates. Another contributor, she says, could be her anxiety over her youngest son's screaming at her the day before the group, insisting he be allowed to stay alone in the house when she and Mark go on vacation in a week. She sighs. "It just gets me in my stomach, and I feel like I'm all over the place, like I haven't been in a long time."

Sue Ellen has suffered from progressively worsening eczema since childhood, she's told me outside the group, and she's tried every kind of medication to treat it. When her three boys were in grade school, and Mark had just gotten the job he has now, with the four-hour round-trip commute, she was bedridden for weeks at a time, her face broken open, her back scored by a rash, her hands blistered. The sores exuded a "terrible odor," she says, and were a breeding ground for dangerous staph infections. Steroid shots helped, and at times her skin was "fine," but the threat of another outbreak was omnipresent. "I just felt like how could anybody stand to look at me," Sue Ellen says slowly. "I can't even stand to look at me. I think"—she pauses—"I started closing myself in."

Mark first witnessed her eczema in the early months of their marriage. Within days of their wedding, they moved to a small town in Louisiana for his first job out of college, with the U.S. military. They had to get there in time for him to join a ship for a three-month research mission in the Pacific. Sue Ellen, who'd never been away from home before, was not allowed to accompany him and knew no one in her new hometown. Upon his return, Mark was "shocked" by her skin, he says—"she went to everybody, dermatologists, allergists, you name it"—but to no lasting avail. As soon as he could, he found a job back east (he hated the government gig, anyway) so she could have the help of her sisters.

It had occurred to Sue Ellen that her condition had emotional roots as far back as their stay in Louisiana, but it wasn't until a good twenty years later, around the time that the couple and their son were referred to Coché, that Sue Ellen's long quest to cure her eczema led her to try something called the "emotional freedom technique." EFT is based on the belief that many illnesses are caused by unresolved negative emotion—and eczema has long been linked to stress, even by conventional doctors. It involves lightly tapping various spots on your face and hands while repeating some version of what Sue Ellen says: "Even though my skin is broken out, I deeply and completely love and accept myself." She calls the calming of her skin "awesome," and she has come to use EFT not only to treat episodes of eczema but to manage the upsetting feelings that she believes precipitate them.

Sue Ellen also is a fan of the bestselling author and alternative medical practitioner Louise Hay, who's known for linking a list of ailments to various metaphysical causes. For eczema, the culprit is "breathtaking antagonism," but you don't have to be a New Age healer to believe that the terrors and neglect of Sue Ellen's childhood drove her to choke back her feelings, to keep herself as small and unobtrusive as possible, only to have her body betray her, to erupt red and raw. The sad irony is that her painful, unsightly skin only pushed her further inside herself, so that the already nominal allotment of confidence and assertiveness she'd taken from her girlhood, which flowered briefly in her late adolescence with Mark, retracted into a hard kernel.

So now, in her late forties, it might be considered a modest victory for Sue Ellen to simply sit and tell ten people she feels ashamed that she risked the wine, humiliated by her face, as mild as the outbreak is, and to allow herself to sop up their compassion. For some people, this kind of confession would be routine, or even the very opposite of progress. For Sue Ellen, it's a shoot of green.

"I just feel for you," Leigh says, her voice breaking. Yesterday Sue Ellen was "radiant" during the Pilates, she says, and then to have this happen. "And I'm just sorry you're so hard on yourself."

Mark starts to say something, but Coché shushes him. "Wait, what Leigh's doing now is *beautiful* emotional leadership, so let's just let it happen."

"I really . . ." Leigh begins. She looks sadly across the room to Sue Ellen. "I really feel badly."

"Who else in here feels badly?" Coché asks, and the group is nodding, except for Marie, who looks like she's sleeping. "For Leigh to reach out and capture the sentiment of the group is just very lovely," Coché continues. There is a long silence.

"And it makes me uncomfortable," Sue Ellen says. "It just confirms that I look as bad as I feel." Mark has taken her hand.

"No, it doesn't confirm that at all," Coché says. "It simply confirms that people care deeply about you and wish you weren't so hard on yourself."

"Yeah," Sue Ellen says, sounding unconvinced.

Finally, Coché asks the question the rest of the group is sitting on: Does Sue Ellen think her skin reaction has anything to do with what happened with Marie yesterday?

"I don't think that's—" Sue Ellen begins.

"You don't think that's it," Coché talks over her. It's like she thinks Sue Ellen is being obstinate by refusing to entertain the possibility.

"No, 'cuz I—"

"Would you tell us a little bit about what happened when you [tried to talk to Marie], just so it's out on the table?" Coché probes.

"Um, I'd rather not," Sue Ellen says. (And later she'll tell me that she hadn't wanted to look in on Marie at all—Marie told everyone to stay away, didn't she?—and she *does* think her eczema may have been provoked by her self-recrimination about being unable to refuse Coché. The thought crossed her mind when Coché was quizzing her, but Sue Ellen kept it to herself. She's not sure why.)

"Okay, okay," Coché says, resigned. She's not going to unlock the cage of what she'll later call the "elephant in the room" that way.

The group spends the rest of the morning on weight, the most engaged, if tortured, segment between Rachael and Michael. Once again, he gets perturbed that none of his proposed solutions to her problem, this time her inability to lose weight, are "good enough"; she's at a loss to say why he's missing the point, only that she feels handled or managed more than "supported"; he feels blamed and lashes out with a "joke" about how Rachael can never eat just a bowl of ice cream, she has to shovel in a whole quart. Ha, ha.

"You're not responsible for *everything*," Mark rumbles to Michael, whose eyes widen for a split second, like Hey, I never thought of it that way.

Mark looks almost professorial today, peering through the half-glasses on the tip of his nose. Ever since Mark played Michael's bullying father in the second group, Michael has seemed to look up to him, or at least listen to him with an extra measure of respect. The younger man's regard may also soothe Mark in some small way. Mark's face slackens and his eyes fill at any allusion to his rampages and his lost time—working, always working—with his now-grown sons.

Coché has an idea. "Michael, can you stand up for a moment. Can I joke?"

"Sure," Michael says.

"You'll like this. Raise your right hand, repeat after me: Send me."

"Send me," Michael repeats, dopily raising his right hand.

"Your tired," Coché intones, holding up her own hand.

"Your tired."

"Your poor."

"Your poor."

"Your huddled masses."

"Your huddled masses."

"Who are you?" Coché asks.

"I'm the Statue of Liberty, I think."

"Who are you responsible for?"

"The huddled masses?" Michael ventures.

"Uh-huh," Coché says. She's not referring specifically to Rachael here. Michael's wife is only one of the masses whom he tries to patch up (so as to divert any claims), though in the next session Rachael *will* appear huddled and pitiable, unfortunately.

Part of Michael's task, Coché goes on, is to figure out where his I'll-help-you-get-better/get-better-or-else impulse comes from and how he can learn "to make some new decisions, to stop automatically living in the past and live in the present." Michael admits he doesn't always understand how he's hurting Rachael but wants to do better, and just before lunch, I notice they've gone from stonily staring at each other to holding hands.

Before the group breaks, Coché takes another pass at Marie. "We just want to invite you to share with us where you are. How can we help?"

Marie keeps her head in her hand. The only reason she came today, she says, is because of the "contract," prompting Coché to ask why she'd told her she was "fine" before the group began.

"Because I wanted you to drop the situation immediately," Marie says.

"Why?"

"Because I don't want to discuss it." (As Coché would tell Marie more than once, "If I'm the person you engage to help you when there's a mental health disaster, I can't just ignore you when you seem traumatized.")

"Are you angry with me?" the therapist asks.

"Yeah, a little bit. There are just times that I have to regroup."

"Did I push too hard yesterday?"

"When I want to go off and be alone, that's when I need to be alone. When I say I'm fine, that means just *drop* the subject."

"Could you do me a favor," Coché says, as calm and collected as if she were asking Marie for the time, "and instead of saying you're fine, could you say, 'I need to be by myself'?"

"Um, no, I find that when I say that, the response is the exact opposite," Marie says, seemingly referring to the ghosts of her father and brothers that Coché believes are lurking in the room.

The discussion of weight wasn't a total bust, and Coché will tell me that she, indeed, offered it as a kind of balm. "You could've gotten me to talk about anything, I think," she says, with a laugh. "As I felt Marie in the room, it seemed so heavy to me, and I'm thinking, How are we going to get through this next six hours, who's going to talk about what? Is she gonna run out again?" Put another way, she was tending to group "cohesiveness," which Coché defines in her book as the "degree to which the group is attractive to its members." There is a circular relationship, she says, between the level of honesty among members and their desire to show up and participate: People aren't going to reveal themselves if they're sour on the group, and the more they reveal themselves, the more sweet, or cohesive, the group becomes to them.

Some of Coché's gambits with the group that to me seem the most silly or tangential—for example, next month she'll make a point of having Leigh pass out Hannukah gelt—are her efforts to encourage cohesiveness. My perhaps ticklish radar for mawkishness aside, I'm not sure the gestures work. Then again, I'm not sure they don't. Coché is like the mother who insists that her Thanksgiving guests go around the table and say something they're grateful for. The teenagers and Grandpa may squawk, but secretly everyone feels better for the ritual.

Along similar lines, I'm taken aback at how strongly Coché praises people in the group, especially for their intelligence. I mean, they all seem smart, but they aren't a bunch of geniuses. Coché says it's her way of focusing on the positive without having to prevaricate. "It's my way of saying that these are good folks, these are special folks—you can trust them. If I thought they were a group of warm people, I'd say that, but it doesn't feel like that to me."

She hopes that her readiness to exalt what's decent in the members will not only build cohesiveness in the group but serve as an object lesson for at-home use. The benefits of appreciating one's husband or wife sound obvious, but as anyone who's long married knows, gestures of affection and regard don't come easily in the domestic fray. Yet when one spouse manages to rise to the occasion, to give glowing notice to the other, the goodwill that ensues can seem of a much greater magnitude than the puny words that precipitated it. (Assuming, that is, a couple isn't in one of those cognitive traps where even the good is interpreted as bad.)

As the twisty, penetrating thinker Adam Phillips, a London psychoanalyst, muses in his 1996 book of aphorisms, *Monogamy:* "What if our strongest wish was to be praised, not to be loved or understood or desired . . . ? We might find ourselves saying things like: the cruelest thing one can do to one's partner is to be good at fidelity but bad at celebration? . . . Or it's not difficult to sustain a relationship but it's impossible to keep the celebration going. The long applause becomes baffling."

Coché seems to instinctually grasp the value of wild clapping for one's spouse. The group has overheard her on the phone calling her husband "my hero" for fixing the office plumbing; she regularly credits him for a miraculous revamping of the office computer system. To me alone, she calls him her "rock," "a worthy opponent," "a strong, powerful man"; she brags about his various accomplishments. It could be construed as a bid for reflected glory, but it's also a way to keep the celebration going.

Before Marie's defection, Coché planned to spend the second day of the two-day meeting digging back into the couples' sexual relationships. Carlson's movement exercises—and an afternoon last month the group spent with a massage therapist—had seemed like a neat segue into the physical. Since sex was sidelined in the second group, Coché has felt like the couples have been treating it as *her* topic, "rather than one of the central pieces of a marriage."

Coché's new priority is to "bond" the group. At least with weight, she reasons, people will be brushing up against how they feel about their bodies, which potentially could lead to the delicate matter of sexual desire. If it doesn't, so be it, because what's most important now is to show the members that they can "get through tough situations," she says. "We all survived, and we're able to sit and talk. We're a little bit wounded from what happened, but not *so* badly, and we can move forward together." The crises of marriages require the same steadying, the same forbearance, though in this case the battle will sooner or later have to be reengaged, Coché believes. The group will have to return to Marie and her "inappropriate behavior." Likening the group to a family, Coché says that you can't ignore the "tempestuous adolescent" in your midst forever, no matter how fearsome she looms.

Coché doesn't have to wait long. After lunch, Marie is missing. She went to her car to eat alone and hasn't returned. When Coché declines Clem's offer to try to fetch her, Mark begins: "Maybe you can help me with this, Judith, because I'm not feeling good about it." His arms are folded across his chest.

"About Marie?" Coché asks.

"Yes," he says. Mark can't (or won't) explain his reaction to her behavior much beyond that, which is typical, but in this group "not feeling good" passes for murderous rage.

"Well, usually if one person in the group feels that way, then other people do, too, so you're probably representing a silent subgroup," Coché says. "So let's talk a little bit about this. We're not going to talk about Marie." Her demurral rings false; she knows that they are going to talk about her and, in fact, she thinks they *have* to do so to move on. Coché asks the group to consider how they cope with silent, smoldering presences in their own lives.

Immediately, they get into Marie's claim at one point this morning that she had a migraine. Did she or didn't she, they're asking, the implication being maybe she could be forgiven her sulkiness if she had a *physical* ailment. They go on like this, circling, loath to admit they feel like throttling her for paradoxically controlling the group by refusing to participate. For waving them off when they inquired into her well-being but then sitting here with "that look in her eyes," as Clem says, like a queen disgusted with her court.

"I'm hearing the door," Clem says. Shhh! The group looks like they've been caught in the act. Marie is *here*! She's in the waiting room! Even Coché blanches: Has she broken her own policy? she seems to be thinking. Never trash a member who's not in the room to defend herself? Well, that's not really a *policy*, and this group isn't capable of truly trashing anybody (to their credit or not, sometimes I'm not sure).

Coché shifts to the middle of her chair, plants her feet on the floor. Who knows when Marie will grace the group with her presence? Coché will not be intimidated.

So what's it like when someone gives you the silent treatment? Coché picks up, glancing at the door, before focusing on Mark. Sue Ellen has mentioned her parents' epic silences, and how she had been mortified to find herself attacking Mark in the same way.

"It feels manipulative," he says, when Marie walks in. Without a word, she heads straight for her seat on the couch, next to Bella.

"Marie, people are still working with how they feel about you today," Coché says.

Oh Christ, you can hear her thinking.

"That's what you walked into. So they're not talking about you per se; they're talking about what it feels like in a community when that happens. That's what you've walked into. And Mark led it off and said,

'I need some help. This feels really hard.' So that's what you've walked into." Coché is repeating herself, I think, out of nerves. "So what people said was that the 'fine, thanks' felt dismissive."

"It was," Marie says, with knifelike economy. "I wanted to move on."

"I understand that," Coché says, "but . . ." And on it goes, with Leigh saying Marie is reminding her of father's "abusive" retreats from her family, how the man acted like a "six-year-old," with Coché saying that "if someone is present, they can't be *absent;* the energy is too high." Bella goes so far as to thank Marie—and sounds like she means it—for helping her to realize how pained she was when she recently called home and her father picked up the phone and passed it wordlessly to her mother. ("He loves you even if he doesn't always show it," her mother had stammered.) Her father falls into prolonged silences when he's angry or just tongue-tied with emotion, Bella says. The problem is figuring out which is which. This time Bella assumes he's worried about her, that he doesn't want her to get pregnant again too soon after her miscarriage.

As the discussion grinds on, Marie's eyes just get narrower, her protestations more verbose, until Coché offers that maybe, just maybe Marie is "transferring" onto group members, transforming them into siblings, such that she'll never be persuaded that the people surrounding her here thirty years later aren't merely attacking her.

"Okay," Marie says simply. It's as if she has returned from a nasty fugue.

This day, as others, Coché is trying to keep Marie from monopolizing the proceedings, but she's equally concerned about her becoming the resident scapegoat, a common danger for people like her in group therapy. Many of the other members, Coché believes, still are uncomfortable about confronting themselves or their spouses. They're perfectly happy, at some level, for Marie to chew up the time and take the role of the "bad" one. Call it round-robin projective identification, with the group's aggression and anger being dumped on ever-ready Marie. Or, Coché says, think again of the tempestuous adolescent, and how systems therapists would perceive her as expressing the subtler but no less damaging dysfunction that the rest of the family avoids. This isn't to say that the teenage savage isn't a pain in the ass, just that she's not *only* that.

And although I wonder if I'm trying too hard to make this group fit the stages Coché has laid out, it does seem that Marie's abrupt desertion, the crisis, cracks people open a bit. Marie gets the group's "juices flowing," Joe observes, if only because she stokes everyone's ire.

For him and Bella, that means revisiting the miscarriage, which Coché says is "hanging out there, unresolved." Joe opens the door, saying the couple had the worst fights they've ever had in the weeks following the miscarriage. He thinks it's because he has been stifling his sadness, to protect Bella. She actually *apologized* to him for losing their baby, Joe says, and if she'd realized how upset he was, she might have blamed herself all over again. Anyway, he continues, he's not really worried it will happen again.

"Why wouldn't you worry?" Coché asks. "That doesn't make sense."

"From my perspective, that was our one," Joe replies. "We've had it, it's over."

Bella shakes her head—add this to her bill of particulars about how her husband bends reality. Instead of addressing her, however, Coché draws Michael into the conversation. It turns out that not only did a miscarriage come between Rachael and her first husband—as she told Bella in the last group—the same is true for Michael in his first marriage. The only difference is *he* was the one who put a cone of silence around the subject. "It drove a wedge between us," Michael says. "I mean, there were a lot of issues, but this was ultimately the one that made us go our separate ways."

"Yes," Coché says solemnly. She first saw him when he and his former wife were divorcing. "So it's crucial that the two of you"—she's addressing Rachael and Michael now—"figure out this support issue." She's referring to Rachael's feeling that Michael was dismissive about her struggle with dieting. "It may be that not talking about something difficult creates more of a schism than talking about it. Just as not flushing what was going on with Marie today was harder than flushing it." ("Flushing" is one of Coché's favorite locutions.) Now she's back to Bella and Joe. Does Joe understand why Bella took umbrage when he said he wasn't worried about her having another miscarriage?

"No," he says.

"I just think it's not true," Bella blurts. "There are so many risks, so many possibilities. Nothing's happened yet, so we don't know. We could be here in another year and never be able to have children ever again, or we could have twins."

"These are the kinds of thoughts that people have when an accident happens," Coché says gently, "and a couple needs to be able to work them through." Instead of telling Bella he's not worried, which may well be true, Coché agrees, might Joe consider saying something like, "If it happens again, we'll deal with it"?

He turns to Bella on the couch and speaks to her inaudibly.

"When I saw Joe turn around and start to say—it made me cry," Rachael says. Her shirt is splotched with tears. "Because I didn't have that."

"You didn't have what, Rachael?" Coché asks.

"Because my first husband"—she's weeping now—"just blocked everything out."

"So you didn't have—" Coché says.

"I guess just the acknowledgment." She laughs, embarrassed. "So I want to say to you as a couple, don't block it out, 'cuz I don't want to see you have that breach. Don't live in a fantasy world, Joe." She laughs again, kindly.

"I don't understand what to say or how to react," Joe moans. "I've been walking a tightrope, trying to give her space, not stir up the issue, so I'm sorry if I mishandled it." He turns to Bella again; she smiles sadly.

"I don't think you mishandled it," Coché says. "I think both of you couldn't *figure out* how to handle it. You know what's a good thing to do, Joe, dip in and see how you feel."

"Okay," he says.

"So how does it feel to lose the promise of a child, once, even just once?" Coché asks.

Bella's dark eyes fill with tears.

"How does it feel to lose the promise of a child?" Joe repeats. "I mean, let down, depressing. It's like it's your birthday party, and no one shows up."

"Lonely," Coché says.

"Lonely," Joe echoes.

"Empty, disappointed," she continues.

Joe is still around, he says, plodding through his days, "but something is supposed to be going on, and it's not." Bella's face falls, settling into the softer planes of grief.

"The metaphor of a birthday with nobody there is perfect, brilliant," Coché says. "So, Michael, had you been in touch with your feelings, how might it have felt [when your first wife had a miscarriage]? Or should it happen now, how might it feel?"

"I can't—I can't go back to the past. I, you know, we've talked about it ourselves." Michael is squirming under Coché's gaze. "And I kind of always told Rachael, let's not talk about it until it happens."

"It's not dangerous. It doesn't make anything bad happen if you talk about what you're afraid of," Coché says. "Joe, when you began to speak from your heart, Bella's face changed, and she began to feel a level that has been hard for her. By giving yourself permission to feel, it allowed *her* to feel. Michael, I'll model for you." He twitchily pushes the hair from his face.

"Rachael, what are you worried about if you get pregnant?" Coché asks, playing Michael.

"Going through this again," Rachael answers.

"Going through what again?"

"A miscarriage, and the pain."

"Tell me what that was like for you."

"It was lonely, and very, very painful."

"And how was it lonely?"

"Because my husband was in pain and couldn't talk about it, and I was in pain." She pauses. "And it was made worse by my family."

"How did your family make it worse?" Rachael had called her parents in Australia to break the news.

"Because my father said that if I was a cow, and that happened to a cow, he'd shoot it."

Some people gasp; I burst into tears. Rachael is such a good soul—what kind of monster would talk to her that way? No wonder she moved seven thousand miles away.

Coché asks for Michael's reaction, and he says, laughing, "I can't understand why she still talks to her family with all the horrible things I've heard through the years." The group understands fumbling for the right words, they understand the awkwardness of comforting a spouse in front of other people, but Michael's wooden response is of a different order altogether. It's his Dukakis moment, and you wish you could switch off the TV.

"All right, so don't tell Rachael what to do," Coché says roughly. "And get the laughter out of your voice. How do you feel?"

"It's—it's overwhelming," Michael says. His white teeth are cruel. "It's—it's my nightmare, too, that my parents wouldn't love me. And yet it's . . . it's so complex." He laughs again. "I mean I can't even express it."

I might dismiss Michael as a total jerk if it wasn't so obvious that Rachael cherishes him. It's really not just that I trust Rachael's appraisal, though. For some reason I can't put my finger on, I don't think Michael's jerkiness is "global, stable, and internal," as the scientists of cognitive attribution would say. I do wonder, however, if the group is ever going to understand Michael's aversion to his wife's suffering—and to his own anger, for that matter. He has recoiled from Rachael like he's just tasted something rotten—and all behind that rictus of a grin.

CHAPTER 10

―――――――――

The Attachment of

Michael and Rachael

It's the first weekend in December, and nonpracticing Jew that she is, Coché is wearing a silk scarf printed with nutcrackers and Santa Clauses, but she's anything but jolly. She's through playing good cop, it seems—this group had its crisis, now let's get down to it. The group stages are a heuristic device, not a map she expects people to follow, but nonetheless she radiates impatience.

Michael receives the first blast. Coché has just started going around the circle, asking people what they "need to take home today."

"I don't know," he says, fading.

How about the way you won't let your wife mention the *m* word unless and until she loses a pregnancy, I think, or your detachment when Rachael related how her father compared her to a cow due a bullet? Nah. What Michael says is that with his busy holiday schedule at the store, he's actually a "little resentful" that he and Rachael are here rather than taking his rare day off to "bake cookies, decorate the house, do the traditional stuff."

"That's the third group out of nine or ten that you've said, 'I'm not sure why we're here,'" Coché says. "So take a look at that. Are you angry that you signed up for this format, or are you angry at Rachael because she thinks you need this, or at yourself because you actually *do* need it?"

"I'm the one who really pushed, 'Let's do this,'" he says, "sooo . . ."

"Yeah," Coché says, "I remember." That doesn't mean you're willing to come to grips with the troubling aspects of your relationship, she tells Michael. "We have these wonderful kaleidoscopes in our head, and we shift reality to continue to remain the same." She pauses. "Well, since you're here, is there anything you want to take home?"

Michael stares back at her.

"Okay," she says flatly. "Rachael?"

"Um, we kinda talked about what we wanted to work on today, and we really couldn't come up with anything." She seems to have amnesia about the last group, too. Maybe they can discuss a potential visit for Michael to meet her family in Australia? Rachael offers. The group understands why that prospect would put her on edge—it's hard not to beg her to disown her parents, *now*, before they do any more damage—but the trip is too speculative for her comment to have any bite.

"So you're both in agreement that there's not much that feels bad," Coché says.

"Not right now," Rachael says. The two almost seem allied against Coché, which is unusual for Rachael at least. She is not the gushy sort, but she can't conceal how much she looks up to her therapist: the mother she didn't have.

Coché has more in store for Rachael and Michael, but for the moment she moves on.

"I think we can touch on issues about the holidays," Aaron says, "just dealing with behaviors of other family members who—"

"Why would we handle family members who aren't here?" Coché interrupts. "We're dealing with *your* reactions."

"Yes, we're dealing with the reaction of family members," Aaron says, "and the stress that you see when family members get together. It's not things I—"

"The stress that *you* feel," Coché says.

"Yeah, yeah, yeah."

"That you, *Aaron*, feel."

"I, Aaron, feel as part of a couple. Yeah, and—"

"We don't feel things as part of a couple. We feel things as individuals," Coché corrects. "I'm sorry to—"

"No, that's all right," Aaron says over Coché.

"I'm just trying to—"

"No, no, no," he says, speaking over her again.

"—get you to the place where we can actually work."

"Um, also maybe touching on—" Aaron blunders on.

"Wait. Stop. We don't feel things as part of a couple." Coché's words are pinging off Aaron like hard, little SuperBalls. "I don't know how to feel something *with* my husband. I just know how *I* feel something."

"But you can get a sense of his feelings, right?" Aaron asks.

"That's not what concerns me," Coché says. "What concerns me is managing my *own* feelings. He's gotta worry about his."

The couple had a session with Slowinski that they might "touch on," Aaron begins anew, "and, um, the grudges as it relates to anger." (The theme for the day was "Grudge Collection," Coché announced earlier, "the internal, fleeting thoughts of 'Oh, here she goes again, or here he goes again.'") Then there's a quarrel he and Leigh had in the car on their way to the group, Aaron continues, "which, uh, we could touch on."

"So pick one," Coché says. "What feels like the hardest?"

"Um, probably the latter one."

"The grudge from the trip down?"

"Yeah."

"Good, okay," Coché says.

"We can touch on that," Aaron says.

"But, we, we're not going to *touch* on it." If only Coché could rise up to her full height, stalk over to Aaron, and shake him by the knobby shoulders. "We're a *therapy* group. We'll *work* with it." (When Aaron an hour later tees off with one of his monologues about his "repressive background," she'll cut him off again: "Leave it, we know your background.")

Marie and Clem get a pass—Marie seems to have recovered from the bump debacle; the couple says they have a specific incident to discuss, and after last time, there is no way Coché is going to get bogged down with them right away. Interestingly, Marie had her hair cut sometime between this group and last, the one seemingly inhabited by her boorish father and brothers. Her once waist-length hair is now just below her shoulders.

"Dealing with grudges is great," Joe says, when his turn comes. "I think I could teach a course in it, on how to hold 'em, how to create 'em." He's generically self-flagellating again, but Coché doesn't pick up the switch he offers. She wants to know why he has failed to make an appointment for a medication evaluation with a psychiatrist, as he'd promised her. In her consultations with Bella and Joe between groups, she's become "concerned about some of the unevenness in his behavior," she tells the group.

Joe strokes the side of his face. Wellllll, he says, he was hoping to get the results of a blood test he took for an insurance physical (to forward to the psychiatrist, so he wouldn't have to get another one), and he'd been trying to contact the insurance agency, but then he realized that he never really *had* a blood test for the physical, and, and . . . Now he just wants to start from scratch with the blood test.

"So tell me why you didn't communicate that with me," Coché says. Leigh regards Joe with furrowed brow.

"I didn't realize it till yesterday," Joe says, scrambling. "I—I finally spoke [with the insurer], it was Thursday."

"So how is it that it took you two weeks to call the insurance company, when it was obvious that I was really worried about it?" Coché asks.

"I apologize."

"I'm not asking for an apology. I'm asking you to think about what happens inside you. I appreciate the apology, but you wouldn't be getting [the blood test] for me."

"Right."

"I just had finger surgery, I got a piece of glass in my finger," Coché expounds. "If the surgeon tells me to do something, I don't wait around. I just do it. So what happens with you?"

"Good question, I don't know the answer."

"Let's start with that. This is an example of how group work in the here and now can give you the opportunity to deal with a live issue, which is: How come you didn't get back to me? And you can then translate that into your real life, especially if you've gotten feedback recently that sometimes you drop the ball. Have you gotten that feedback?"

"Yeah, mm-mmm." Joe's lapses seem to have something to do with the restaurant. Neither he nor Bella is giving any details, however. (Though later Coché practically screams that they should. Joe and Bella have "a lot, lot, lot, lot, lot, lot, lot" going on between them at the restaurant," she says. By the seventh "lot," you want to clamp your hand over Coché's mouth, but Joe and Bella hang tough. They don't crack.)

And what does Bella want to address?

"Um, I think the area of the baby and weight and stuff like that would be good."

"Say it more specifically," Coché says, "because if I said it that way, I wouldn't know what I was talking about."

"*I* know what I'm talking about," Bella says.

"I know *you* know what you're talking about," Coché responds with matching pique. She just wants the woman to stop cosseting herself with generalities or obfuscatory psychobabble. Bella's appearance suggests she's ready (or should be ready?) to try another tack. Two groups in a row, she's been rumpled and bleary, which is out of character for her.

Mark comes in for similar treatment from Coché when the couples review their goals for the year. He says he still needs to "gather more tools and sharpen the tools I've got so I can deal with situations in a productive way without causing pain for everybody involved."

"Give us some real-time examples," Coché says.

"Um, when I'm in a situation that could make me angry, how I could react to that situation without blowing up."

"Are you still blowing up?"

"No," Mark says forcefully.

"Then why do we need to work on that?"

"Uh, well, even though I'm not blowing up, I don't think that's completely gone. Things are going well at home, so I don't get tested as often, but I feel like I could easily slip back."

"So can you think about, with Sue Ellen, resentment that builds up that you don't talk about very much?"

"Hmm, toward *her*?" he says.

"Yeah, her," Coché deadpans. "Sue Ellen, who at all times approaches perfection—that one."

Coché hopes to *raise* Mark's level of anxiety, to give him a shove to change, or at least to consider whether he or his marriage still need to.

It's not that she is unimpressed with the strides the couple has already taken in their close to two years with the group. Since Mark confessed his transgression with his son to Coché, he hasn't gotten physical, or even particularly loud, with any of his children. Mark is the "poster boy for therapy," Coché has said to me. "He takes what he hears and runs with it."

Coché also isn't a therapist who is suspicious of the power of positive thinking, which is dispositional for Mark and which Sue Ellen is trying to cultivate with her affirmations. Coché once told me how in college she'd been thrilled to be selected for an elite singing group but found herself terrified to sing solos: "I decided I just couldn't be shy, it wasn't going to work." Pondering how to change, she hit upon the word "poise" and walked around campus repeating to herself: "p-o-i-s-e, p-o-i-s-e." It worked, she said.

Her faith in can-do optimism notwithstanding, Coché worries that as a couple, Mark and Sue Ellen have a tendency to coast over rough spots—really, he pulls her along for the ride—and then wonder how things got so bad. Something like that happened with their son's drug abuse.

So for the first time, Coché utters the word "resistance" with the group. "It's what your body does when you want to change, it's what your spirit does, your emotions do. They push back. They go, 'We're not changing. We're gonna do Christmas, we're gonna play. We're gonna talk about other people, take care of everybody else. We're gonna go intellectual, or we're gonna say, 'Let me help you, darling, because there's nothing wrong with me.'"

Everyone in the group can recognize themselves in there somewhere. And eventually, as the day goes on, Coché shakes loose a few authentic interactions from the couples. Aaron says, for instance, that he resents it when Leigh "barks" at him.

"Most people would, Aaron," Coché says, laughing appreciatively.

"Well, I mean, 'barks' is probably not the right word," Aaron balks. He's not sure how to take Coché's teasing.

"You're running away from barking!" Coché exclaims.

He *was* on the right track. He tiptoes a little further. "Well, I feel, uh, diminished when Leigh barks at me."

"Yeah, I bet," Coché says, nodding. "Anybody in here feel diminished if their partner barks at them?" The chorus does its job.

"So if you tend to be anxious by nature," Coché says pointedly, to Aaron, "you internalize feeling intimidated by your partner's anger pretty easily. And we kinda live like this." She cowers behind her upraised hands, like a sinner before a wrathful God. "So do you tend to be a little anxious by nature, maybe you think?"

"Yeah, yeah," Aaron says. "And that can cause resentment, obviously."

"It *does* cause resentment. Who wants to live like this?" Coché cowers again. "And it's hard to feel sexy when you're living like this." Cower. "So how would it impact feeling sexy?"

"It—it would retard that process totally."

"Not *would*. It does."

"Yeah, it does."

"How?"

"By not wanting to be around the person, much less touch and feel them in any way."

Aaron is speaking his own words, breaking free of the bobble-headed mimicry of Coché. I know from talking to him outside of the group that he's an educated, relatively worldly man, but he can be so mechanical in the group, a product of anxiety in part, that I find myself forgetting that. So I'm surprised not only at his directness but at the precision of his vocabulary. He came up with "bark"; he came up with "diminish"; *he* said he doesn't want to "touch and feel" his wife in this situation. Anxiety can make you stupid.

"So can you turn to Leigh," Coché says, "and tell her, 'When you bark at me, I don't want to be around you sexually for a while.'"

"Leigh, when you bark at me I don't want to be around you in terms of intimacy and sexuality." (*In terms of intimacy and sexuality?* He's backsliding, alas.)

"Thank you for sharing that," Leigh says without reservation. "It helps me when you speak up and tell me what I'm doing." The group believes her—despite the fact that she's thanking her husband for finding fault with her, despite the "sharing" lingo. The group is as grateful as she is.

As Aaron and Leigh talk, Coché is watching Bella out of the corner of her eye. "Bella," she says, "your face was wonderful. What did it feel like when you heard Aaron say that?" There are indeed tears in the young woman's eyes.

"It was touching," she says.

"Tell him," Coché says.

Bella looks at Aaron full-on. His bumptious speechifying has prompted many a stifled yawn from the group, but perhaps Bella is seeing a more complex person in this moment, a man deserving of new respect. "It was very straight, and honest," she compliments Aaron.

"And then it was also how well you received it," Bella tells Leigh. "It's moving."

"It's very liberating when your partner is holding up his end to make a couple," Marie jumps in, addressing Leigh. This is Marie's idée fixe. In her own marriage, she continues, it would be "so lovely" if she could state her position, Clem could state his, then together they could formulate "our position." "*Our* position," Marie says again, as if savoring a rich chocolate on her tongue.

Near the end of the day, Rachael says she wants to return to a comment Michael made in the morning about the insistent internal mandate he feels to please her, which includes not taking any time for himself after work. He's overdoing it, Rachael says. She likes time alone, too. They're straining to talk it out when Coché stands up from her chair. "I'll be right back," she says, with a verbal wink.

The earlier discussion began when Michael said that his remaining goal for the year was to become more "emotionally greedy" for himself, "to stop being so giving." Of course the group knows him to be emotionally stingy with his wife almost to the point of inhumanness, but they'd also heard about the guy who abruptly dropped his dream of having a motorcycle because he couldn't bear upsetting Rachael.

To get underneath the two seemingly contradictory states, Coché had first instructed Michael to say that he had "needs that deserved to be met," then add that if he didn't get what he deserved, "he'd be impossible to live with."

Michael mouthed the words like a bewildered kid. His pale, water-color eyes were smooth reflecting pools, blinkingly turning from face to face. *I'm a martyr, not a persecutor. I'm a martyr, not a persecutor.*

Trying another tack, Coché recalled from the last group how he pressed fattening food on Rachael, even though he knew she was trying to lose weight. Why would he do that? Maybe because he believes he can't need anything, so he's in a perpetual state of depri-vation, the group suggested, and covertly, irrationally "punishes" his wife for it.

"So I make Rachael try the food because I'd feel bad if she didn't get an opportunity?" Michael asked, off by a mile.

Coché reconnoitered once more, suggesting to him that while he "loves to play," he feels guilty unless Rachael plays with him. "You get to enjoy without her," Coché declared.

"Because you . . ." Bella coaxed.

"I deserve it," Michael said, sighing deeply. It wasn't that Michael refused to admit to any aggressive impulses, it was as if he was unaware he had them.

Now Coché pokes her head back in the room. "Michael, come with me. I promise I won't hurt you." He drags himself out. A minute later, he reenters wearing a navy T-shirt that reads ANGER IS MY FRIEND. Coché evidently has a stash of these in her closet.

"Blue is really my color," Michael jokes, humorlessly. He takes his seat next to Rachael. "Now that I'm labeled," he says, sounding, well, a touch angry.

"How are you labeled exactly?" Coché asks.

"It's—"

"Oh, your label is *angry*," Coché says.

"Yes," Michael replies.

"No," Mark says. "It means that you don't recognize that anger can be your friend." The obvious is eluding Michael.

If you don't note your anger, Aaron says, you'll "schmolder." He's unintentionally turned the "smoldering" to which Coché has referred into Yiddish—the group howls, affectionately.

"Anger lets you know when something is not correct," Marie tells Michael.

"It's your body's way of saying things are not all right," Coché piles on. Feelings, including anger, are harmless in and of themselves; it's how you manage them that matters. "But when you have been raised as disconnected from your negative feelings as you have, anger is in charge of you. It disconnects you from yourself; it puts a smile on your face. It leads you to do things that aren't good for your wife.

"If you're angry and your automatic reaction is to not know that you're angry," Coché continues, "then it will catch up with you and act like a tornado before you know it. And the tornado may be a sweet smile, a passive stance, something that just seems slightly out of step, like why would you offer somebody french fries if they're telling you they don't want french fries." She is zeroing in on Michael again, and she notices how grim he looks. He's never looked so sad—or is it mad? He's wearing this stupid T-shirt, and being picked apart like a turkey after the big meal.

"I'm sorry to do this, because I know it's not very pleasant," Coché says to him. "But anger really is your friend, and we have to help you connect to the pipeline that is anger, because, like Aaron, you are probably good and angry about stuff that has happened." She shakes her head sympathetically. "Good and angry."

Apart from the callousness Michael's father displayed after his son's car wreck, the group doesn't know what "stuff" she's referring to, but it sounds specific. "Is that possible?" Coché asks softly.

"Yes," Michael says, subdued.

"It's possible," Coché affirms.

"Most likely," Michael says, almost imperceptibly.

As soon as the focus shifts away from him, Michael slips off the T-shirt and folds it into a neat square—he's been working retail forever. Watching him, I feel hollow.

"What I learned from my parents is that to have control in a relationship you need to devalue the other person," Michael begins, in the next group. He clears his throat. "And then, if that doesn't work, use sarcasm and emotional detachment to distance yourself from what you can't control—"

"Wow!" Bella says.

"—what *I* can't control," Michael finishes with a flourish. He's even correcting his own distancing pronouns.

The group is agog. New year, new you, like the magazines say. It's January, and between the last group and this one Michael has gone from bovine self-awareness to describing his own modus operandi with plain-spoken eloquence. Michael can't say exactly how he came to the realization; he thinks it might have been inspired by a questionnaire Coché gave the couples in December's grudge-holding group—he measured high in resentment—but he's really not sure.

"Wow!" Now it's Coché doing the parroting. "That is beautifully understood." Insight may be only half the battle for change, but this particular insight has been a long time coming. "Say it again," she tells Michael.

"I use sarcasm or emotional detachment to distance myself from what I can't control." Michael is not smiling, he does not look self-satisfied. He looks sober, like it really stinks to believe this about yourself.

"And it works like a dream," Rachael mumbles sullenly.

New, too: Rachael isn't stroking away her husband's discomfort with her it's-okay-baby half smile. She looks like it stinks to be married to him, or rather to be who *she* is, which makes her suit him so awfully well. What she learned from her family, Rachael says, was that "men are in charge, they take care of everything, your feelings don't count." Coché began the group asking everyone to reflect on the family-sculpting exercise they did last spring and then write a few sentences about what their parents taught them about relationships.

"You're what used to be called a 'neurotic fit,'" Coché says to Rachael and Michael, "where you have two people who are slightly off balance who managed to find each other and can continue off balance in that combination forever." The group laughs.

"A love story," Mark cracks.

"No, no, that's what we're here to figure out," Coché says. "Does that feel bad to you?" She's talking to Rachael, whose eyes are pink. "I hope that doesn't make you feel worse, you're so sensitive today."

"I don't know what to make of it right now," Rachael says, confused and sagging. She'd been so sure that fun-loving, malleable Michael was unlike her former husband, who, though well intentioned, was controlling and remote. "The great irony of many relationships," writes the psychoanalyst Stephen Mitchell, "is that the presenting feature of the other person, the quality for which we chose that person, often operates in his or her own psychic economy as a defense against precisely the opposite." An emotional bait-and-switch if ever there was one.

Michael has his own bait-and-switch to contemplate. He has spent his life believing that he is passive and accommodating, the antithesis of his father. "I don't want to be a bully or domineering or controlling, but it's just happening that way," he pleads to the other men in the group. (Coché has broken them into single-sex subgroups; she's leading the husbands, while her guest coleader for the day, her psychiatrist daughter Juliette, takes the wives.) "I always, I—I think about all the times I correct Rachael, like, 'You should do the wash this way, you should cook like this . . .' I didn't learn how to form a loving relationship; I learned how to form an economic alliance, and—and—it's just scary." He'd met his first wife while he was still living at home, he says, and *she* was the authority figure. She knew exactly what she wanted—to become a doctor—and Michael followed her from college to grad school to her first job. His attitude, he says, was "Yes, ma'am."

"Well," Coché says, "as I only half jokingly said that my hope for Bella was that she'd trust us enough to become a member of the group—which I assumed would take a while because she is so accustomed to being in charge—my wish for you was that you'd feel safe enough to begin to use your intellect to notice how awful this feels."

"It does feel bad," Michael replies. "I'm like tearing up constantly, so I know it's there." In an early group, he got into a snit when Rachael said in passing that she adored it when he cried during movies. She *had* sounded patronizing, but his reaction registered as disproportionate for a second-millennium therapy group: Boys still don't cry, dammit!

There is also a new wrinkle in Michael and Rachael's lives: She has sunk into a moderate depression. In the December group, she'd enthusiastically related how she was on the verge of being hired by an employment agency to help foreign workers acclimate to the United States, but the offer didn't come through. (Her last exciting new job has not turned out like she'd hoped.) She's known she is vulnerable to depression but has not wanted to believe it, chalking it up in the past to PMS or, as Coché says, "a bad marriage" (to her first husband). But, "since this job thing happened, I've just been seesawing. Um, and it's really scary, 'cuz"—she sighs—"because I feel out of control and um, um, I just want the old self back, I just, 'cuz one morning I woke up and I said to Michael, 'Where am I? Where have I gone?' That bright, bubbly person who used to just do stuff." She's crying.

Coché summons the group to care for Rachael, particularly coleader Juliette, who as a psychiatrist has been schooled in the use of psychotropic medications, and Marie, whose own depression has been severe. The two urge Rachael to stop beating up on herself for something she can't help, and coach her toward taking a few steps to feel better. It turns out that she is taking an antidepressant—prescribed by a psychiatrist to whom Coché referred her when she and her first husband were splitting up—but the dose is so small that many doctors would consider it "subclinical," or not enough to make any difference. She can't remember why her dose is so small. Maybe her psychiatrist was acceding to her reluctance to pop pills for what she's long considered a deplorable "weakness." Or maybe he kept the amount low because during the throes of her divorce, she was taking an antianxiety medication, too, and she couldn't take too much of either. In any event, she agrees to consult with the doctor again.

"It's not that a psychiatrist can give you more Celexa so you don't have to deal with the fact that you didn't get the job," Juliette soothes, "but so you can get back to a more balanced sense of Rachael, so you can *handle* the fact that you didn't get the job."

"But I think I can, the fact that I didn't get the job," Rachael says brokenly. "There's other stuff."

"So, Rachael, tell us the other things," Coché says lovingly.

"Well, this all is affecting us," she whispers, not looking at Michael. "We're just withdrawing from each other."

"And that's really scary?"

"Particularly because tonight we're going to Michael's work party, and I'm supposed to be this bubbly, fun person"—she is crying so much she can barely get the words out—"and I'm just not there."

"Would it help if I told you that it's not going to affect our relationship—or *anything*—if you don't go tonight?" Michael says. They're not on the couch. They're on separate, wide-seated chairs, and he has reached across the divide to hold her hand.

"I think it would've helped if you said it earlier," she says. "For example, last time I was like this, you said that I'm like most women, who cry to get out of stuff."

"He said *what*?" Coché asks.

"Something to the effect that women cry to get out of things," Michael acknowledges.

"And I found that really offensive," Rachael says, "because I couldn't control my crying." And she starts weeping again.

"So it leads you to worry that he's judging you," Coché says, "like your mother did." (Rachael remembers her mother's response to her emotional lability as "Snap out of it!")

Michael turns to his wife, still holding her hand. "Rachael," he says earnestly, "I wish you could be in my head so you could see that I'm not judging you."

"But can you understand why I would feel that way, given that comment?" It doesn't seem like a mistake for Rachael to keep at him; rather, it seems like a positive development.

"It wasn't last night that I said it, though," Michael says. "It was a long time ago, before the depression started." His tone has remained undefensive. "I've had a lot more education in depression than when we first got together. I understand it a lot better than I did before."

"In other words," Coché says, "you're sorry that you said some of those things—"

"I am sorry," Michael says, "there's a lot of things—"

"Then you can just say that," Coché says.

"I'm sorry that I said those things, and that they hurt you." He looks into Rachael's eyes. "And they were said out of ignorance."

"It was like you put a knife in my back," Rachael continues. She pauses, staring back at her husband. "I know [my depression] is very difficult for you, but it's very, very lonely." The group can barely hear her. She is clutching a soggy napkin in her hand, crying again. "I need you, but I'm scared to reach out to you. It's just that the things you say to me when I'm like this can hurt me even more."

"I don't know what to say," Michael replies, not taking his eyes off Rachael. He has admitted before that he gets undone by Rachael's emotions, but with an air of indignation. Now he seems humble, as if he'd like to learn to say the right thing, he really would.

"Sometimes it's best to shut up," Rachael says softly.

Michael smiles, with what looks like genuine remorse.

Rachael smiles feebly back. "Just be there," she says.

One way of seeing Rachael and Michael's exchange is that they didn't get sucked into one of their typical negative spirals, and if observational marital research has proved anything, it's what an accomplishment that is. "It was as if thousands and thousands of little roots and threads of consciousness had grown together in a tangled mass, till they could crowd no more, and the plant was dying," D. H. Lawrence wrote of the doomed alliance of Clifford and Lady Chatterley. Rachael and Michael had managed to pull a root clean.

It seemed like more than that, however, more than an avoidance of the old. There was heretofore unseen feeling passing between Michael and Rachael: a quickening. Your chest clutched with it, and you imagined the couple collapsing in a heap when they got home, exhausted by the arduousness of the day.

In the argot of attachment theory, which has become one of psychology's central preoccupations in the last twenty years, what happened between them might be called a "bonding" moment. The father of attachment theory is London analyst John Bowlby, who, like Winnicott, was formatively influenced by his work on the impact of maternal deprivation during World War II. From this evidence and his later direct observations of infants, Bowlby inferred that to love and seek love are evolutionarily adapted survival techniques, designed to optimize survival of oneself and, later, one's progeny.

What attachment theory is known for in the public mind is the "strange situation" experiment, in which Bowlby and his colleague Mary Ainsworth had mothers briefly leave their infants, then classified the children according to their reactions to the separations and reunions. There were the "securely attached," whose primary caretakers were thought to relatively consistently meet their needs; the "anxiously ambivalent," whose caretakers were more erratic; and the "avoidant," who couldn't count on their caretakers much at all.

Bowlby always asserted that attachment needs organized our existence from "cradle to grave," but he never investigated what that really meant for grown-ups. It wasn't until 1987, when University of California at Davis social psychologist Phillip Shaver and his then graduate student Cindy Hazan published "Romantic Love Conceptualized as an Attachment Process," that so-called adult attachment was born. And with it, another prism through which to view marriage.

The article was part of Hazan's dissertation, and she'd come to the topic when she happened to be reading about the aftermath of divorce while simultaneously taking a child development course featuring Bowlby. She was struck by the similarities between children's reaction to being separated from attachment figures and that of spouses ending a marriage. First, there was a kind of panic. In the child, that meant lots of screaming and crying, frantic searching for the missing parent. In the adult, the corollary was obsessive rumination about the lost partner, physical agitation, anger. Then lethargy set in, accompanied by sleep disturbances and a dwindling appetite—for young and old alike—until, eventually, adjustment: The child or newly single person returned to normal, though to some degree scarred by the experience.

Convinced that Bowlby's theory of relationships best accounted for the emotional intensity and interdependence in intimate relationships, Hazan and Shaver endeavored to imagine what attachments would look like in adulthood. "We made up a description of an avoidant adult, we made up a description of a secure adult, and an ambivalent one," Hazan says. Since then, their "made-up" categories, as they disarmingly call them, have been refined, but they're the foundation on which adult-attachment experimentation and theorizing are built.

Shaver encapsulates what secure attachments look like in grown-ups this way: "When one person is down or worried or uncertain, they rely on the other person to be their supporter, their caregiver. And that person is able to suspend their own dependency needs to be the caregiver. Then, the way sexuality plays out over time, it's partly putting yourself in another's hands"—trusting that your partner will be available and responsive—"and partly being a caregiver, a sexual caregiver." The big difference between mother-child and adult attachments is that the latter are mutual; husbands and wives depend on each other *and* care for each other. (What the other two attachment styles look like in adults in their purest form is rather predictable: the anxious ambivalent is desperate for approval and affection, yet sends confusing signals. The avoidant fends off intimacy.)

Twenty years, and ten thousand studies since Shaver and Hazan inaugurated a new field, they and their colleagues across the country and the globe have covertly watched how spouses and lovers separate in airports as an adult approximation of the infant "strange situation" experiment. They've tested subjects' ability to suppress thoughts about a painful breakup, confirming that the avoidant were better at it. Interestingly, however, the "defensive strategies" of the latter group broke down when they were asked to simultaneously remember a seven-digit number—the idea being that under a certain level of stress, even the avoidant can't push away an attachment threat.

The research is impressive in its scope and creativity, though the conclusions of adult-attachment theory can seem at once overdetermined—couples depend on each other for emotional support and sexual solicitude, big whoop—and inadequate. For example, investigators who've followed subjects over a couple of decades haven't found a very strong link between attachment security in infancy and that in early adulthood. This raises the question of what is unique or especially powerful about attachment versus friendship or mentorship or kindly attention. Indeed, at least one psychologist has argued that true attachments in adulthood can only be with God or a higher power. Romances lack the necessary dependency dynamic, Bowlby's "stronger and wiser figure."

Hazan brushes aside such criticism, saying that it was foolish to ever assume "perfect stability" between babies and adults. "It's better to think of security as a developmental process with a *tendency* toward stability," she says. She also wants to change the subject a bit. Attachment research has gotten hung up on the whys and wherefores of how the less healthy styles play out in adults rather than explicating the basic human processes. The questions she wants to answer are, for example, how does sex motivate people to initiate and maintain attachment relationships? To suss this out, Shaver et al. recently have subliminally exposed subjects to naked pictures of attractive strangers, then used various methods to test whether the images strengthened attachment-related thoughts about their actual partners. The erotica worked, with qualifications: Don't expect super-duper subliminal computer graphics for commitment-phobes and those who love them to hit the market anytime soon.

Getting out of the lab and imagining attachment systems thrumming inside all of us, ready to awaken with a vengeance when our security is threatened, goes some way to accounting for the terrors (and afore-mentioned terror*ism*) that surface in a gasping marriage. The violence of emotion—or, in Michael's case, its chilling absence—suggest that somebody's very survival is at stake. It is this intuition that led a Cana-dian clinician, Susan Johnson, to use attachment theory in her project to reorient the field of marriage therapy, at least as it's taught in graduate schools and compiled in textbooks.

Owing to its family-systems origins, as well as the popularity of behavioral methods such as contracting and communications training, couples therapy has been unique in that shifts in behavior tend to be sought as the precipitants of fundamental change, as opposed to insight or fresh emotional experience: The agoraphobic wife is "cured" when her husband instructs her that she dare not leave the house. Yet at the same time, there is now broad recognition that many couples can't seem to behave differently, no matter how transparent the wisdom of doing so (or even how clever the paradoxical directive). In psych jargon, couples' "skills deficits" often seem less a problem of "acquisition"—they know what they *should* do—than of "performance." They can't make them-selves do it.

Johnson's answer is her own "emotionally focused therapy," which is a pretty funny name if you aren't up on the brand distinctions among competing couples therapy schools. Who knew you could corner the market on emotion in *therapy*? Johnson gets her own joke: She came up with the name, she has written, as "an act of defiance" against her field's distrust and disregard of emotion. "I used to have huge argu-ments with Neil Jacobson, who for a long time was the king of couples therapy, or at least he thought he was," Johnson tells me in an interview, fondly remembering the now deceased promoter of behavioral couples therapy. "I mean, he would always say, 'Emotion is epiphenomenal. You just ignore it. Change the behavior, change the cognitions, that's what you need to do.' And I'd say, 'Lots of luck doing that. How do you do that?'" The model Johnson developed is part Carl Rogers's humanism, part systems (in its attention to patterns of interaction, not its reliance on behaviorism), and, perhaps most importantly, part "experiential."

Experiential techniques are designed to get the client to encounter something new during the therapy session rather than merely spending the time jawing about that possibility. It's what Coché is agitating for when she exhorts the group to stay in the "here and now," to concentrate on their immediate feelings and thoughts rather than extemporizing about their philosophies on life, love, and happiness. (Proving once again that Freud is the sun no matter how loudly his descendants curse the heat, the psychological profession's use of the phrase "here and now" began with a onetime favorite of Freud, Otto Rank. Rank, who eventually was ousted from Freud's inner circle, argued in his book *Will Therapy* that a patient's defenses could be dismantled in the "here and now"—and thus it is unnecessary to excavate childhood sources. That heresy wasn't the one that got him bounced, however. It was Rank's first book, *The Trauma of Birth,* in which he suggested that *pre-*oedipal issues of separation from the mother, including the physical rupture of birth, might contribute to neurosis. Rank, then, sowed the first seeds for relational therapy.)

Returning to Johnson (who sounds rather like Rank when you think about it), she says about a third of couples come to her with "attachment injuries," in which one partner has violated the expectation that the other will offer care in times of danger or distress. The injuries become the "focal point for all the insecurity in the relationship; they come to stand for all the little hurts," and block progress. The only way to break the impasse, Johnson contends, is to create equally intense moments during therapy sessions.

Which isn't to say that she helps spouses to yell or wail in each other's company. Part of the reason working with emotion has gotten a bad rap in the broader therapy world, Johnson conjectures, is that it has become associated with pure ventilation—primal scream therapy and the like—which easily can perpetuate rather than relieve pain. Johnson's task is to shape strong feelings, with the goal of getting partners to send new, more positive emotional signals to each other, to generate good to crowd out the bad.

In one videotape of her work with couples, a woman named Sarah tells about a miscarriage she suffered several years before. She lost the baby in the bathroom, and when she called her husband, Sam, to come help, he just stared at her and at the blood all over the floor. Her sister drove her to the ER, and Sarah tearfully recalls "sitting in the back of the car, feeling totally alone and holding this butter container filled with my baby." Since then, the wife says that the couple's daily interactions seem to reflect that event—she needs help, he goes cold—and she's become convinced she can't trust the man she married. Seeing how upset his wife is—and with Johnson sitting there so the "couple doesn't do anything too weird," says Shaver, who's watched the tape at conferences—the husband gradually admits that he was so horrified by the bloody scene that he just withdrew. (An avoidant attacher, perhaps?) He is ashamed of himself, Sam says. "I, well, I guess I was just so scared, I—I—I tried to step back and manage the situation, you know." At this juncture, Johnson's "softening" occurs, which is the "culmination of a hundred little realizations, risks, and new perceptions." The couple acknowledges each other's pain, and Sam tells his wife that he doesn't want her to be alone anymore. "I am here for you," he says. "I want to hold you. I want to take care of you."

Intriguingly, considering the upheaval that miscarriages have caused in the group, Johnson says they're a common cause of attachment breaches, right up there with infidelity. It makes sense, she says in our interview. "For the man, a miscarriage is a medical emergency; for the woman, it's the death of a child. Attachment injuries are all about life and death and wanting somebody to stand beside you. There's a dragon coming for me—are you there for me or not?"

And, again, spouses can't talk their way past such ruptures, she says. They have to, in a sense, relive the nightmare while emotionally reconstructing the way it went down. It's *Groundhog Day,* where Bill Murray discovers that only when he reveals himself to Andie MacDowell, in all his perfidy, will the time loop be broken and his love requited. Or as Johnson writes, post-softening, "The couple can do what securely attached partners and children can do in relationships: they can accept and articulate their attachment vulnerabilities; they can ask clearly for their needs to be met, rather than attack or withdraw; and they can take in another's love and comfort, and translate that love into a sense of confidence in themselves and others."

That may sound too good to be true, especially when you consider that Johnson's protocol for getting to this moment takes a mere eight to twelve sessions—but she, and a few others, have conducted studies that show it works as well or better than other models. Still, there is a bit of grandiosity in her claims, if only because a fair number of couples therapists don't genuflect before a single model. As a result, like Coché, they haven't thrown emotion overboard, and they're versed in the power of experiential techniques, one of the most venerable of which, by the way, is family sculpting.

When Rachael asked Michael to "just be there," her words were not met with a pregnant pause in the group, as there would be in the movies—or in staged therapy videos. Coché recognized the momentousness of what had happened, however. By her existentialist reckoning, Rachael had reached the point of despair that paves the way for change, perhaps, ironically, abetted by her depression. In her previous marriage, Rachael would begin to speak up about her needs, Coché says, but then quickly backpedal, or trail off in bewilderment. The group has seen her do that, too: In charged moments with Michael, Rachael more than once has said she feels "confused." Coché ascribes her muddled state to the anxiety incurred by the effort to change; then, too, what better defensive strategy than to retreat inside a mental haze.

This time, of course, Rachael plunged into the clear. Maybe it was because Michael signaled he was ready to hear her by admitting to his own will to control and vindictiveness when he couldn't. Maybe it was because the group and Coché were there to buoy Rachael up. Whatever it was, this was the first time in the group when Rachael didn't immediately lap up the thin gruel of contrition Michael put before her. She took the risk of expanding upon Michael's transgressions: She said how abandoned she felt by him, and asked him to care for her in the future.

Equally noteworthy, Michael stayed with his wife through her sadness; he didn't check out behind a smile or a mean-spirited joke, even when she directly criticized him. He let himself absorb how he'd hurt her, and, not incidentally, to Johnson or Coché—or anyone who'd sat with him over the last eight months—he revealed a weakness: He didn't have the answer, he didn't know what to say.

CHAPTER 11

Joe's Humiliation

Though largely ignored in the aftermath of their miscarriage, a red flag has been waving wildly behind Bella and Joe for some time now. First, there are the strange goings-on at the restaurant: As the manager, Joe has two bosses, Bella and her business partner friend, Tara. And while Bella and Tara may be united in believing that it's only a matter of time before the place is going gangbusters, there has been a steady stream of indications that Joe is not with the program, or is actively messing things up. Or maybe it's that Bella is unfairly blaming him? One time I wrote in my notebook, "Bella seems more married to Tara than to Joe!"

It's true that the last time the couple discussed the business in detail, Joe seemed nearly as upbeat as his wife. With a little swagger in his voice, he talked about how he was dancing with his waitstaff and burning through to-do lists. But that hasn't stopped the flag from whipping around above his head, no matter that the couple is blind to it, or pretends not to notice.

Second, and not unrelated, Bella's condescension toward Joe has continued unabated. Coché definitely notices it, and like *Madeline*'s Miss Clavel awakening with a start in the dark of night, she periodically proclaims, "Something is not right!"

An exchange between Bella and Coché from a few months ago is typical. "At times I'm angry *for* Joe, because he's put himself in a position that doesn't help him," Bella said congenially, like she was discussing a finicky orchid that refused to flourish, "and then sometimes I'm mad I even let him do it in the first place."

"Your use of language—although sophisticated and controlled, there still is the undertone of 'I'm in charge of Joe,'" Coché observed. "I *never* hear that from Joe. So think about authority issues and equal relationships. Because the last thing you need is to be in charge of another adult."

"Yeah," Bella replied, "I've got to make sure he's in charge of himself."

"That's just it," Coché said. "*You* can't make sure he's in charge of himself."

Joe either barely seemed to register Bella's treating him "like a little boy," as Coché said another time, or grinned it away—"that's my wife."

The first time Joe twists around in his chair to acknowledge the danger sign is when it's just him and the other men, with Coché as their leader. Juliette is across the hall with the wives. "One of the hardest things about growing up male" versus female, Coché begins, "is that there is not the same level of respect and dignity associated with knowing one's own heart. The hardwiring is different—we know that—but I am saddened sometimes as I hear some of you talk about the lack of emotional fluency that you grew up with."

She appraises her small group: Clem, with his hands clasped, hanging between his knees; Mark and his confident, mildly bemused demeanor; Michael shifting in his chair, jumpily; and Joe's grave expression. So grave, in fact, it's like he's deliberately arranging his facial features. *Now I'm looking serious,* you imagine Joe saying to himself. It's like he's a silent-screen star doing his first talkie—the mannerisms seem slightly overdone.

The four men (Aaron is home sick) listen carefully to Coché. They all treat her with deference, except perhaps for Michael, who occasionally takes a swipe at her. Since husbands are often hauled into couples therapy by their wives, one of the more important tasks for the therapist is to hook the men, and Coché is good at it. As in this speech, she manages to suggest that it would be smart for the husbands to tune in to their feelings without leaving the impression that they're deficient. Her forcefulness and matter-of-factness also probably help with the men.

Outside of the group, Coché has told me that, of her own parents, she identified most with her father. In 1902, six-year-old Louis Milner emigrated from Russia to Philadelphia with his jeweler father, mother, and seven siblings. When he was twelve, his father died, leaving Louis and his older brother to support the family. The eldest boy took over the family jewelry store, and at the tender age of nineteen, Louis gave up his dreams of becoming an English professor and opened an "apothecary," Coché says. With so many brothers and sisters to support, Louis decided to forgo marriage to devote himself to his business, which quickly thrived. "My father—there was nothing show-offy about him," Coché says, "but he was a big, expansive person, and people really cared about him. His drugstore became known as *the* place to find medicine you couldn't find anywhere else."

Only when he was forty-two—after he'd fulfilled another dream, taking a six-month round-the-world trip—did Louis marry Coché's mother, who was eighteen years younger and a Juilliard-trained pianist. Coché is obviously proud of her mother, for her willowy beauty, for her musical talent and "rebellious spirit"—she tells me her mother studied Schoenberg's twelve-tone music in the 1950s, when the modern form was widely scorned. But she adored her father, who died in 1990 at the age of ninety-four. "My father had a phenomenal sense of humor, and a certain kind of wisdom, a human wisdom that made him a psychologist long before there was such a thing," Coché says.

After her remarks about the trials of "growing up male," Coché tells the men she wants each of them to talk a bit. They glance at each other for a split second—who's going first?

"I—I'll start," Clem says. He's been doing that more, going first, "exercising leadership" as a veteran member of the group, as Coché has been coaxing him to do. She is giving the isomorphic process a push, hoping that if Clem steps up in the group, he'll do the same with Marie.

Coché said earlier that the group would use this session to return to the family influences they'd begun unpacking six months ago, and Clem seems to have metabolized what everybody else noticed from the start: He says he's "amazed" at how he has carried his parents' marriage into his own. To illustrate, Clem embarks on a convoluted story of laundry contratemps between him and Marie, before Joe intervenes. Now Joe is

taking the helm. With brisk Socratic questioning, he guides Clem back
to the underlying dynamic, to how "he puts himself in a position to get
beat up," as if blindly following in his beleaguered father's footsteps.

Then Joe smacks his own forehead with his palm. "Oh, for the love
of God, I'm doing it, too. Are you kidding me?" he says. "I didn't get
until now how much of my parents' relationship I'm striving to re-
create. This is all the crap I couldn't stand! My father was probably one
of the most immature, irresponsible people on the planet, and got yelled
at all the time."

"By your mom?" Clem asks.

"By my mother, yes. And she pretty much yelled at everybody, so
getting yelled at, dressed down—it may be hurtful, but it's kind of,
weirdly, comforting."

"How 'bout 'familiar' instead of 'comfortable'?" Coché says. Getting put in his place is second nature to Joe, she goes on.

"If it doesn't happen, then you're not actually married," Joe says.

"That's what marriage means," Coché echoes.

"That's what a relationship is, right," Joe replies. He's fired up.

"So marriage is getting dressed down," Coché says, "being angry all
the time and not knowing what to do with it."

"Find a hobby and go do it. When you come home, you kiss your
wife on the cheek, eat dinner, then go do whatever it is that you do. My
father had a garage and two cars, and he spent every moment out there."
Then, on the weekends, when his mother gave his father a list of chores,
Joe says he learned that "you should be angry that your wife is telling
you what to do, and do it pissed off."

"So marriage is a matriarchy where the male gains power through
indirect anger," Coché says, hanging on to the "marriage is" game.

"Yeah," Joe mutters.

"Mark, you're nodding," Coché says. "Is that true for you?"

"I don't think it's true for me, but that's a lot of what my father
did." Mark's father was in his refuge, his woodshop, when he slashed his
daughter's portrait.

"Here's what I want to say: A matriarchy feels horrible," Coché says.
"And what happens is the battle goes underground."

"The cold war," Mark says.

"The cold war," Coché affirms. "It's 'Go ahead, let her try to take charge, she'll see.' Or, 'Yeah, she can take charge all right, but she can't control how I feel, I've got that.' So you think of it in terms of family of origin." She's addressing Clem now. "What happens is you remain the unappreciated, helpful guy, and Marie becomes the males in the family she grew up in: dominating, harsh—"

"Total control," Mark says.

"And nobody's soft and loving," Coché says.

"I didn't get enough of it," Joe says, referring to the wifely roughing up. "My marriage actually is a kind of partnership, so I went and made my wife my boss, just to keep that stuff going. It wasn't conscious or intentional, but looking at it, I'm, like, of course I'd end up working for my wife."

"And you could be angry about it," Coché says.

"And I could be angry about it," he repeats.

"Specifically when you're in the restaurant, I guess?" Clem says.

"Yeah."

"It's not just in the restaurant," Coché corrects Joe, "but you've been very open—and this is a nice quality in a way—you've been very open to Bella's leadership." She becomes Bella: " 'Think about it this way, sweetheart.' Or, 'Why don't we do it this way—wouldn't that be a good idea, Joe?' " (Unlike Joe's mother, Bella specializes in eminently reasonable coercion.) "And you tottle off and say, 'Oh, okay, that would be a good idea,' " Coché continues. "But what's going on inside of you?"

"It's humiliating," Joe says. Finally. Joe finally acknowledged the flag.

There's a rustling outside the office—Coché's husband has arrived to pick up Whitby, who's gotten sick. She jumps up and opens the door. "My hero," she says to John, who appears briefly in the doorway. "Thank you, hero. One dog . . . Help yourself to some chili on the way out," she calls to her husband's back.

While I've taken a lesson in Coché's readiness to flatter her husband, I wonder if this time she's at some level trying to show the group's male contingent that she isn't one of those awful matriarch types. After all, the men overheard her calling John at home to come get the diarrheal dog, lickety-split. But now they couldn't say she wasn't grateful to her man; they couldn't say she didn't appreciate her husband's prompt compliance.

Back to the group, back to Joe: "Yeah, with your intellect," Coché says, the way Bella talks to him sometimes would feel "absolutely humiliating."

The real humiliation is yet to come, but first things first. When the husbands and wives reconvene, Coché tells them that they're not going to explicitly review the discussion from the single-sex groups; if it arises naturally, fine.

Sue Ellen starts, relating the good news that she, Mark, and another relative are going to buy the motel that Sue Ellen has been managing for some time. The group praises Sue Ellen up and down, and she allows herself to be proud, in her turtlelike way: A third of the business will be in her name, she says, and she helped engineer the sale from Mark's mother.

"So while we're doing career stuff," Coché says, "because some of you have this as your core issue, um, who else is doing big career stuff?" Her gaze lands on Joe. "Joe, tell us what's happening."

"All right, so I'm officially out of the restaurant," he says. Huh? The group didn't know his departure had even been under consideration.

"So now I'm a full-time corporate lawyer." He's smiling.

"Really?" Marie says.

"You look relaxed, and just, I—" Clem says.

"Look at Bella," Coché says.

"She's glowing," Rachael says. Bella does look closer to her old self. She's still heavier than she was before her pregnancy, but she's chic in a black V-neck sweater, jeans, high black boots, and pink lipstick.

"A happy husband," Bella says, grinning. Everything is all better, except the group doesn't really know what was wrong in the first place, what instigated Joe's departure.

"It's great, the office is about five blocks from my house," Joe says. "I get up in the morning, I buy the *Wall Street Journal*, a coffee, and I walk there. I can actually read the paper for ten minutes, and I don't have to worry about whether the kitchen staff is gonna show up. I can just call clients—and it's a completely different experience.

"And it's exciting because the gentleman I'm working for is one of the top litigators in the city. But he doesn't have a clue about the whole corporate law world, which is the reason I'm there." Joe is brimming with enthusiasm. "He has six thousand clients. We're just going to go out and meet them and say, 'By the way, we now offer [corporate services].' So it's been working very well so far, and he's very well connected. He represents [a famous civil rights leader], whom I hopefully will be meeting on Wednesday."

"And what did you file last week?" Bella prompts.

"My very first lawsuit," Joe says, "after ten years." (Litigators, not corporate lawyers, are the ones who usually go to court.)

"Now, not to throw cold water on this, because this is very exciting," Coché says. "But what we know, Joe, is that you can sometimes have shifts. So when you first went to the restaurant, you were very excited, you loved it, you loved that it wasn't the law, you loved that you didn't have to wear suits."

"Right."

"So as we now predict that [your attitude] may shift," she says, "how do we deal with that in advance? So we're not as surprised by it." He told the group at one point that he never wanted to be a lawyer, that his parents guilted him into it.

Bella is nodding vigorously. "So you're not pissed off, and you know, depressed and—"

" 'I hate these damn clients,' yeah I know," Joe says.

"The Italian Irish in you: I'm mad, and I'm sad," Bella says fondly. Everyone laughs.

"Uh, I don't know," Joe says. "It's difficult to say, because I've never felt how I feel right now about being a lawyer. I've gained a new appreciation for it: for the ability to use my mind, compared to anything else I've done. But more importantly, I value my time, and just from a time-money standpoint—"

"Right," Bella says. "The only thing, just anticipate that there will be moments when you hate it just as passionately. So what Judith is inviting you to think about is how might you prepare for that, so it doesn't take you out of the game so much?"

Coché suggests he jot down a list, "nothing flowery," of what advantages he sees in his job now and what disadvantages he expects to see, which he can consult when his "emotions throw [him] out of balance." It's worth a try, she says.

Joe likes the idea, and the group moves on to Rachael, and her latest job woes, without finding out why he abruptly left the restaurant. Another question lingers, at least in my mind: Why would a "top litigator" hire Joe—whose legal experience is ten years as an associate at two midtier law firms in another city—to spearhead an ambitious corporate practice? Joe seems smart and competent and all, but . . .

Before the morning is over, the group does get one question answered. The new manager of the restaurant is none other than Bella. "It's amazing," she says, "because my business partner and I are really getting our hands dirty. And it feels like we really should have done it in the first place." If her breezy dismissal of Joe's tenure offends him, he doesn't let on. His eyes look a little glazed—maybe he's taken cover in a corner of his mind beyond Bella's reach.

"And we made a decision to move our real estate offices into the restaurant, because we have extra space there and so it's like a phenomenal business decision," Bella says. "And Tara and I have virtually assumed every process. There are a few things that Joe knows that we don't know yet." He's been gone for barely a week.

"And is he helping with that?" asks Coché, who has been consulting with the couple over the phone.

"Now he is," Joe replies.

"Now he is," Bella repeats.

Apparently, Joe initially refused to show the two women the ropes, he was so angry. It's time for lunch, and still, no one has said *why*.

There are only two groups left in the year, and Coché begins the afternoon by asking each person to give a fifteen-minute progress report and indicate whether they're planning on "graduating" or continuing for another cycle. But as usual, the group members aren't hewing tightly to that format, and when Joe's turn comes around, Sue Ellen asks him how it happened that he'd refused to return to the restaurant. This is why group therapy works; inevitably someone will ask the question that needs to be asked.

"That wouldn't feel very supportive," Sue Ellen says, "if Mark refused to come over to the hotel—"

"I *have* been back," Joe says, but "for a few days I was being a five-year-old, an absolute, unmitigated five-year-old."

"Wait, Joe, back up," Coché says. She—and everyone else in the group—is onto Joe's inclination to cut off inquiry with promiscuous self-blame. "I think you felt demeaned when you were at the restaurant, so I think it's important for people to understand what happened, and for you to say, 'I cannot allow myself to be treated that way. And I will do whatever I need to do to get myself out of that situation.'"

Joe sighs. "I don't think anybody 'treated' me any way. I think I took what I was experiencing and felt as if I was being humiliated."

"Nevertheless, can you explain to the group what transpired, because if they understand they'll be able to help you work with the issues?" Coché clearly wants Joe to tell the group something only she and Bella know—she tried to dislodge the information in the last session, when she observed that the couple had "a lot going on at the restaurant," and repeated "lot" seven times. Now she is taking the direct approach.

Joe shuffles some papers in his lap; he looks up. "You want examples?" He *really* doesn't want to answer the question.

"I'm trying to help tell the group some of the events that transpired such that you—who are not a completely unreasonable person—said to your wife, 'I'm not going back there, and you can't make me!'"

"Um, so one of the things that happened—well, a coupla things, uh." Joe fumbles. Then he launches into a lengthy account of what he has said before, but in more detail: The restaurant has been hemorrhaging money since the day they bought it, nothing he did seemed to make a difference, and then, without breaking tone or pace, he says: "Tara sat me down and accused me of surfing porn on the office computer."

No one says a word. You can almost hear the group stop breathing. That was Tara's explanation, Joe continues, for why he wasn't turning the business around: He was too busy looking at dirty videos. "She then said I should go see Judith about 'my problem.'"

"That's not entirely true," Bella says. "Because she checked your personal computer, and found evidence of porn on your personal computer, too." She *what*?

"Oh yeah," Joe says gruffly. He lent Tara his laptop for what he thought was a business presentation, and she searched it for porn sites and found a couple.

"So is it fair to say that you were accused of being sleazy?" Coché asks.

"Sleazy and irresponsible," Joe says. The group is letting Coché do the talking, but everyone's eyes have gone hard. They look outraged on Joe's behalf, but it's almost as if they fear if they speak, they'll prolong his public shaming.

By going through the computer's history and painstakingly showing that he hadn't even been on the premises most of the time that someone was logged onto "BigTits@hoes.com," or whatever, Joe was able to prove that it was actually another employee who was entertaining himself on the restaurant's dime. (Bella fired the guy.)

While Bella says Tara made a mistake, she doesn't seem sufficiently affronted for Joe. "You had porn on your own computer," she says to him. "You made yourself susceptible by not ever telling me you watched porn. I didn't really care that you watched it, but it caught me off guard." Moreover, "It's a little hard when you have these lapses in competence, and then you won't just admit when you didn't do something."

This is the crux of the matter for Bella: Life with Joe can feel like a daily free fall down the rabbit hole. The restaurant may be beyond rescue, but he's the kind of guy who says yes, I paid the bill, no, I haven't touched the restaurant's rainy day fund, yes, I made an appointment for psychological testing, when indeed he'd done none of the above. The couple lost a chance to refinance the mortgage on their home because he missed a payment without mentioning it to Bella. Joe's knee-jerk tendency to "tell people what they want to hear," as Bella delicately describes it, can manifest when the stakes are absurdly small. One day, Bella says, she asked him whether he wanted to play his old college sport, rugby, again. "Nah, I'm done with that. I'm really tired of getting hurt," he told her. The next day the couple went out with a friend, and Joe said how excited he was: He'd found a rugby team to join.

Joe's screwups seem like they might be an unconscious means to strike back at the supreme leader, Bella, but Coché later tells me that she doubts that is the case. What she thinks happens is that when Joe gets overwhelmed, he becomes "paralyzed." So instead of diving in and trying to do the best he can in a bad situation, he just lets the bill sit, loses track of it under a stack of mail, "forgets" about it, then "forgets" to tell his wife. Or something like that.

And it's becoming evident that Joe and Bella are under greater financial pressure than the group knew. For nearly a year, the couple has been living off their dwindling savings and a small salary Joe took from the restaurant. It's January, and Bella has yet to make a single real estate deal, despite her midsummer prediction that by "August, September my money will kick in, and then we won't have to worry ever again for the rest of our lives."

Whatever Joe's failings, Coché is taking this opportunity in the group to help him restore his dignity, or stand up for his rights, as Marie might frame it. It's actually what Bella says she wants. Like Marie, she insists she's anxious for her husband to be an equal partner. Whereas early in the group Bella boasted that she could manage everything herself, no problem, now she seems on the verge of terror: at Joe's slipperiness, his unsteadiness on the job. And while the group still isn't sure Bella could countenance a Joe who challenged her authority, Coché thinks a change in the system, so to speak, would bring out the young woman's better side. If Joe could gather himself, come into his own, both of them would benefit. That is the hope, anyway.

"Will you try this on and see if it fits?" Coché says to Joe, assuming his voice: " 'I am tired of being the fall guy, and you guys, [Bella and Tara], actually believed that I've done a lot of stuff I haven't done, and I'm tired of it.' Is that the way it feels?"

Joe pauses, then rephrases her slightly: "I'm tired of being the reason the restaurant is not succeeding."

"And who said—" Bella begins.

"Nuh-uh, nuh-uh," Coché says. "You're gonna get a turn. I need to know what's inside of him." She asks Joe to talk about other times he's been the fall guy.

"I'm tired of being the reason the restaurant's not succeeding," he says, "just like I was the reason that New Year's Eve"—a special party at the restaurant—"wasn't successful."

"Go earlier in your life," Coché says. "Just like the reason that . . ."

"Like I was the reason the car jumped into [my dad's Corvette] and crashed it up," he says.

"Is there more?"

"Just like I was the reason my sister doesn't feel confident about herself."

"So are you ready to stop being the fall guy?" Coché asks. "Don't answer too quickly."

That is what Joe usually does, after all, agrees with others too readily and resolutely. "I'm supposed to be purple today, so I better be purple" is the way Coché explains his stance. It's as if he feels so fundamentally deficient that he needs to instantly "become" something or someone else. The same goes with his preemptive apologies; he throws them out as a screen, before anyone can see the rot. "A contrived sense of guiltiness," wrote analyst Stephen Mitchell, "can serve as a psychological defense against a more genuine sense of pathos or sadness for oneself."

To relinquish being the fall guy, Coché goes on, would be a "very big shift" for Joe. So is he ready?

"I'm scared to say yes," he says.

"Because?"

"I don't know what else to do."

CHAPTER 12

———

Marie's Revolt and Mark and

Sue Ellen's Good-Bye

Whatever happened to Marie and Clem? They've been there all right, every group; she in her calf-length denim jumper, he in his button-down shirts and khakis. But for a while following the Pilates weekend, they dominated less than they had, and Marie—she was downright cheerful. Was it because the couple had been doing better, as they both said? Or was it that Marie's pride had been wounded by the scene she'd made? That she wanted to show the group that she was still a force to be reckoned with: She wasn't going to stay in the role of the traumatized female, undone by an errant bump, forever?

There was one stretch during the December and January sessions when the couple did take the floor, and it was remarkable for what it was *not:* a chance to feel for noble, long-suffering Clem and silently condemn the harridan Marie. This time, the group deeply imbibed how crazy and demoralizing it would feel to live with someone whose main weapon was to become *more* passive, *more* (spitefully) a good guy.

It came after the husbands and wives returned from their respective single-sex groups: Clem and Marie got into a protracted debate about why he'd "disregarded" her and taken a basket of dirty clothes to the basement, when the night before she unambiguously stated that she wanted to do the laundry herself. She couldn't follow his system, she told him. This was the laundry contretemps that Clem had previewed for the men, and the full group spent nearly an hour batting around how Marie could have made the request more kindly—with Clem chiming in to say he was just trying to help out.

Finally, rather suddenly, Clem changed his story. He conceded that in this instance Marie *had* made her preference known civilly, and that she *had* thanked him for taking sole responsibility for the job during the months she was taking a class. He'd picked up the basket to "poke back" at her, because he felt demeaned by her disdain toward his laundering methods. And, he blurted to his wife a few minutes later, "Some of it might even stem from a week ago. I felt insulted when you said [I] didn't work that hard in the group." An insult about which he hadn't said a word at the time.

Fights about the toilet-paper roll (or laundry) are never about the toilet-paper roll, everyone knows. And, incredibly, there is hard data to corroborate this marital truism. Researchers videotaped more than 118 couples having a Gottmanesque conflict discussion, then immediately afterward asked them to watch the tape (alone) and report at twenty-second intervals what they remembered thinking or feeling in the moment. Less than a fifth of the thoughts pertained to the content of the argument, whereas a full 58 percent were judgments about the other person or the communication process, and these were largely negative and firmly held. Not, "I think maybe he's shading the truth," but "The bastard is lying"—that kind of thing. Another disquieting finding: "Although the discussions themselves were occasionally quite confrontational," the investigators noted, "they were mild by comparison to the internal dialogues." If the group only knew what went on in their fellow members' heads—though maybe it's better they don't.

Marie said she understood, in retrospect, why Clem took offense at her comment about his wayward participation in the group, but she was practically frantic about how to ever get her point across, how to be heard by Clem. Eventually, she started to sob, which she'd never done.

"I can't make things clear enough," she cried.

"And gentle enough," Coché added. She—and everyone else in the group—regularly pointed out to Marie how harsh she sounded.

"And, yeah, if I make it more gentle, I'll dilute it even more."

"For those of you who are passive," Coché said, shifting from Clem's point of view to Marie's, "who control by withdrawing, this is what it feels like to your partner. This is why they try to boss you around, because they don't know what else to do."

For Marie to cry was like Michael saying he didn't know how to care for Rachael and Joe confessing that he might be unable to stop viewing himself as a failure-always-in-progress. It was a small breakthrough, a change in the system that could beget other changes (for a systems thinker) or a "softening" (for attachment therapist Sue Johnson) or necessary despair (for Coché). She also might call it a "therapeutic moment," one sip of a medicine Marie has to keep taking if her marriage is to be removed from the critical list.

That doesn't happen, however. In the second-to-last session, in February, old Marie comes clawing back, not in her dealings with Clem but with Coché and the rest of the group. Before adjourning the month before, Coché told the group to come the next time prepared to discuss whether they planned to enroll for another year, as well as to make recommendations to the other couples. Those who choose to return also must attend two extra sessions Coché decided to add to this year's cycle, she told them. The therapist doesn't want anyone to lose their momentum while she's locating reinforcements.

Now the moment of truth has arrived. Sliding into it, as usual, Coché first asks everyone to reflect on the fact that this exact set of people likely will be together today and only once more. She pauses.

"It feels great," Clem says. Not exactly the bittersweet lament Coché was trawling for. It's great, he says, because he's seeing some changes in his marriage, and he's realized he's part of the problem. Recently he's even managed to assert his displeasure or frustration in the moment, rather than leave Marie hanging (and vulnerable to a later good-guy attack). The laundry lessons may be sinking in.

A bit later, when Michael says he's feeling scared and anxious because "looking at yourself objectively is not easy to do," Clem reassures him. "I'm just thinking how good you'll feel in a few months or a year from now. I see some big changes in Marie that really are exciting for me."

The group is familiar with Clem and Marie's swinging, but this time Clem is kicking for the trees. "I'm really appreciating just talking to Marie, and, almost like I haven't, I didn't appreciate her much." He turns to his wife, sitting next to him on the leather couch, not, notably, on a separate piece of furniture. "Now I look back and I see the things you do at work, and how smart you are, and I'm really, uh, feel lucky to be married to you."

"Sheesh!" Marie says, drawing back in exaggerated surprise. "Thank you."

"That's a big statement," Rachael says to Clem.

"Yeah, I'm very happy the way we've been going," he says. "I—I would, I think I would like to go on with the group." What's the stuttering about?

"I'm sort of looking forward to the group ending," Marie says minutes later. Oh, *that's* it.

As expected, Bella and Joe and Michael and Rachael have announced that they're continuing. Both couples have been laid low in the last few months and as much as said last session that they were staying on. Leigh and Aaron are out of here—he's been talking about "graduating" since day one. And the same goes for Mark and Sue Ellen, who seem, who've *always* seemed, relatively happy.

"There are other alternatives out there that would be a better fit for me," Marie goes on. "Not that you all aren't lovely." She glances around the group, a thin smile on her lips.

"So you're feeling glad that it's ending?" Coché says. She's shifting around, screwing herself more firmly into her chair.

"Relief, yeah," Marie says. "I was ready for it to end six months ago."

"I'm just curious," Coché says, "how is it that you haven't told us that?"

"Uh, because I had a contract here." Marie says she figured she'd "grab" what she could from it, and then "pursue other avenues." She seems to be referring to individual therapy, but she's not spelling anything out.

"Okay, so I guess we'll hear more about that as we go through the day."

Ding. Ding. Round one is over, but round two begins minutes later. "So let's move on to progress reports," Coché says, "but before we do that . . ." She'll do this many times this day, announce that the group is going to "move on," then return to Marie.

"I just want to flush out the group," Coché says. "I'm a little surprised, Marie, that you felt impatient and bored for six months. Did anybody else see that?"

"Yeah," Rachael says. She seems less depressed than last month—she's taking more medication now—though she has the look of a patient just out of the hospital after a long illness. Her cheeks are streaked with a rusty blush, like she tried too hard to hide her malaise with makeup, or was too weak to blend it in.

"There's been many times when I've had to really push for what I needed out of the group," Marie says to Coché, ignoring Rachael, "so I don't see that it should be as much of a surprise—"

"No, I'm not surprised that you think you had to push to get what you wanted."

"All right, well . . ."

That's different from saying the whole group has been a bust, however, Coché says. "So if you understand that the model of therapy is to say what's in your heart, and this has been in your heart, how is it that you haven't told us?" She is essentially asking the same question she just asked, but with a one-two combination that hits Marie where she lives. If Marie knows the proper action, she takes it—at least that's how she presents herself. And Marie *knows* therapy—or again, that's how she presents herself. So when Coché makes the issue a matter of Marie abusing the rules of the therapeutic road, well . . .

Well, Marie just rejects Coché's whole premise. I *have* told you I've been unsatisfied, she insists. They go back and forth like this, with Marie throwing up a new objection to the group every time one of Coché's swings almost lands. Finally, Marie gets around to what she considers the group's real problem: Coché. She backs into it. The group has been overly "fluffy," Marie says. "I mean, fifty minutes into a five-hour session," and we're still talking about how people *"feel"* about the group's ending.

"So this feels fluffy," Coché echoes. She keeps repeating Marie, buying time to contemplate her next move. "Does this feel fluffy to anybody else?"

"It feels a little fluffy to me," Rachael pipes up once more, now on Marie's side. (I was thinking the same thing.) Despite that, Rachael says, she has come to believe that Coché's efforts to "bring closure" are important. (Hmm, I'm with Rachael again: how often my husband and I fail to acknowledge each other's comings and goings, an endless series of small gashes.)

"The way one says hello and good-bye in relationships makes a huge difference in terms of how one feels about the relationship and oneself," Coché says.

"Oh my God, to me this is so refreshing," Leigh exclaims. The alleged fluff quells her anxiety about not being in the group for the first time in a decade.

"Well, let me just say that I didn't say the group wasn't meeting *y'all's* needs," Marie says. "But it feels too 'Kumbaya'-ish, for myself."

So what's Marie's take on Rachael's comment about the importance of closure? Coché asks. Is it "possible" there are reasons Marie wants to leave of which she herself is unaware?

"No."

"It's not possible?"

"There's always the possibility, but I've always had a good sense of what parts need to be met for me to make the progress that I want to see." And just with this conversation, Marie complains, "the constant, it's not discounting—"

"I discount how you feel, is that what you're saying?" Coché asks.

"No."

"My disagreeing with you?"

"Well, just even saying, 'How does it feel that Rachael said that?'"

"I didn't ask how it feels; I asked *Is it possible that . . . ?*'" Coché can play this game, too, maybe too well. "I'm interested in whether you will consider that you might be incorrect?"

"Yes, I would be happy to consider that. But I'm also going to consider that I might be correct."

"Of course you might be," Coché says. "So let's move on." Ha! The group isn't going anywhere.

"I don't want to spend a whole lot of time on this, but I'd like you to consider a paradigm shift, that the way you enter a family, a group, or a couple, and the way you leave it is crucial to your sense of well-being in it. And when you're sitting on dissatisfaction," Coché says, changing the subject, "it seeps out through your pores." (Is she channeling Freud? "He that has eyes to see and ears to hear may convince himself that no mortal can keep a secret. If his lips are silent, he chatters with his fingertips; betrayal oozes out of him at every pore.")

Veiled belligerence and indifference toward the rest of the group have never stopped emanating from Marie. Even when she was at her most jaunty, like in her comeback group, following the Pilates weekend, she snubbed the other couples—some of whose names, she has told me, she can barely recall. When Coché asked Marie in that session if she'd help Bella understand her contempt toward Joe, Marie paused for what seemed like forever, then said: If by help you mean letting Bella listen "as I explore this issue," fine, I'll help. But don't expect anything more from me.

Had Marie aired her "dissatisfaction" as it arose, Coché says, the group wouldn't have to be dwelling on it now.

Au contraire, Marie says.

So again, Coché says, what you're really objecting to is my leadership, right?

"I thought it slowed the group down. It's almost"—Marie sighs, like, can you believe how dense this therapist woman is?—"diverted the group."

Before you conclude that, Coché replies, surely you'd like some feedback on the matter from the group?

"No, I don't want some feedback."

"Well, I'd like to give some feedback," Rachael says. Her depression notwithstanding, she has never seemed meek with anyone but Michael.

"Please," Marie says, "I'm not asking for feedback."

Rachael scoots forward in her chair, toward Marie. *"I* have felt like you were just here for yourself. If it wasn't focused on your needs, you weren't necessarily here for the rest of the group."

Bella doesn't care if she has an invitation, either. When she first met the couple, "Clem, you were like so shut down, and so like, you'd absolutely wait until everybody else talked, and to see you so alive and vibrant . . . it's miraculous." The group earlier noted that Clem's posture seems to have improved; he's stopped slumping on the couch like a teenager being scolded by his mother. Bella is again giving Clem a pat on the back, giving him what she can't give Joe.

Now Bella looks at Marie. "And then there is how you consistently feel misunderstood, and it feels like you get bitchier—I don't know how else to say it—you get nasty when you're trying to be heard." And yet, Bella says, Marie sometimes seems to learn from what others say, to benefit from it. "I don't know where else you'd get that," Bella says, because "like me, you're very confident in your own view of things."

"I also think what's going on," Leigh joins in, "is that when men in your life spoke up, you couldn't hear them, because they were so abusive. And now that Clem is speaking up, it's just too scary for you."

It goes on like this. Coché and the group ask Marie in a dozen ways to reconsider her decision: Maybe she's resisting Clem's new forcefulness because part of her still wants to be in charge? (No.) Maybe the couple is "splitting the ambivalence" (the year before, it was Clem who wanted to leave the group and the marriage, but Marie wanted to press on)? (Absolutely not.) Maybe her discomfort with the "fluffy, 'Kumbaya'" aspects of the group reflects her discomfort with softness in her marriage? (No, no, no.) "Don't you think I've considered and reconsidered all these possibilities?" she says, incensed.

Bella and Joe and Michael and Rachael are coming back, and Clem wants to, but the session ends without Marie committing to anything. She's never seemed more bitter.

A month has passed and this is it, the final regularly scheduled session. For Mark and Sue Ellen and Leigh and Aaron, it's really over, no more group. (Marie and Clem's plans are still unknown.) The departing couples will never again huddle on Coché's midcentury modern love seats, never squint to read the titles in the library of psychology books lining one wall of her office, never look to her liquid brown eyes as if to say, "What's next?" Or, "Do you think I'm right here?" Or, "You've gone too far, Dr. Coché." Or, "Help me, *please*."

How do the graduates feel about leaving? Coché begins, smiling. She's wearing a bright turquoise cowl-neck sweater, festive for commencement day.

The professions of excitement and nerves and regret have barely subsided when Coché asks, rather abruptly, "Joe, how many minutes did that discussion take, do you think? Did it feel like we wasted time?"

"Uh, no," he says, perplexed. He's alone today; Bella stayed home sick.

"What about you, Mark, did it seem like a waste of time?" Coché asks.

"No," he says.

"You, Sue Ellen?"

"No."

One by one, Coché asks everyone the same question, and they all murmur their assent. "Marie?"

"It was okay," she says, with a smirk.

"Honestly?" Coché asks, her tone not rising an iota.

"It could have been done faster, yes."

"How many minutes do you think were wasted?"

Marie stares back at her.

"Why am I making a point of this?" Coché asks. Could it be because the therapist is pissed off at Marie? Perhaps, but the group will see that there is a method to her madness, so to speak. "Anybody?"

"Because Marie brought up [in the last group] that we've been wasting time," Clem says, his voice careering into the higher registers.

"Right," Coché says. Later, she will tell me that her plan going into the group was to take the first opportunity she got to bore in on the global dissatisfaction with the group Marie expressed the last time. For one thing, Coché thinks Marie and Clem definitely need another year. Coché could see them alone, but she imagines sitting in an empty office with Clem and Marie, swatting at one tortured bit of logic after another: flies that just keep landing. The group helps "keep it real," Coché might say if she were forty years younger. Instead, she says that a group can "hold up the mirror" to Marie's behavior better than an individual therapist can.

Except that this group hasn't done that, Coché concedes, at least not consistently or firmly enough. Which leads to the other reason she says she's determined to "get underneath" Marie's scorn, lately effluent, for her fellow members: to make a last stab at getting the group to take her on, for their own good as much as Marie's. "Everybody felt it when she left emotionally, physically, and as long as it remained untouchable, the message was that we are not strong enough as a clinical entity—or as a family or as a couple—to deal with the tough stuff."

Marie is not pleased with Coché's impromptu tactic. "I think you railroaded us. When you are down to exact minutes, it comes across as very critical, as 'how dare you have those feelings!'"

But why didn't Marie answer honestly, admit she thought the group was frittering away time on niceties, the first time she asked? Coché inquires.

"There are times where it's almost not worth the effort to bring it in," Marie spits.

"But isn't that what got your marriage into so much trouble in the first place," Coché beseeches, "that you gave up being honest, and became so angry and so resentful and so withdrawn that you were unable to participate?"

"No, no. It was that I didn't [feel] I had the *right* [to be honest]."

Okay, I got that, Coché says. What she wants Marie to do now, however, is to examine her own "lens." "If you're furious with me, that's perfectly fine, but then this is the forum where you need to address that, because I can't work with you unless I find out how you think I'm incompetent, or what you're angry about."

"All right," Marie says. "It comes basically down to a matter of trust. I don't trust you any longer." Mark's eyebrows rise; the rest of the group exchange holy-shit glances. In her battle of wits with her shrink, Marie has exercised the nuclear option.

"Good," Coché says, too quickly. "Let's get this out on the table."

In our private talk, Coché will admit that she was extremely nervous about navigating Marie's instigation. There was the breakdown in group cohesion to worry about, in the final session, no less; the therapist's conviction that Clem and Marie would founder without the group; and the fact that "a reporter was watching." At the same time Coché felt some confidence she might be able to engineer a decent outcome because of her long experience with Marie, "the energy between us," and because of Marie's "terror of not changing."

The only signs of Coché's unease are a few deviations from her usual verbal pacing, like the too rapid answer, and, once or twice, a twinge of defensiveness in her tone. Being unpopular or impugned seems to threaten her less than the average person (or even the average therapist), the product of both temperament and nearly three decades on the job, I'd guess. This morning, she also gets a hand from the rest of the group: What does Marie *mean,* they ask, when she says she doesn't trust Coché?

The therapist has her own "agenda," Marie responds cryptically. The situation isn't "safe and secure enough."

"Does that mean you think I'm dangerous?" Coché asks sweetly, but not faux-sweetly.

Marie's eyes widen, before they narrow into slivers. "I—I really am taking a step back, yes, mm-hmm."

Coché draws Clem in. Did he know about this lack of trust? Yes. Why didn't he say anything? Well, he thinks Marie has been speaking to it herself, and he and his wife "have been talking more lately, and it seemed like you were kind of beating up on her sometimes, you just keep focusing it back to Marie." Clem's neck is bright red. His alliance with Marie might be a welcome development, except her ultimate aim is the opposite of his. He wants to return to the group.

Groups must address a member's lack of trust, Coché says. "Because if anybody has suffered a level of dysfunctionality in their childhood that would lead them to be naturally distrustful, if that gets kicked up as part of psychotherapy, it needs to be worked out . . . Marie, you're smiling, can you help me out?"

"I just think you're so way off base." She shakes her head, disgusted.

"Can you correct me?"

"Well, I'm not sure if I want to, to take the time and effort at this point."

"It's a lot of waste of *our* time," Rachael says. She has had her hair cut into a short wedge, and she has on red lipstick.

"Yeah, I mean I'm getting annoyed," Leigh says, "because this is our last group, and talk about time spent." She and Aaron have been trudging to the group for so long, and it's looking like there is not going to be much time to mark their accomplishment.

"Why is it, if I didn't bring it up, and Judith did," Marie demands, "you're annoyed with *me*?"

"I'm annoyed with both of you, to be honest," Leigh replies.

"But I'm saying I'm not willing to pursue it. Didn't I just say that?"

"In a roundabout kind of way," Leigh says.

"No," Coché says, "she was clear. I asked her to pursue it. The reason I see it as necessary is that I don't know how, I mean, Marie and I can sit for hours—"

"Right," Leigh says, "so sit for hours without us here."

"No, no, no, no," Coché says over Leigh. "Marie and I can sit for hours, but I don't know how to help her quickly move beyond where she is." Coché looks across the room to her nemesis, and blows her nose. She has an awful cold. "I think you've made remarkable changes, absolutely remarkable, and I think you'll continue to, but this must get worked out. So if we're not to discuss it here, where are we to discuss it?"

"We probably could do it individually," Marie says.

"Okay," Coché says, "then can we do this? Will you and Clem agree to come to April and May"—the two extra groups for this year—"and can you and I meet sometime between now and April?"

No, Marie says, sipping from her travel coffee mug. She won't agree to the extension *before* she has a one-on-one with Coché.

That won't do, Coché counters. Bella and Joe and Michael and Rachael need to know who is coming back.

"All right, then: no," Marie says. She's not coming back.

"So you're not willing to continue in this format until the end of May?"

"Correct." This is excruciating.

"Can you people just react to that?" Coché says. And they're off again, Mark saying how unfair Marie's evasiveness is, Rachael complaining that the group is being "hijacked," Joe disagreeing and arguing that everything the group does "brings up something that each of us has to deal with." (Which is pretty much what Coché believes.)

Betrayals of trust are the "foundation of difficulty in forming a healthy emotional attachment with someone," Coché goes on. She wants everyone to think of someone who betrayed them, and how it affected them. Mark interrupts; he can't concentrate on the question because his mind is "racing." The aggrieved silent routine—it's what Sue Ellen used to do with him. Sue Ellen nods in agreement; she mentioned during Marie's first insurrection, four months ago, that she recognized herself in the other woman. "Is something wrong, Sue?" Mark would say. "I'm fine," she'd say, meaning, "You have failed me miserably yet again."

Leigh can't attend to Coché's question either, because she feels "belittled" by Marie's dismissal of the earlier graduation talk, though come to think of it, she says, that goes to a past betrayal. Her father used to treat her like Marie is doing now: "I was made to feel that I didn't have a voice, yelled at in a very inappropriate way."

Michael and Rachael exchange a meaningful glance. "That's exactly like my family," she says.

Coché tries to coach Marie to empathize with why Leigh feels demeaned, but Marie keeps to her pedantic rap: "I think I presented what I needed to present in a way that was nonthreatening."

She doesn't want to insult Marie, Coché says, but she needs to show her what her nonverbal brush-offs look and sound like. Coché plays Marie, "Um," she says in a pinched tone, "why don't you guys just go ahead." Coché's arms are crossed and her lips pursed in a simper. Marie glowers at her.

"The nonverbal cues are like yelling and screaming," Coché barrels on. "Just like a bully is a loud coward. So this is quiet yelling and screaming, and it affects everybody. And it's not Marie's fault." It isn't? "It's that this group has not figured out how to work with this kind of communication pattern, with this level of affect."

It goes on like this for well over an hour, with Clem at one point pleading, "We just keep beating this same horse, and if Marie says she doesn't want to talk about it—"

"But we can't *not* talk about it," Coché squawks.

But finally they do, they stop talking about it. The beginning of the end is when Mark and Leigh say that since Marie has lost trust in Coché, they assume that whatever new therapeutic "avenue" she chooses won't involve her. Both Marie and Coché profess surprise at this—suddenly they're on the same team again.

"So just out of curiosity," Coché says to Marie, "what do you think the likelihood is that you and I are going to work this out?"

"Oh, probably very good," Marie says.

Then Coché offers her an "ultimatum," essentially the same deal she offered nearly two hours earlier: She and Marie can have an individual session to hash out the alleged distrust, but only if Marie will agree to attend the two sessions added to this round. "So, Marie," Coché says, "let's say by one o'clock I need an answer from you about April and May." It's almost noon.

"All right," Marie answers pleasantly. You gotta be kidding me. After lunch, Marie will agree to return to the extra two groups, but the announcement is anticlimactic. Coché had her at "all right," the group knows.

"People have different styles of changing," Coché tells me. "Marie, she's a bit of a dramatist about it. She has a temper tantrum, fights it off, has a temper tantrum, fights it off. And then she slides through."

That's fine for Marie, but it raises anew the question that's hovered over the group since the beginning: Is it actually *she* who has slowed everybody else down, she who has interfered with the other members' marital-improvement projects? Outside the group, in conversations with me, almost everyone gripes about how Marie goes round and round the same topic, about how she never listens to what anyone else says. "It just makes me crazy," Bella says. "I go home pissed."

"Ohhh yeah," says Joe, her genuinely funny sidekick, "and then we talk about it the entire ride home."

Yet, Bella says, she hasn't given up on the group—after all, she's coming back again, with Marie. "I go back to trusting the process, that something will be revealed."

I know what she means; the question of Marie's impact on the group can't be given a definitive thumbs-up or -down. At the simplest level, the dismal state of Marie and Clem's union might motivate the other members to change, especially Bella and Joe. The dynamic between the two couples is similar. "If Joe feels like Clem in twenty years, that would be *horrible* for me," Bella moaned to me once. "If that's where we're headed . . ."

And, as Coché has said, the group *could* have challenged Marie earlier but didn't: for fear of confrontation, for fear of having to delve further into their own mishegas if time opened up, for fear of who knows what all. It finally happened, Coché says, though she wishes it wouldn't have taken so much pushing from her, or so much time—until Mark and Sue Ellen and Leigh and Aaron were on their way out the door. (On the other hand, Coché says, if early on Bella had said to Marie, "'Will you please shut up?' Marie probably would've stormed out," maybe for good, which certainly wasn't what Coché was aiming for.) The therapist isn't sure what she could have done to speed up the process, but she will believe by the time the group ends that the majority of the members made real progress, whether in spite of Marie, or, in some instances, because of her.

Though the confrontation with Marie takes most of the morning, the level of honesty and urgency within the couples increases almost immediately afterward, as group theory would predict. She gives the group its second crisis, perhaps, and this time the momentum will not dissipate, as it had before. "All of a sudden my blood feels like it's flowing again," Joe says a few minutes after Coché and Marie "make up." "It feels like we've gone from first gear to third." And the "deepening" that will occur in the upcoming two sessions, to use Coché's lingo, when the group is pared down to three couples, is almost incredible.

But first the group has to get through today's meeting. "All right," Coché says, letting her gaze rest briefly on Leigh and Aaron, then Mark and Sue Ellen. "There are four hours left in this group. How do you feel about moving beyond this? Let's just talk a little bit about how we say good-bye."

"I'm excited," Mark says.

"What are you excited about?" Coché leans toward him expectantly.

"About carrying with me what I've learned, and excited about our relationship, between Sue and I."

"You've said that time after time." Coché nods. "Who else in here is excited?

"Yes!" Coché says, cheering the big grin on Leigh's face.

Except, except, Leigh says, she is really glad that she and Aaron aren't abandoning therapy altogether—they're going to meet once a month for maintenance with Coché—because of, well, because of incidents like what happened with him last month. She feels bad even bringing it up now, in the last group. Her voice cracks. Next to her, Aaron peers out at the group, scrunching up his eyes, once, twice, three times.

"Go ahead," Coché says gently. This graduation party just can't get off the ground.

The other day, Leigh says, she was walking by the bathroom where Aaron was taking a shower when suddenly she heard him shout: "Those dirty Goldbergs." Goldberg is Leigh's maiden name.

"What?" Coché exclaims. Even she can't help herself. Rachael was a cow, and now Leigh is a dirty Jew?

The rest of the group is equally aghast, or maybe it's just flummoxed. What was Aaron *thinking*? they ask. Was he angry? Leigh's eyes are wet.

"No, no," Aaron says. "It could have been anxiety. I don't know, I'm not sure what it is."

"Do you hear yourself when you do it?" Coché asks. It almost sounds like Aaron has Tourette's.

"Yeah, I think so, yeah." Okay, so he's not in some kind of altered state.

"Is it within your conscious control never to do it again?" Coché asks.

"Yes," Aaron says, shifting on the couch.

"Are you *positive*?"

"Yes."

Aaron assures her it is "because quite frankly, I—Leigh has never brought it to my attention, like this." He's done this before?

"Yes, I have," Leigh insists.

It seems like Coché is moving too quickly, and Marie intervenes. When Coché was extracting the promise from her to reveal her plans by 1 P.M., she also told Marie she wanted her to be in charge of "collecting" her mistakes, and it hasn't taken long for Marie to embrace her assignment.

"If you're by yourself in a room," Marie demands, "why can't you say whatever you want to say?"

"Why are *you* getting so mad?" Joe shoots back. "She's the one who's upset." He gestures toward Leigh.

She's mad, Marie says, because she disagrees with Coché's cease-and-desist strategy for Aaron. "Why do you have to be politically correct in the damn toilet!"

That's one way to look at it. Marie's perspective rubs a little tarnish off freaky-deaky Aaron. Also important, it keeps the discussion going, because the group hasn't touched what might be behind his outburst. While Aaron and Leigh are both Jewish, he's of German descent, she of Eastern European. German Jews traditionally looked down on their less educated, supposedly coarser counterparts.

"Yeah," Leigh says through tears, "there's this attitude in his family—"

"Right, right, right." It's Aaron's blocking maneuver.

"—of highfalutin"—Leigh keeps talking—"but believe me, where I'm from is just as highfalutin as—and for you to say that, but not directly to me." At other times, she adds, "He'll be talking to the dog, and he'll say, 'You better be good because your mean mother is not going to like you if you're not.'"

"No, I don't say that," Aaron says.

"Yes, you do."

"No, this is the first time you've ever brought this to my attention."

"That's not *true*," Leigh says.

"I'm being honest; otherwise, I wouldn't have reacted the way—"

"That is not true—"

"It absolutely is the first time," Aaron mutters under his breath.

"Honey, it is not true," Leigh says. Rachael and Michael take each other's hands across adjoining chairs, as if hanging on for dear life.

"Instead of calling each other liars," Coché rebukes, "can you simply acknowledge that this is a really tough thing and you haven't figured out how to handle it?"

"Right," Aaron says.

Yeah, Leigh says, when we visit Judith once a month, it won't just be for a social call.

"Why are you worried about that?" Coché asks.

"Because that has been some of your pattern," Leigh says, glaring at her husband. "We've spent months and months with Julian [Slowinski], and you would just coast or put the sessions in my lap. I made the ultimatum last year about the divorce to wake you up, and you heard me, so I'm not, I'm not—" The truth is, this year in the group Aaron seemed to be coasting as well, and Leigh hasn't acknowledged it until now. While in the first two sessions, she let it be known that attention still needed to be paid on the sexual front, she pretty much dropped the topic after that. That could have been because all was well, but the group didn't get that impression.

"You seem very angry, Leigh," Aaron says now. Wow, he's pulling out the active listening.

"I *am* very angry."

"I'm sorry you're angry, I'm sorry you're angry. I—I repeat this is the first time you've brought this to my attention." Not this again.

"Maybe it's the first time you *heard* it," Marie says.

"I do, I do feel like it's something we can work with Judith on and resolve," Aaron sputters. It's like he sees the vaudeville hook coming for him: It can't be, don't *tell* me we have to come back to the group for an eleventh year.

But he's safe. Nobody is going there. Aaron admits, under Coché's questioning, that his family has "a history of feeling intellectually and financially superior toward people who are Jewish and come from other places." He, the boy who ate dinner in the kitchen while his family was in the dining room, doesn't consciously share their snobbishness, but maybe he couldn't help but absorb some of what was around him. In fact, he says, maybe his shower fulmination was prompted by Leigh's criticism of his parents, of how they treated him.

"But I was *supporting* you," Leigh says. Coché laughs her raspy laugh, which devolves into a cough. What's going on, apparently, is that Aaron has described his parents' despicable actions to Leigh through the years, and she has too heartily joined in dumping on them. As psychologically astute as Leigh is, she is refusing to see that her husband might have bridled at such "support."

"What he's saying," Coché tells her, "is that you would compare his family negatively to yours."

"No, I didn't, I wasn't," she says.

"That's what he heard, Leigh," Coché replies.

"No, I wasn't comparing—"

"That's what he heard."

"That's what I heard," Aaron chimes in.

"But you didn't say, you didn't tell me—"

"He's telling you now," Coché says.

"You should have—"

"I'm telling you *now*," Aaron says. Maybe he's being self-serving, trying to take the focus off his bafflingly bad behavior, but at least repressed anger gives some *reason* for his eruption.

"So, Marie, do you feel comfortable now to move on?" asks Coché, who hasn't forgotten that this discussion was born out of Marie's flagging the therapist's "mistake." Leigh isn't ready, however; she's crying. "I just wish that I didn't have to bring this in here, because it's so painful to even repeat it. It makes me very, very upset, like a blow beneath the belt." And she hates that she always has to be the one who problem-spots.

"It's really hard when you think you've addressed something with your spouse, when you keep saying it, and they're not hearing it. It is very frustrating." That's Marie talking, but her words aren't being bitten off to berate Aaron-cum-Clem; they're being draped comfortingly over Leigh.

"Marie!" Coché says with a start. "This is the way you were in the women's group."

"That's just what I was thinking," says Sue Ellen, who was also in the women's group. Her hand is resting on Mark's knee, while he's absently stroking her arm. They could be watching TV together in their living room. Sue Ellen says she noticed the change in Marie the second Leigh started talking.

"Yeah, you're so different," Coché says again. "You're kind and you're warm and you're friendly." Not to put too fine a point on it.

"Well, that's not—" Everybody laughs. Sue Ellen would never be that untactful. What impresses her, she says, are Marie's unique "insights," like suggesting that Aaron had a right to privately vent. "I just never would have thought of that, because of the words he used."

Coché nods, then turns to Leigh and Aaron again. "So are you two ready to move on?"

Yes, yes, they are, but Leigh, in a pale gray cashmere sweater and gray slacks, looks slightly stricken. Where is her happy ending?

Mark and Sue Ellen are the only ones who have one, so far. Their ride into the sunset began last session. About a third of the members had weighed in on the pluses and minuses of the group's ending, when Sue Ellen spoke. Her voice seemed to come out of nowhere, as it often does.

Oh yes, there she is, there's Sue Ellen: in her pale blue fleece, nestled in just behind Mark. He sits forward; she stays back.

Sue Ellen's disciplined stillness can be disconcerting (does she think I'm ridiculous?), even though the group knows by now that it is staggering self-doubt that silences her. When she does go beyond one or two words, it feels like a full-body effort: She gathers her thoughts, wills herself to speak from somewhere in her gut.

"I feel good about leaving, about it ending," Sue Ellen said, "because I feel so comfortable . . . with Mark." She stole a glance at her husband, next to her on the leather love seat. Did his gaze embolden her? The group has seen her blanch under Mark's undisguised admiration, yet it is also, undeniably, a source of strength and comfort and wonder for Sue Ellen. "Um," she continued, "there is an unbelievable peace over me about Mark."

The group was quiet for a beat, in tribute. You want the very best for Sue Ellen.

Would she call what happened in her husband a "transformation"? Coché broke in. She was seemingly referring to Mark's newfound ability to treat his wife and sons less like extensions of himself, who best not defy him—or else.

"Yes," Sue Ellen said, "but . . ." Coché never gets it *quite* right for Sue Ellen. Correcting the therapist is Sue Ellen's aggressive act.

"I think a lot of the [transformation] is in *me*," Sue Ellen said. "Mark hasn't really—he's changed, but he's always been . . . a good guy." Her voice grew husky. "And I just had to . . . recognize that."

It was moving to hear Sue Ellen talk so explicitly about her enduring love for her husband, but there was actually little outward change in the couple during my time with the group. Only Leigh and Aaron, who'd been with the pair since they started two years earlier, had any sense of what Coché meant by "transformation." Sue Ellen, by Leigh and Coché's telling, had been virtually shut down, enfeebled by her eczema, and with Mark at a literal and figurative remove from the family, left on her own to handle her sons. Granted, Mark would swoop in to get his wife and boys in line, but he was like a boy arranging the figures in a neglected dollhouse. As soon as he stuck his large hand under the roof, he angrily realized why he'd stopped playing. *They won't stand up straight!*

For Mark, changing meant letting up, backing off, listening. Even when certain his solution was the "right" one, he told the group, he'd come to realize that no one in his family was going to give him the time of day if he merely issued orders. He had to seek their input, encourage it, and with Sue Ellen establish clear limits and consequences for their sons so he wouldn't be reduced to helpless rage. He had to "soften his power," as he said once.

Sue Ellen, meanwhile, had to find hers. In her, you see the reason why low self-esteem has been blamed for all manner of misery and failure. Sue Ellen was the genuine article: someone who *should* give herself a lot more credit, who not only deserves to do so but who could be counted on to spread the good feeling around were she to accrue it. "I actually was afraid," Sue Ellen says. "I felt like the boys knew better than I did, like I wasn't very smart." (She blames this on failing a grade as a little girl, though that's like blaming a single termite for toppling a mansion.) Only with a measure more confidence could she think creatively about how to help her troubled son and maintain her resolve against his inevitable protest. In her marriage, her task was to figure out what she wanted (needed? The distinction between the two words often is irrelevant) from Mark. The worthless don't want, so she had no choice but to give herself some respect.

This describes the changes Sue Ellen and Mark made, but not really *how* they made them, with relative speed, when others can't. There is no single answer, but several of the relationship models underlying the practice of marital therapy tell a plausible story. For starters, while much of the last half of the twentieth century in psychology has been devoted to understanding the human animal as part of a pack, in the last two decades couples therapists have shown renewed interest in understanding how individual pathology can sully the "in-between." The word "pathology" is apt because the focus on the individual has been motivated in large part by the explosion in the use of psychotropic medicine and the corollary construct that mental disturbances of all kinds are biologically based (which came first, the idea or the drugs, is hard to say).

This sort of middle-ground view, that intimates together become something new *and* maintain some essential parcel of self, has the virtue of more closely capturing reality for Mark and Sue Ellen, and for many of us, surely. When Sue Ellen said *she* was the one who had to change most, she was only in part being generous. Her commitment to figuring out how to do that—she saw her task mostly in cognitive terms, altering her thinking—has to account for some of the couple's success. In addition to the couples group, she joined Coché's women's group, attended Al-Anon meetings, and eventually began her near-religious practice of positive affirmations. This entailed a massive amount of self-disclosure and introspection for someone as inhibited as Sue Ellen, a middle-aged woman who last sought psychological help as a young bride wrecked by her skin—even if she did do more listening than talking. As for Mark, Coché considers him one of those rare creatures who actually has the will, and the relatively uncomplicated conscious and unconscious agendas, to quickly benefit from insight and education. Once he was coached by the group and his wife about how to be a better husband and father, he became one, more or less.

What is most awe-inspiring about Sue Ellen and Mark may have made changing easier: After twenty-five years of marriage, they still seemed—how else to put it?—*in love.* John Gottman, with his affinity for ratios, talks about a condition he calls "positive sentiment override," in which there is enough goodwill between spouses to cushion them in fraught moments, to keep them from automatically demonizing the other and instead give the benefit of the doubt.

"We had the goal of coming out of this together," Sue Ellen says.

"It was just, how could we do things better?" Mark adds. "Get the tools we need to encourage and help our children rather than the situation we'd been in." Other members of the group offered up statements like this, but they seemed aspirational rather than actual. For Mark and Sue Ellen, there truly seemed to be little of the internal chatter of the is-he/she-right-for-me, could-I-do-better variety. A core of affection between them survived the years. Thus, when their son's addiction exposed the weaknesses in their marriage, there weren't the "thousands and thousands of roots" to untangle before any new growth could appear.

Yet what about systems theory and its principle of unintended consequences? Is the theory just irrelevant for the couple, in that it would seem to predict that when Sue Ellen started speaking up, Mark would try to put a sock in it, no matter how much he'd detested her censorious silences? He didn't. In fact, he pretty much applauded Sue Ellen's new forcefulness, in handling him and their affairs.

There is another reading of the system the couple has going, however. When Jay Haley contended that "who is to tell whom what to do under what circumstances" lies beneath all serious marital conflict, he meant not that power has to be shared fifty/fifty, but that a couple can't fundamentally disagree on its distribution—and through all their troubles, I'm not sure Sue Ellen and Mark ever did. She has been content, even grateful, to stay behind the scenes and run the household, leaving the major decisions, such as where the couple would live, to her breadwinner husband, whose casual comment about "softening" his power (not relinquishing any) speaks volumes.

"The world demands too much of undemanding women," Peter Kramer wrote in his couples book, *Should You Leave?*, reflecting on how modern culture insists on a kind of equality that some women and men prefer to live without. Tightly defined, old-fashioned roles aren't for many of us, at least not for a lifetime, but Sue Ellen isn't one of those. She just wanted more support on the home front, an ally in a trying time, and didn't know how to go about asking for it. So when she told Mark what she expected him to give her and her sons, she was in a sense just doing her job . . . but better.

Finally, I think Mark fell blithely into step with the new, somewhat more willful Sue Ellen because he'd never quite been living with the old one. An inveterate optimist, he didn't see Sue Ellen as she saw herself, or as she was perceived by the rest of the world. (You might say, then, that he existed partially outside of the system, or at least that in this case the system was *not* greater than the sum of its parts.)

Of course, Mark's very subjective vision probably explains why it took him forever to recognize that his home life was in shambles, as Coché suggested, but it had an upside. "When I got to know Sue," Mark says, "she had goals, she talked about wanting to do photography, we were both active"—they have biked and jogged together throughout their marriage—"and beyond that, she was so beautiful and fun." Mark noticed the toll her skin condition took on her, her turn inward, but, he says, "I always felt Sue had such potential that I expected her to get over it, to grow out of it, to put it behind her."

She did do that—she didn't let him down. Sue Ellen became the woman Mark married. Or maybe it's the other way around: By never losing faith in his wife, by contracting so she could expand, by becoming her helpmate as opposed to her benevolent dictator, Mark created the woman he married.

I think of the couple when I'm reading *A General Theory of Love,* written by the neurobiological enthusiast Thomas Lewis, who argues that what we call love is basically how we were treated as children, however unlovely that might have been. "Most people will choose misery with a partner their limbic brain recognizes over the stagnant pleasure of a 'nice' relationship with someone their attachment mechanisms cannot detect," he writes. "And yet on a planet of six billion personalities colliding and meeting the improbable is occasionally bound to occur."

There are exceptions to the "general theory," in other words, the lucky few who end up with a spouse who takes his or her hand and grins. As a girl, Sue Ellen certainly was loved in a most unlovely way, and then, one summer evening near midnight, she collided with a tall, curly-haired boy outside of a bar: "The instructor fate provides," says Lewis, "is often amiably unmoved by the other's problematic emotional messages. Through the reach of their relationship and the utility of his relative imperviousness, he can gently and incrementally dissuade his student from headlong flight down paths that terminate in sorrow."

CHAPTER 13

"I'm Ambivalent about Staying

Married."

I don't know if I'm doing the right thing," Bella says, "by staying in
this marriage." The new, stripped-down group is not an hour old; Joe
announced minutes ago, "My wife's pregnant again" (Coché had asked
each person to share a "wonderful thing" from their lives); and now
this. It's like a boulder has thudded onto the middle of Coché's decorous
Persian rug. One second passes, two, three.

"That's a *very* courageous statement," Coché breaks in. The group
blinks, unfreezes. *What?* But in the next instant, they get it. Finally,
Bella seems to have dropped the facade of the "perfect, successful young
married person," as Coché described her once. But Joe, poor Joe. I want
to go sit between him and Bella on the love seat, throw my arm across
his wide shoulders. He is staring at a spot in the center of the room,
holding his beefy, white hands tightly in his lap.

The group knew that Bella had become increasingly disturbed
by Joe's tenuous relationship to the truth. And they knew she wasn't
pleased at how he'd botched some things at the restaurant (while also
being blamed for misdeeds he did *not* commit). But to hear that she is
considering divorce comes as a shock. The restaurant supposedly had
been eliminated as a source of contention: Bella, with her partner, Tara,
had taken Joe's place and was relishing her new gig, the group learned

two sessions ago. Joe, meanwhile, was a lawyer again and couldn't wait to get to the office in the morning. How had the situation deteriorated so quickly, to the point that Bella, replying to Marie's request for clarification, says, "I'm ambivalent about staying married to Joe"?

The answer, the group gradually learns, is that the restaurant has continued to collapse, despite her energetic ministrations; the couple has run through their savings; and there is a hitch to Joe's great new job, after all. The reason he was hired to start a new corporate practice, despite his relative lack of experience, is that he's being paid entirely on contingency. The fancy litigator who signed him up isn't taking any risk. The guy has a few potential cases for Joe, and if Joe manages to settle them or successfully take them to trial, he'll earn a cut of the proceeds; otherwise nothing.

In sum, Bella—expectant mother Bella—is discovering that no matter how positive and industrious she is, she can't handle everything herself (hardly, since, as the group will come to realize more clearly than ever, Bella bears her fair share of the responsibility for getting them into the fix they're in). It's not that she doesn't love Joe, she says; she does, though in this context, the words dissolve, *poof,* as soon as they hit the air. *What is love again?* The issue is the couple's incompatibility "in business and professional life," Bella tells the group, the "mismatch" between them. And it's recently dawned on her that she's becoming the stereotypical wife who is forever trying to change her husband. She doesn't want to be that person, she says, for Joe's sake or her own.

More than the rest of the group, save Coché, I know the couple's backstory. Between this session and last, I interviewed them at the restaurant. When Joe drove me up to the place around five-thirty in the evening and ushered me through the front door, I wanted to laugh. From the peculiar vantage point of therapy, the restaurant had become gothically dark: stalactites poking from its ceiling, bats flying under the eaves. But no, everything seemed so normal. The long wooden bar was crowded with what looked like after-work regulars and a few ruddy-faced drunks. Bella came bustling out of the kitchen in jeans and heels, and the three of us took a seat at a table in a large, empty dining room. That was the only disturbing aspect, that no one was eating, but it was still early. Tara, by the way, never flew in on a broom.

Sitting next to Joe, Bella filled in details of their joint past. She had immediately fallen for Joe's "loving, generous spirit," his sense of humor and of adventure—he'd traveled alone in Africa after graduating from law school. They'd been dating for about six months when she took him home for Thanksgiving. Joe had explained to Bella that he was starting his own business, building a solo law practice that would give him the freedom to golf some days but still earn a good living. So over the holiday weekend, she asked her executive father to help her new boyfriend with his marketing plan. Dad—whom Bella describes as "military, engineer, CEO, he doesn't BS anything, he can smell it"—concluded that Joe didn't have a clue, and let his daughter know it. Bella's aunts, meanwhile, adored Joe; they thought she'd found a keeper. Bella was torn, but she ended it with Joe. "I was really worried that he wasn't up to being successful," she said as Joe listened on, occasionally making a comic face. *What ya gonna do?*

Later, with just me in the car, Bella said that after she broke up with Joe, she tried getting back together with her previous boyfriend: an investment banker whom she'd originally left because of "strip clubs and calls from other girlfriends." The two spent a week together on vacation. "I was alone on the beach one day, and I realized that if I married him, this would probably be my life: beautiful kids, beautiful clothes—but alone." That's when she returned to Joe. He moved in with her, and the couple got engaged.

In other words, Bella made one of those calculations successful thirtysomething women supposedly make all the time: Instead of going for the type A *macher* who was as ambitious and driven as she was, she'd picked funny, loving, devoted Joe. But while she was sharing an apartment with her fiancé, Bella's reservations came rushing back. Joe was eating oatmeal every day, she said, "for *dinner.*" At her insistence, he came clean about how much he was making. "I don't think I could've imagined how little it was," she said, laughing ruefully. Now she knew why he had so much time for golf.

Joe didn't dispute any of this. "Look, in my world, if I could, that's [the business] I'd want to create. The reality is I'm not particularly good at generating clients. I rented furniture, found an office, bought a Nissan Sentra, and was trying to figure it out."

Bella urged him to get a no-brainer job to pay the bills and work on building a law practice simultaneously, but instead, after about six months, Joe pulled down his shingle. He just couldn't make a go of it. He found a stable job, as an associate at a corporate law firm. It was the job he'd eventually leave to follow Bella.

"Joe?" Coché says to him now, in the group. "How's this for you?"

He glances at her, then fixes his eyes back in the center of the room. His hands are still clasped between his knees, like he's holding himself back.

The group waits: Rachael and Michael, Bella, and Marie (Clem is absent, at a job-training seminar). The expression "our hearts go out to you" seems literal; it's like everyone is sending out skeins of compassion to Joe, offering to draw him close. I not only feel bad for Joe, I feel a little guilty, because Bella told the group that it was my interview of the couple, probing their past and her relationship with her business partner, that brought her dissatisfaction to a head.

"The phrase I'm repeating over and over to myself," Joe says slowly, "is 'anger is my friend.'" This is the slogan on the shirt Coché gave Michael a few months ago. "I'm very mad right now. 'Angry' is probably not a good word. I'm furious. I'm hurt, and I'm spitting mad."

"[Mad] specifically because?" Marie asks.

"He's about to say," Coché says, sounding a little irritated at Marie for not just letting Joe's story unfold.

"Reasonable people will differ with what I'm about to say, but in my world"—Joe keeps using "my world" to signal that he's realized he's capable of convincing himself of things that don't jibe with reality—"I've been organized around this relationship since I met Bella. And now it feels like I'm the only one." He is wearing a long-sleeved cotton T-shirt and dark cotton sweatpants, and so is his pregnant wife. They look like sporty twins.

"That's fair," Coché murmurs. "That's fair."

For all his faults, Joe says, he thinks Bella is not making sufficient "allowance" for how stressful the last two years have been for both of them: getting married, moving to a new town with no regular source of income, starting a business that has failed to deliver anything close to expected returns, a miscarriage, and now another pregnancy. "I did not come to a couples group for an entire year to hear that now we're gonna cut and run. I'm sure I'll have a more thoughtful reaction later, but right now I'm just angry." If he wasn't angry, I'd think he was dead.

"Has Bella said she's going to cut and run, or has she said, 'I'm not sure what to do'?" Coché asks.

"She's threatened it," Joe says.

"I know that, yeah." Coché nods. She seems to realize that she mis-stepped: Joe, understandably, isn't ready to sift through his wife's words.

"We've been working for some time on being a team, and I think I have made a substantial amount of progress," Joe says tightly. "I am a stubborn jackass sometimes, and my first instinct is to lie anytime I'm cornered. I won't do what I say I'm gonna do all the time—in fact, I won't even do it sixty percent of the time. I tend to dream a lot and be in my own world about how things are going to go, and I get that it's really tiring to be around somebody like that. But I've always been like this. I don't think there's anything wrong with it."

What is there nothing wrong with? Coché asks.

"How I live my life." Joe is all over the place, throwing out words like confetti at a funeral. His lack of follow-through and readiness to fabricate are undoubtedly real, but then so is his histrionic flair: He's making himself sound worse than he is, the upshot being that when he defends his way of life, he sounds ridiculous. Joe backtracks. "I know there are areas for improvement. I have a lousy self-image, which I'm working on, and that might help clean up a lot of this." He sighs.

So you don't have ambivalence about being married to Bella, like she does about you? I ask. In the shrunken group, I'm talking more than I ever have. It seems like my perspective is more necessary with fewer participants, and the group and I are easier together. Long ago, Coché likened my role to that of an intern, but now I'm half that and half something else. As a journalist who is coming solo, I'm still considered to have the objectivity of a third party, like a student therapist, but because I occasionally share information about my own struggles as a spouse, I have real married-person cred, too.

"I've never been ambivalent about being married to Bella," Joe answers ardently. "Before I met her, I was never going to get married. I was very happy dating and being single, and I could've done that till I was fifty." There is a pause.

"Is that true?" Bella asks.

"Yeah," Joe replies, miffed. "I was never going to get married until I met you."

"You were *engaged* before," Bella says.

"Yeah." Joe sighs, and Rachael suppresses an incredulous giggle. This man will never cease to amaze.

Joe has an explanation, of course. He'd always thought living on the West Coast would be a gas, so when his girlfriend got a chance to move there, he asked to come along. Sure, she said, as long as they got engaged. Joe produced a ring, with no intention of making good on it. So in his mind, he was telling the truth because he never *felt* like he wanted to marry fiancée number one. There is still the niggling problem that he explained one "lie" by recounting another. He's digging a hole so deep, the group almost expects to hear him say that, well, he actually did marry the old girlfriend, and although he never got around to divorcing her, he's not a bigamist because it didn't mean anything.

Even so, people are giving Joe the benefit of the doubt. It's easy to contradict yourself, Marie says, in the heat of emotion. Yeah, I add, I heard Joe's "I was never going to get married before you" as a cry from the heart, like, "Bella, this is killing me, you're the one, you've always been the only one." The group is lining up behind Joe, but it's not like they don't empathize with Bella. Joe may not be acting out of malice, but he is practically gaslighting his wife. And if he doesn't drive Bella crazy, who could blame her for doubting the content of his character, when all she keeps knocking on is shell?

"Joe," Coché says, "can you talk a little about the hurt that's underneath the anger? If I put myself in your spot, I'm really devastated." Joe doesn't say anything. His mouth is set in a grim line. He *still* doesn't say anything. People shift in their seats. Michael puts his arm around Rachael, and she leans into him, her legs stretched out in front of her, like in the early days. Is Joe going to answer? What skewed but somehow trenchant observation is going to pop out of his mouth?

After thirty seconds that seems like an hour, he says, "It feels like betrayal." That's direct, all right. Joe sucks in his breath.

Bella doesn't flinch. She is sitting with one leg crossed on the chair, watching Joe almost curiously. She looks neither guilty, on the one hand, nor like she's straining to keep from correcting her benighted husband, on the other.

Does Joe understand, Coché inquires, that when he says one thing and does another, he's trampling on Bella, even if he's motivated by roiling emotion or a desire to please? "It's like sliiiiiding into home base, sliding from one position to another in order to have everything be okay," she says, adding that Michael and Clem surely know of what she speaks.

Joe sort of gets it, he says, but Marie cuts Coché's questioning short. You can't expect too much of the guy, she says. He just had the "wind knocked out of him."

Bella shakes her head no. She's kept quiet since firing the shot over the bow, but now she wants to correct the record. This isn't the first time she's told Joe "where she stands," she says. At least five times in the last three months, she's told him she's had it. (When I asked the couple at the restaurant how they decided to reunite after the breakup during their courtship, they had this mordant exchange: "She didn't [decide]," Joe said. "Well, I married you, didn't I?" Bella replied.)

But in the past, Joe objects, Bella hurled the divorce threat in arguments, or wedged it into a long list of complaints. "This morning, it's no longer 'concerns.' This is a solid position."

No one doubts Joe's read of the situation now. When Bella volunteered to go first and then announced, "I don't know if I'm doing the right thing by staying in this marriage," it was frightening precisely because she wasn't ranting and raving. Her tone was even, devoid of recrimination or rancor.

"There's a difference in your presence," Coché says to Bella.

She nods; she knows.

"You're really calm, and it's different from hearing you say"—Coché speeds up—"'I question this, I question that, I'm really having trouble with this, I'm really having trouble with that.' That's different from a slow sigh, 'I don't know if I'm doing the right thing.' But I don't know that you intended—"

"No, I'm that serious," Bella says. She refuses Coché's bid to soften the hit for Joe.

There is a therapeutic method for ailing marriages that is almost an inversion of Sue Johnson's emotionally focused therapy. In this manner of thinking, troubled couples, rather than being poorly attached, are poorly "differentiated." To fully understand the idea, it's best to turn to the writing of Murray Bowen, the systems therapy star of the 1950s and 1960s who coined the term.

Like many notable clinicians of the era, Bowen began his research with schizophrenics (partially because schizophrenia is among the most debilitating of mental illnesses, and so its sufferers are likely to end up in psychiatric care, and partly because just about everyone who was seriously screwed up sixty years ago was labeled schizophrenic). From the first, Bowen pioneered unorthodox research and treatment protocols, such as bringing mothers, and later both parents, of adult schizophrenic children to live together on psych wards for as long as two years.

His meticulous observations of these families were the raw material for his later work, and what most impressed him was the symbiotic relationship between the schizophrenics and their mothers. The classic configuration, in his view, was that of a mother who projects her weak self onto her son or daughter, so that she becomes totally strong while the child devolves into the opposite. The mother can then "mother her weak self," Bowen writes, while preserving a powerful self-image.

In today's climate, where schizophrenia is assumed to be a strictly biological defect, Bowen's focus on family dynamics can sound heretical, like the worst kind of mother bashing. But, in fact, he was rebelling against the mother bashing of an earlier era—yes, Bowen, too, was a recovering Freudian. As such, he did not traffic in ad hominem (or ad *mom*inem) attacks. Rather, his attitude was systems are systems—all a mother, or anybody else, can do is recognize his or her contribution, and if you're gumming up the works, try to change it.

In person, Bowen had a neutral stance, at least judging from a tape I watched of his counseling a couple, one Mr. and Mrs. Welford. Legs crossed at the knees, taking languid pulls on the cigarette always between his fingers, Bowen asks one pointed question after another with a beguiling combination of formality and frankness, and in a slight country twang. To her: "Miss Welford, what's the difference between being sick and not sick?" To Mr. Welford: "Ain't it awful to end up a failure?"

While Bowen believed the degree of "borrowed functioning" was greatest among the mentally ill, it was characteristic of all relationships, not least between husbands and wives. "In the emotional closeness of marriage, two partial 'selfs' fuse into a common 'self,'" he wrote in the book he considered his crowning achievement, *Family Therapy in Clinical Practice.* "One of the selfs in the common self becomes dominant and the other submissive or adaptive. Said in another way, the dominant one gains a higher level of functional self and appears 'stronger,' at the expense of the adaptive one, who gave up self and is functionally weaker."

The underlying point is that people choose spouses at roughly the same level of differentiation as themselves. Bowen, who was nothing if not sure of *his* self—though with a southern boy's good manners—even developed a one-hundred-point scale to capture the concept. On it, zero represented "no self" and one hundred "the highest theoretical level of differentiation," theoretical because the score was beyond the attainment of mere mortals.

So what does self, of which the best differentiated claim an abundance, look like? (Bowen's use of "self" makes for some awkward syntax.) It's illustrated, he says, by such stances as: "'These are my beliefs and convictions. This is what I am, and who I am, and what I will do or not do.' . . . The basic self is *not negotiable in the relationship system* in that it is not changed by coercion or pressure, or to gain approval, or enhance one's stand with others." The reasonably well-differentiated person, Bowen goes on, is "free to engage in goal-directed activity, or to 'lose' self in the intimacy of a close relationship." By contrast, so-called low-scale people are psychologically enjoined to pursue others to buffer their fragile partial selves; they avoid "emotional fusion" only by avoiding relationships altogether.

Bowen's notion of it taking two spouses to make one whole person is a leitmotif of our culture, often taken as the ideal: The ancient

Greeks searched far and wide for their other halves—an angry Zeus had chopped every being into two; the Bible tells us that "two shall become one"; for Keats, love was "two souls with but a single thought, two hearts that beat as one." The perils of such mergers aren't ignored, either. In *Jane Eyre*, there is the wonderful example of the matched set of Reed sisters, whom Jane comes to visit a decade after they and their cruel mother cast her out. The pretty sister, Georgiana, babbles about parties and potential suitors, is bereft without constant attention and possibly on her way to penury; the less attractive Eliza does not want for intelligence or diligence but has become a misanthropic recluse. "Feeling without judgment is a washy draught indeed," Jane concludes, "but judgment untempered by feeling is too bitter and husky a morsel for human deglutition." The writing is delightfully visceral, but seems just off. The young women both seem to lack real feeling *and* real judgment. What they're ultimately missing, Bowen would say, is self (and perhaps it's the rare mid-nineteenth-century woman who wasn't so afflicted—though, come to think of it, the heroic Jane could've been the first ever hundred-point differentiation winner). Eliza is merely the superficially functioning one. She has to avoid others, lest she slip into her sister's indiscriminate entanglements.

Yet while Bowenian thinking has been part of the scenery for centuries, he was the first to name and describe a sort of grand systemic design, based on a close study of human behavior. (It's similar in kind to how John Bowlby "discovered" attachment from watching mothers and babies separate and reunite.) Another piece of Bowen's theory was what he called "multigenerational transmission." Based on genealogical information he gathered for twenty-four families—in a project that took ten years, he traced one as far back as three hundred years—Bowen argued that parents pass down their own differentiation quotient to their children, and the children pass it down to their children, and so on. In what he called his most enriching personal and professional experience, he struck at the root of his own family tree by waging a years-long campaign to differentiate from his parents and four siblings.

In a speech to his fellow family therapists in 1967, he laid out his secret differentiation battle plan (none of his small-town Tennessee relatives knew what he was up to) in all its astounding detail. It involved, among other machinations, slaving to establish a one-on-one relationship with each of his parents; sowing surface conflict with one brother—"a tempest in a teapot"—to reveal buried emotional patterns; writing numerous individual letters to his siblings, their wives, his nieces and nephews; and immediately telling family members what *other* family members said about them. This last was an ambitious attempt to "detriangle" himself, which goes to perhaps the best known of Bowen's insights. When two people are under stress, he said, one of them always recruits a third. The two originals either scapegoat the new guy to make peace, or one or the other aligns with him or her. The inside/outside positions are ever-shifting, and Bowen reportedly loved to ask his clients to go to the blackboard in his office and diagram the interlocking triangles in their midst.

The uproar Bowen's experiment engendered in his family is predictable, but at the end of it, everyone was at his or her "best overall level of adaptation in many years," or so he said. He hastened to add, however, that he hadn't done it *for* his family. One must differentiate, he instructed, solely to build his own self. If the effort works, intimates likely will "pull up" to the differentiator's new level, but there is no such thing as differentiating "to help others" or seek their approval or admiration. If you're doing that, you're actually aspiring for "togetherness," and, Bowen only half winkingly wrote, "An emotional system does not appreciate such stressful nefarious maneuvers in the service of togetherness."

Bowen came to believe that a differentiating blitz on one's first family was the most efficient means to acquire more self—and thus trigger improvements in relationships with spouses, children, and colleagues—but his practice was hardly limited to blueprinting multigenerational operations. His primary occupation was counseling couples and families, helping them differentiate their way to better relationships. Which is more or less the course Coché—after some initial hesitation—seems to be taking with Bella and Joe.

They couldn't seem more ripe for a dose of differentiation. There is the dramatic difference between Bella's hypercompetence and Joe's spacey bungling, suggesting that some borrowing and lending of functioning is afoot. There is the neon-lit triangle Bella has formed with her business partner and, to some extent, her father. There is also, as I realized in a flash of recognition during a conversation with Coché, the fact that while Joe admits to taking refuge in fantasylands that distort the truth, Bella sees her own mirages as well. She leaped into a speculative business venture fully expecting to get rich in six months. "It's a personality dynamic with Bella," says Coché, who has known her since she was in her early twenties, "an unrealistic sense of what's feasible, a romanticized sense."

Finally, Bowen says that a marriage between the lesser differentiated can go along swimmingly until the couple hits rough water, which Bella and Joe were in as soon as they married—and if anything, the waves have only gotten higher. In addition to having a baby on the way and a total household income of zero dollars, another new fact emerges: The couple has a massive mortgage on the town house they bought when they moved. To make the payments, they've been living in the basement (which flooded a while back, recall), and renting out the top four floors, but it's barely enough. Oh, and guess who they bought the place from? Tara.

Coché puts the couple's challenge in existentialist terms. One way groups and couples build cohesiveness, she says, is to lighten the mood when the tension is high, to joke during a fight. (I'd remarked on how during my conversation with Bella and Joe at the restaurant they both could make fun of themselves, despite the gravity of what we were discussing.) "An equally important but much less enjoyable skill is to face the terror of what you people are going through right now," the therapist continues. "You're not talking about whether you can laugh, joke, go out to dinner. You're talking about whether this baby is going to have a secure future. When you get into children, financial security, sexual compatibility, it gets pretty dicey, if people are honest."

Several times in the group, Coché has mentioned a contemporary popularizer of Bowen, therapist and author David Schnarch, who happened to be the focus of a lengthy magazine piece I wrote about sex therapy. Schnarch is all Bronx-born bluster to Bowen's wry, understated aplomb, and Coché sounds like Schnarch now in her bluntness, even her diction: "To be able to say to another person—" She stops. "Rachael, can I borrow you for a moment?" Rachael nods, and Coché looks at her full-on. "I don't know if I can be married to you for the rest of my life. I haven't reached closure on that, and I'll let you know when I know, but I wanted you to be the first to know [about my ambivalence]—after me."

Rachael looks horrified, though it's only a role play. "I'm speechless," she says.

And what exactly is Bella insisting upon for herself and her marriage?

"I'm committed to an authentic relationship that is nurturing for both people," she tells Joe. "And I don't care if you want to be a teacher or a social worker or a lawyer—I really don't care. I care that you have something that is paying the bills, giving you confidence."

Schnarch might have paraphrased Bella something like, "So what you're saying is, 'Joe, number one, stop bullshitting me, and, number two, get a job with an actual paycheck.'" Then Schnarch might have addressed Bella. "And, please, Bella, drop the 'nurturing' crap. That's you wanting your husband to validate you because you can't validate yourself."

But Coché isn't Schnarch, and she asks Bella how it feels to have plainly told Joe she may want out of their marriage.

"It's more peaceful," she says.

"It feels more peaceful," Coché repeats.

"You should see my world," Joe cracks.

Everyone is quiet. Joe looks bleak.

"Would it have been better not to say it?" Bella asks unrhetorically.

"No," Joe says, "it needed to be said."

"It needed to be said," Coché repeats, "and it hurt."

"It needed to be said, and it hurt," echoes Joe. "And I need to have the reaction I'm having right now."

"Okay," Bella says simply. Bowen (and Schnarch) would approve. The way to tell whether a differentiating step has been taken, Bowen writes, is if it elicits a strong emotional response—you can't declare yourself over taking out the garbage—and the endeavor can only succeed "if the differentiating one can stay on course without defending self or counterattacking."

Coché and the group aren't going to just let the conversation stop there, however. Having seen this couple in action, they think Joe might want to lay down a few bottom lines himself. Earlier, when Bella said she wanted a partner who was authentic, nurturing, and financially stable, he muttered, "We had that."

Now Coché gets Joe to fill in the last dots. He was making $130,000, on a law-firm partnership track, when Bella came to him around the time of their wedding. She was quitting her job, she said, and joining her friend in a new real estate business, which happened to be a couple hundred miles away. Joe could come with her or stay put until her money started raining in—she didn't think it was a "big deal" for them to be separate for a while. Joe decided to remain back at first, and within a few months Bella called to tell him the good news: Tara had a house she wanted to sell them. It was a great investment, but they had to act quickly; in fact, the deal was already in motion.

And where was Joe with all of this? Coché asks him now, though she pretty much knows the answer. While the two were living in separate cities, they visited Coché for couples therapy occasionally, and she saw Joe alone once or twice. "I'm inviting you to remember what you told me, Joe, and see if you can be emotionally honest with Bella. She's being emotionally honest with you. She's centered, she's calm. Her words are carrying what's going on inside her."

"I don't think I mentioned a thing about myself," Joe says. "I think I said, 'Bella has dark circles under her eyes and she needs to do this.'"

"Well, what *I* remember you said is, 'I've never seen this house. It feels like a big house, I'm not sure we can afford it. I'm not sure their partnership is going to work out. The business plan doesn't look solid to me. Yeah, I'm not crazy about being an attorney, but it's good money,'" Coché says. "Am I remembering incorrectly?"

"No," Joe replies.

"And I said something like, 'Joe, did you try to talk to her?'" Coché recalls, at which point she says Joe replied, "'Wellll, I think it'll be all right.'"

Coché turns to Bella. "What would have happened if he had said, 'You can't ignore me, I won't allow it. This is our marriage, and we make these decisions together'?"

"Well, we had a conversation," Bella says, sounding defensive for the first time this morning.

"You did?" Coché asks.

"Mm-hmm," Joe says.

"Uh-huh," Bella joins in, "at which point he agreed, because if he hadn't—"

"But I can't believe you really had a *conversation*," I wail. "It's hard for me to imagine Joe saying, in the same way you're saying, 'I'm ambivalent,' with real force behind it. I think he would have been petrified to tell you. This was how you were gonna get rich, really quickly, and I think I'm not—I would have had a hard time standing up to that." My passion is greater than my fluency, unfortunately. "I'm sure you had conversations, but since we know so often the conversations involve Joe just saying what he thinks you want to hear—"

"My understanding of what I said is that I agreed to move," Joe says, as if he has a multiple personality and he's not sure what his alters are up to.

"You agreed," Coché says, "but you can agree and *not* agree."

But what *could* Joe have said or done, the group wants to know, since Bella was dead set on proceeding?

"If Joe had said, 'I'm not signing the deed to this house, and I'm not handling the restaurant deal the way you want to, because my mind tells me that it's going to be a financial disaster, and I don't know that this partnership is going to work very well. But I can't stop ya, so go down there, and then we'll duke it out.'" If Joe had done that, Coché continues, the couple would now probably be negotiating their differences. "So we're going to practice this, so you can hear it," Coché says to Joe. "The sentence is—and you say it very sweetly: 'Not and be married to me you can't.'"

"Try it," she says to Rachael. "You can go off and build tents in New Zealand," Coché say, feeding Rachael her line, "but not and be married to me you can't."

Rachael fumbles; she can't get it out.

"You really can't say that as part of a fake exercise?" I say to Rachael, as in *what's wrong with you?*

"No, I can't say it," Rachael answers, unsmiling. I feel like a jerk.

Marie offers that when she's clear about what's nonnegotiable for her, she can easily express it to Clem, but so much of the time "there's this wide gray area that I can't figure out." If she accedes to Clem's wishes, "Am I selling myself short?" But if she refuses him, "Am I just self-centered and not committed to the marriage?"

Put another way, differentiating from your spouse sounds straight-forward and noble when sitting with a therapist (assuming you've got the guts). On the outside, it's murkier. Yes, Bowen writes that "a reasonably differentiated person is capable of genuine concern for others without expecting something in return," but how do you know whether you're defining yourself over something foolish? When you should be flexible rather than tough-minded? Yielding rather than, as Marie said, "self-centered"?

"That's why you often hear me say that couples therapy is individual therapy for people who decide to stay together," Coché crisply replies, "because until you know yourself, it's very hard to convey how you feel to another person."

But what if what you know about yourself is that you're ambivalent? I press.

"Then that's the statement: I don't know what I want," Coché says. "It would feel completely authentic for Joe to have said to Bella, 'I can't stop you; I don't think it's a good idea, and I want to be with you, but I don't know how to do it. So for right now, I'm completely stuck. And I'm furious that I have to make these decisions. These feel like really poor choices. What I want is to sleep next to you and have some money coming in and for you to be happy, and I don't know how to do all that.'"

"Okay, I'm sorry," Bella says, irritated. Moving together *was* the couple's answer: "We're in the same city, we sleep together, we don't quite have the money flow, so that needs to be worked on—but there's a happiness."

There is?

"Is it possible that *your* answer was moving?" Coché asks Bella.

"I get that he's retracting, or whatever you want to call it—flipping," Bella says.

"I'm not flipping," Joe retorts. He wipes sweat from his brow. "We talked, we agreed, we moved. I've now [been in therapy a year], and I realized I wasn't forthright when we had that conversation, and that was a mistake." Talking it out might prevent a repeat performance, he tells his wife.

"Okay, Bella," Coché says, "so would you have married Joe if you thought you could boss him around?"

"No."

"Why not?" Coché asks.

"Uninteresting, boring."

"Are you sure?"

"Mm-hmm," Bella replies, flashing Coché an enough-already look.

"Positive?" Coché persists.

"Positive."

I remember something Coché told me about her own experience in marital therapy, with her first husband, Erich. While she was "extremely clever" and "adept at getting her own way," the therapist told her, it wasn't paying dividends in her marriage. The therapist helped her to recognize "the downside of what I thought were successful maneuvers," Coché explained. Now, thirty-five years later, she might be seeing a younger version of herself in Bella.

Tell Joe directly, Coché says to Bella, that you wouldn't have married him if you thought you could roll over him.

"I would not have married you if I thought I could boss you around," Bella says, complying. "It's boring, uninteresting, unchallenging."

"Do you believe her?" Coché asks Joe. "You look like you're about eight years old." His shoulders are bunched up, his eyes wide behind his glasses.

"I believe that's an authentic statement for her," Joe says cautiously. He thinks his wife is unaware of her own will to control—but he's afraid to tell her so.

Coché ping-pongs to Bella. "If Joe had said, 'Bella, we need time to think this through before we move,' is that what would have happened?"

"Yeah," Bella says. "I say all the time, 'Do you want to move back? Do you want to move to Chicago, do you want to move to California? Do you want to do law, do you want to do'—you know, what *is* it?"

"I don't get that from you," Joe says firmly. He snaps his fingers, being Bella. "It's, 'This is what we're doing, this is what I want to do, bang, bang, bang.' I say, 'Well, wait a second.' You said"—he's switched to the past tense, referring to their move— "'Look, we're a team, you gotta align. And if you're not going to align, I'm doing it without you.'"

"I don't say that," Bella says.

"Okay, then, that's how I hear it," Joe says.

You've talked that way in the group, I tell Bella. I re-create her Gloria Gaynor/Ayn Rand moment from six months ago: I will survive, with or without him. "I think there is a level at which you really will, um, that it's an attitude, the controlling aspect." I'm tripping over my words again. Like Joe, I'm leery of offending Bella—she's been adamant in the past that the "control" word does not apply to her.

"Is there any ring of truth to that for you?" Coché asks Bella.

"Maybe. I'm like, okay, I can see that characterization."

Really? I'm surprised—and then I'm not. Bella's warmth and bursts of spontaneity always undercut her businessy self-certainty; she has an ease with herself and others that makes you assume she can handle honest introspection. Still, I was beginning to have my doubts.

"It feels like I don't know how else to be exactly," Bella confesses.

Coché's shoulders relax—this has been tense. She doesn't back off, however. She models how Bella shoves things down Joe's throat while sounding as obliging as a Methodist minister.

"But," Marie interrupts, pleadingly, "I like your style, Bella. I really do." To her ear, the other woman asks for what she wants, and that is the quality she's seeking in herself and Clem.

But Marie, Coché says, earlier you made a good point, which was that we should let up on Joe because he'd had "the wind knocked out of him"—that's what we're doing. Marie buttons up—she has been really involved this session, and helpfully so, but this is the second time Coché has signaled her to back off. Marie is not the auxiliary-therapist type— that is Bella—it's just that Marie trips over her own contrariness.

"Because if Bella handles her end differently," Coché goes on, "then there will be a new reaction, and we'll get a logjam broken." This is a big moment for Bella and Joe: By "using the crisis" of possible divorce, Coché is getting the two to focus on the core trouble between them.

"The damage that gets caused by me not speaking up for myself is a lot more than I realized," Joe announces. "I'm not thoughtful when it comes to making decisions—I'm knee-jerk, which creates its own little mess each time." It's weird, because he actually is quite thoughtful insofar as his insights can be novel and stimulating. He and Marie, I've often thought, have refreshingly unusual minds.

"So maybe you don't give yourself enough credit to speak up," Coché tells Joe. "And maybe one of the reasons Bella married you is that you *do* have the capacity to think things through carefully and powerfully, so when you back down—and she takes the power and runs with it— you're letting everybody down, including her."

Your intelligence "was probably one of the things that really attracted Bella to you," Marie says. Just as Bella pays special attention to Clem, Marie is stroking Joe.

"Absolutely," Bella affirms.

"Joe, what's that about?" Coché asks. There are tears in his eyes. "What's happening for you?"

"I never got that," he says, never got that Bella appreciated his mind.

"Good heavens," Coché exclaims, "why do you think she married you?"

"'Cuz I made her laugh."

"Well, how do you make Bella laugh if you can't make her think?"

"It's the first time I heard that I had value . . . to someone else," Joe says. "That's why I'm having this very strong physical reaction . . . It hurts."

"What hurts?"

"*I* do," Joe blurts, laughing.

Now Bella's brown eyes are glistening. "I'm thinking about his parents, angry at his parents," she says. "What parents would never tell their kid that they're valued. His family says they love each other a lot, but it's—you don't feel it."

"Can you stand on your head?" Coché says, turning to Joe. "Because you know, you're kind and you're very quick—you know that, right? You *do* know that," she says, as in *if you don't, you'd better figure it out,* now. "This marriage is not going to continue until you take a full part in it. You have a wife—not a parent, not a teacher—and you're about to have a baby. So if we can stand you on your head in terms of your personal history, you would begin to take charge."

"And, ironically," Marie says, by leaving everything to Bella, he "reconfirms" his belief in his own fecklessness.

"That's what I was saying I'm not going to be party to," Bella adds. "If he really wants to prove that he's a failure, prove his father right— whatever that psychological trip is—I don't want to be on that trip."

"Well, then, Bella: You can't do that and be married to me," Coché says, bringing Bella back to the one-liner she was urging on the couple before.

"You can't do that and be married to me," Bella says.

"Okay, and Joe, we need that from you," Coché says. "One thing she can't do and be married to you. There has to be something."

Joe looks blank. It's been a grueling morning—and the afternoon will be equally full, with more startling developments. The group is smaller by five, and five times more intense. It's like the whole year has been building up to this session.

"Do you want to get back to us after lunch?" Marie asks.

"Yeah, I want to take some time."

"You know what, Joe," Coché says. "You get to think about this for the rest of your life: Not and be married to me you can't. You can't say it casually, because it doesn't work. You can't just throw it out there, and pretend. You have to be very, very careful. You don't get many chances at it."

After the session, I can't resist calling David Schnarch to get his take on where the group left Bella and Joe. From my discussions with him in the past, I knew that according to his way of thinking Bella had set the stage for a "crucible" moment for the couple. She wasn't asking to talk anything out with Joe, appealing for compromise, or manipulating him. She gave Joe her minimum requirements for their marriage to continue, and the question was how would he handle the heat? What would he do?

"If he rebounds like a dependent little boy, that's the end of the deal," Schnarch tells me. (Schnarch has some wisdom, but he also seems to have masculinity issues of his own.) "If [Joe] responds by realizing this isn't the time to sucker punch his wife, because she's serious, if he takes the hit, digests it, and doesn't ask her directly or indirectly to prop him up—and she sees that he actually functions better—the marriage moves forward."

CHAPTER 14

Secrets and Transformations

There are a handful of books about marriage that by dint of their wide-ranging intelligence, originality, and sheer eloquence have become Baedekers for my year with the group, and, frankly, for the years yet to come with my husband. Though most of them are written by therapists, the books are more works of philosophy than technical manuals for the professional, or how-tos for the spouse on the street. The authors are hardly cheerleaders for marriage, but in their clear-eyed recognition of the spiny obstacles inherent to the institution, they're oddly reassuring.

One of these, which I've already quoted several times, is *Intimate Terrorism,* published in 1995 by Michael Vincent Miller, who brings a former poet's grace to his prose without losing anything in the way of incisiveness. Miller theorizes that marriage, like childhood, has developmental stages, the most dangerous of which, following the heady romantic period, can be summed up as: This person, or this union, isn't *at all* what I imagined. What can easily happen at this point, he writes, is that because "modern marriage is under so much pressure to provide so much fulfillment," because "love and sex are so thoroughly bound up with one's sense of identity as a man or a woman," people become consumed with feelings of failure, feelings that are so unbearable that they lash out at their spouses rather than apprehend their own panic or contribution to the decline.

The fundamental problem, he goes on, is that our culture doesn't teach us "to fail gracefully or fruitfully." Lacking a model for love other than the Tristan and Isolde/Romeo and Juliet variety (each of whom skirted the travails of domesticity by dying young), "Our notion of a comeback is an attempt to recapture original glory. [I]t hardly chastens one for an acceptance of a life with diminished or different prospects." The husbands and wives who can move beyond terrorizing each other, or avoid doing so in the first place, he speculates, are those who can first acutely encounter their profound disappointment in their inevitably changed circumstances: "Unlike jealousy, cruelty, or boredom, disappointment contains secret hints of mutuality. It is not such a long stretch from disappointment to empathy."

Disappointment—a sort of rueful recognition of the limits of her marriage and tenderness toward the people she and Clem once were—is what Marie, almost incredibly, brings to the new, smaller group. Because of his work trip, Clem isn't here to bear witness, which may or may not be significant, but as soon as Marie arrived this morning, it was apparent something was different. She is wearing makeup and holding people's gazes long enough that you can see she has sparkling hazel eyes.

Granted, Marie left the last session in relatively good spirits, basking in the glow of compliments from Coché and Sue Ellen. Marie was acting like she had in the women's group—so considerate, so warm, so plugged in. But that came after the bilious morning in which she spewed her distrust for Coché, and client and therapist played a cat-and-mouse game over whether Marie would enroll in the group for another year, as Clem wished her to do. It seemed like she would, at least after she and Coché made peace, but the group didn't yet know for sure. Marie and Coché had agreed to meet alone to settle the matter, and the outcome of that congress is as of yet unknown.

After this morning's session, devoted to Bella's divorce deliberations, people are checking out Joe surreptitiously: How's he holding up? They don't want him to feel that all eyes are upon him—the poor dude who's about to be dumped—but they also want to give him a little nonverbal reassurance. Rachael quickly smiles at him; Marie seems to be trying to act like everything is absolutely normal. Joe has the same sickly appearance that Marie had after she fled the Pilates workshop. He and Bella arrange themselves on one of the love seats, an expanse of black leather between them.

Marie and I take the same places we had earlier. We're sharing another of the love seats, owing to Clem's absence, and we joke about being a couple. I throw my arm around her in a mock hug—I can't believe I do it. But she doesn't seem to mind; she laughs. The third love seat is Rachael and Michael's, and Coché sits on her desk chair, between them and Bella and Joe.

Marie is up first. She's been reading a book about the Holocaust, she says, finding it fascinating and wishing she could share it with her husband. Among Clem's favorite pastimes are boating and fishing, the group knows, but he isn't much for intellectual pursuits. "I need a connectedness with him, and I don't have one," Marie says evenly. "I have a support group [in the person of Clem]. I have a spouse in the same house, we're raising the same children. We have many things that overlap, and we're committed to the same goals, but I'm not connected to him at all."

Is it that you think Clem isn't willing to explore life's big questions with you, Coché asks Marie, "or do you think it's just not in him?"

"I don't think it's in him." Marie looks pensive. "And in a way, if it were in him, I'd lose Clem." To hear Marie cherish what *is* in her husband, even in the context of what's missing between them, feels like a miracle.

"Clem was one of the first men that I didn't feel humiliated by, so he really met a need," Marie elaborates, and you can see the Clem she is conjuring, the sweet Clem tending to the bruised Marie, the Clem who noticeably shores up the other women in the group, like what he said to Rachael before her depression lifted: "When I look over I see a bright, young, attractive woman, and you're gonna do *fine.*"

Marie goes on: "I felt comfortable with Clem and not judged and found wanting in all aspects. And had I not changed, Clem would have kept meeting that need." But Marie isn't the same damaged person anymore, she says. "And I—and I want to desperately figure it out so that it feels authentic, at some point in my life, with Clem, but if the feelings aren't there, I need to figure out how to create them," or even if she can.

Months ago, after noting that Mark and Sue Ellen seemed to "share a great love," Coché did some of her "seeding," floating an idea and then backing away, letting it sit in hopes that people would assimilate it when they were ready. What if you don't have what Mark and Sue Ellen have? she asked. Can you generate some of the "tsunami quality," or is that unattainable if you didn't have it to start with, or is it even necessary?

This day, it seems, the seed is germinating for Marie, and the group is stunned. "I've never heard you speak this fully or with this much caring in your voice about yourself *or* Clem," Joe marvels, "and you're discussing something you're not sure he's capable of giving you. It's a loss for you, but you're capable of saying it in a very caring way."

"What I'm appreciative of is that you sound genuinely philosophical and thoughtful," Coché adds, which makes it much easier for the group to help Marie "get wherever it is she wants to go." Because in essence, Marie is casting about for what her second marriage to the same man might look like, her *re*marriage to Clem, the metaphorical version of what Bella's parents did.

Film critic and philosopher Stanley Cavell wrote a book on what he called "comedies of remarriage," a small group of beloved movies from the 1930s and 1940s such as *The Awful Truth, Adam's Rib,* and *The Philadelphia Story.* What distinguishes these dialogue-rich films, starring icons such as Hepburn and Tracy and Cary Grant, is that they're about grown-ups for whom divorce is an option, Cavell writes. The protagonists have lost their virginity, literally and/or figuratively, but manage to cultivate another form of innocence based on a loose gender equality in which the woman can reawaken to her desire and the man can shake off his masculine straitjacket. "The romance of remarriage poses a structure in which we are permanently in doubt who the hero is," Cavell contends, "that is, whether it is the male or the female who is the active partner, which of them is in quest, who is following whom."

What would it look like for Marie to chase Clem? Could she relinquish enough of her strictly guarded dignity to lunge for him? And could Clem ever allow it? Could he give Marie his back for a moment, be on the run, then turn around and beckon her with a wink?

Earlier in the day, Marie was as generous with Bella and Joe as she later is with herself and her husband, which seems important. One of

Marie's signature habits in the group was that she'd be expounding on another member's trouble and then, without transition, she'd shift from the third person to the second. All of a sudden it was you, Clem, *you, you, you* do this to me—Marie almost didn't seem to realize that she'd made the switch. Today, however, she stayed in Coché's "here and now," and her sympathies swiveled from Joe to Bella, then back to Joe. She scooted to the edge of the love seat and literally leaned toward the couple. The pillow was gone.

Marie did bring up her own marriage once. Twenty years before, like Joe, she agreed without agreeing to follow her spouse, to a place where the career opportunities for her were minimal. She and Clem have *both* paid the price in her bitterness and, to an extent, her depression, she warned the younger couple. Yet she stated it as a fact of her life, like the date of her birth, and the group moved on. The book can be closed on dusty old facts, can't it?

In my interview with Bella at the restaurant, she'd attributed Marie's lengthy period of detachment from the group to arrogance. "It's 'I've got it all figured out, you guys can't contribute a thing.' It's sad," she'd added, almost obligatorily. Then she stopped. "But I don't know, I think on some level Marie really wants everyone to care."

The same thought had occurred to me, but it was so Psych 101 that I didn't want to believe it. In his group therapy text, Irving Yalom has a chapter on "problem patients," of which Marie is a subtype. "They proclaim: 'I don't care what [the other members] say or think or feel about me; they're nothing to me; I have no respect for [them],' or words to that effect," Yalom writes. "My experience has been that if I keep such patients in the group long enough, another aspect inevitably surfaces. They are concerned at a very deep level about the group." He gives an example of a woman "who maintained her indifferent posture for many months," until she was "invited to ask the group her secret question, the one question she would like most of all" for them to answer. "To everyone's astonishment," she asked: " 'How can you put up with me?'"

In a discussion of another "help-rejecting complainer," named Betty, Yalom says she was impatient, resented sharing group time, and harped on how she'd be better served by individual therapy—if only she could get the therapist alone. Was she right? Yalom asks. "Absolutely not!

These very criticisms—which had roots stretching down into her early relationships with her siblings—did not constitute valid objections to group therapy. Quite to the contrary: the group was particularly valuable for her . . ."

Yalom could have been writing about Marie, of course, taunted and pushed around by her older brothers and father. In fact, when Marie and Coché met alone to hash out whether she'd reenroll in the group, leftovers from Marie's childhood were a major point of discussion. She decided to give the group another year, she'll tell me later (yes, she is coming back), in the hope that by learning to relate to the other members more constructively, she can mitigate the legacy of "hostile dependency" that Coché thinks she has imported from the past. (As for her lack of trust in Coché, Marie admits, slightly abashed, it had been a bit of a red herring, an "incorrect" use of the word.)

The extent to which Marie aggressively, if unwittingly, cast herself as the thorn in the side of the group, and in her marriage, is evident in her reply to the group's praise about her new bearing: "Well, Clem comes off as such a grrreat guy," she says, rather girlishly, "that I feel very defensive in the group, because if he's such a great guy and we're here, then there has to be a bad guy. I'm the bad guy."

Remember, Marie, Coché lightly chides, everything is not black and white: "It would be simpler if some of us had white hats and some of us had black hats, but in fact that's not the way we are." Marie nods.

The impact help-rejecting complainers have on the rest of the group is obvious, Yalom says: irritation, confusion, anger, perhaps mutiny. What he doesn't address, however, is what can be expected for a group if the members manage, by luck or design, to stay standing through the hurricane of a Marie, if they shoot through the eye of the storm by her side.

I'm setting it up this way, I know, but I still hesitate to compare the camaraderie, the compassion in the group after Marie finally comes aboard, to the feeling people describe after enduring a disaster together. I hesitate to invoke the tight bonds that develop among survivors. It's too perverse. Am I suggesting that winning the allegiance and affection of the hard-to-get is more satisfying than that of the person who trusts and loves more easily? Am I suggesting that human connection must be the product of struggle—no pain, no gain, as my coach father used to say? Or, that you can only feel the good if you feel the bad, as my guidance-counselor mother had it?

A little of all of these, and more. By the eleventh session, the comfort of feeling oneself enmeshed with other human beings—of rooting for them, of being crushed by what crushes them—is palpable. Added to the blessing of Marie, there is the recognition, more visceral for some than others, that we're not alone in our freakishness. At the restaurant, Joe told me that the group had disabused him of the notion that "everybody else has pretty much got life down." He felt less like he "belonged in a corner in the basement." Then, too, the group may have gradually bestowed on its members the sense of meaning that accompanies altruistic effort (there is psychological research on this subject, but do we need it?). To be free from "morbid self-absorption"—that was a virtue of groups cited by Yalom. Here was the community of Coché, the Puritan village of Miller, the emancipating yoke of sharply experiencing one's common humanity.

Into this welcoming fold, with the shadows lengthening in the interior courtyard outside Coché's window, comes Michael. After Marie's mournful recognition of the gulf between her and Clem, Coché asks the rest of the group if there are parts of themselves that they can't bring to their spouses.

"The sexuality part is always there," Michael replies slowly, "and it's acknowledged"—he turns briefly to Rachael—"but it's not really discussed. And that's . . . there's no way to really change that."

Marie, Bella, Joe, and I steal glances at each other. *Did we miss something?* Michael and Rachael are the pair who were late to movie night because they couldn't keep their hands off each other, whose sexual goal was to perfect the blow job. Even when Rachael was depressed, the couple was having sex once a week. The group knew this only because Rachael, to my suppressed amusement, had offered this relative infrequency as a symptom of how sick she'd gotten.

"What do you mean?" I ask Michael.

"Hmm?" Michael asks, as if he didn't expect anyone to follow up.

"What do you *mean*?" I repeat. Now I'm being my journalist self.

"That I've had relationships with men, and"—he stops. Is this called "backing out of the closet"? Michael laughs nervously, while his fellow group members arrange their features in bland curiosity. *Oh, that's all it is, sex with men?* "I mean, that's—that's . . . what it is," Michael says. "Um, I've brought it up before, but I think Rachael shies away from it, from discussing it—"

"Really?" Rachael asks. Her eyebrows arch in surprise.

"Yeah, we've had this exact same conversation many times."

"But I think we've tried to talk about it, or I've tried to talk *with* you about it."

"Well, you're certainly *aware* of it," Coché says to Rachael. The therapist apparently knew about Michael's sexual history, too.

"Oh yeah," Rachael replies. She searches her husband's face. "I don't think *you're* willing to go there, with me."

"No, I think—think it's the other way around," Michael says. (Am I the only one wondering why they need to go there at all—isn't it a little sadistic if it's all in the past?)

"Well, let's stop figuring out who's to blame," Coché says, "and go there. I mean, we're gonna run out of time today, but you both want to go there."

After a bit more tussling between the two about who wants to talk less about Michael's homosexuality/bisexuality/whatever it is, he explains that after he and his first wife separated, he dated several men, which Rachael knew because the two were friends at the time. (She was still married to her first husband.)

"Um, the trouble is," he says, coming back to the present, "Rachael's not a man." He's in a trance of sincerity—normally, he would've heard himself and guffawed. "So there's no compromise. It's one or the other." That being said, Michael wants his attraction to the same sex to "be acknowledged [by Rachael], because it took me a long time to acknowledge it myself." But then again, *again,* he worries about being "offensive" to her. "So I kind of stay out of getting too far into it, I guess."

"It's one of the hardest parts of being married to one person—rather than to a number of different people at once," Coché says. She's going general, probably because the session is drawing to a close, but I'm still confused about the meaning of Michael's homosexual relationships—to him, to Rachael, to their marriage. "What happens when there is a centrally important part of the self that has to go unfulfilled?" Coché asks.

"Isn't that the whole myth of marriage?" Bella retorts. "I mean, can any one person satisfy every element for fifty years?"

"Of course not," Coché says, "but what do you do with the unfulfilled part of yourself?"

What Michael does—or might want to do—will have to wait until next session, as will Bella's sober divorce threat. Also left hanging is the permanence of the new Marie: Will she show up with Clem in May? Her ups and downs over the year would seem to suggest otherwise, that she'd return next month newly smitten with hatred. But no one in the group really believes that. Yes, Clem was away this day; yes, Marie has ticked forward only to race back to where she started, but today she was so different. This time, her change must have legs. Mustn't it?

Miller speaks poignantly about how, with the shift from arranged weddings to romantically inspired ones, no one is deeply invested in most marriages these days besides the two people in them. When trouble arises, as it will, there isn't a mother or father to notice, or a sister to turn to for support or advice. The result is that marriage is both internally volatile and externally vulnerable. "A man and a woman used to make love in a cosmos filled with widely shared communal and religious beliefs," Miller writes. "Now they make love only in a bed, to which they bring all their anxieties and dreams."

We tend to believe the opposite: that moderns, modern women in particular, can't keep quiet about their relationships. Yet even among close friends, there are only two acceptable marriage narratives: the head-over-heels love story and the sardonically put-upon, hopelessly resigned farce (with the characters in "the antipathetic, recriminatory mood of the average husband and wife of Christendom," as Thomas Hardy sardonically put it a century ago). The resigned wife jokes about her sexually and domestically useless husband and only brightens when she's whispering about the guy she covets for an affair—will she or won't she? Or she laments that although she's given up on ever wanting to have sex with her husband, she got what she wanted: a baby.

The exception to the rule that what goes on between spouses stays between spouses occurs when a marriage is in its final throes. Then husband and wife are each permitted to erupt with rollicking, his-and-her tales of victimization and betrayal. But as for the ordinary misery that precedes the abject end—the bewildering combination of anger and alienation; the seeming impossibility of making good on one's good intentions; the earnest, anxious wish to feel love and return it—those topics are too real, too fraught, unfit for polite company.

I'm partial to the argument of Phyllis Rose, who, with tongue only halfway in cheek, challenged people to resist "cultural pressure to avoid such talk . . . in the spirit of good citizenship." It was in this frame of mind that Rose embarked upon *Parallel Lives,* a book that illuminates the present state of matrimony by examining its nineteenth-century antecedents and that is another of my favorite (accidental) guides to conjugal living. Among the couples she dissects are John Stuart Mill and Harriet Taylor, and like Mill in his famous 1869 essay "The Subjection of Women," Rose calls marriage the "primary political experience in which most of us engage as adults," implicating "questions about the role of power and the nature of equality." Which is how she comes to conclude that conversation about marriage "ought to be taken as seriously as talk about national elections."

While the group foregrounds the psychological, the political ripples below: in Marie's decision two decades ago to put her husband's occupational priorities before her own, in Michael's struggle to conceive of a space for himself between master (his father's role) and slave (his own role in his first marriage), in, perhaps, the extra measure of discomfort engendered in the group by the fact that Bella seems to command Joe, as opposed to the reverse.

From the first, then, I've considered the group, with all its fits and starts, with all its exquisite frustrations, an improvement on the usual discourse on marriage. At least these people are *trying* to be honest with themselves and each other, trying to fashion lives that contain less drudgery, fractiousness, and fear, more pleasure and meaning. And their lack of cynicism about the institution impresses me again and again. Just like any world-weary married lady, I smile knowingly at Byron's "I have great hopes that we shall love each other . . . as much as if we had never married at all," but I wonder if the jaded attitude not only reflects misery but creates it—or makes it too acceptable not to interrupt it. The group is brave, I think, to let their marriages matter.

The twelfth session is the last one before a short hiatus, during which Coché plans to recruit a fourth couple. The day is hazy and mild, near the end of May. The group is congregating in the Philadelphia office because Coché hasn't yet adjourned to the beach for the summer. With its wall of floor-to-ceiling windows, she'll have to turn the air conditioner on and off, off and on; eight body temperatures will never align.

Clem and Marie are the first to arrive, as usual. They have a two-hour drive to Philadelphia, but they've never been late. Clem is wearing khakis and a blue button-down, smiling hello. Does he know what Marie talked about in the session he missed? I doubt it. When Marie announced that she and Clem had never truly touched their mutual isolation, Coché replied, "Well, I think Clem would need some help hearing this, I really do." Translation: Let the group help you broach it, Marie.

As people file in, they look relatively happy to be back together, relaxed in each other's presence. For my part, I'm itching to know what happened with Bella and Joe and to hear more about Michael's sexuality. My curiosity won't be satisfied right away, however. Several times I've impatiently asked Coché why she didn't return to this or that matter from the prior session. While she told me she sometimes goes into a group planning to wend around to a specific topic, she won't force it. She takes the couples as they come. "The group never changes the subject," she said, dispatching her own need to know, if not mine.

Michael has a reason for not immediately picking up where he left off: His grandfather, whom he lived a few blocks from throughout his childhood, died a couple of days ago. He mentions the loss to explain why he can't concentrate on the question Coché has asked everyone to consider: Can you be wrong in your marriage without feeling wounded to the core? Her goal is to lodge in the group-mind the idea that a more productive response to "mistakes" is to try to do better next time, just a notch better. It sounds like *All I Ever Needed to Know I Learned in Kindergarten* advice, but Coché wants the group to cogitate on it, absorb it.

In the last meeting, each of the three couples seemed either poised for a major change, or already off the plank, and Coché doesn't want them to drown in self-criticism when the inevitable regressions occur. Two steps forward, one step back, two steps forward.

"I haven't given myself time to think about [the loss of my grandfather]," Michael says. But here in the group, he says, the banked-up emotion is coming to the surface.

That's totally understandable, Coché soothes. Michael's eyes are heavy with sadness. "This is a quiet setting where you can think about feelings," she says. If he can just "hang out" for a while, she tells him, the group will get back to his grandfather.

In the meantime, Marie and Clem are talking about an area where she wants to see improvement, if only a modest one. In a squabble the week prior, Clem spat at Marie, "You'll never be happy." It was not only deflating, she says, but threw her back into the scrum of her childhood, where that accusation was routinely flung. What's worse, she says to Clem, "is that the people telling me that in the past were really mean-spirited. But you telling me—you're such a lovely person." A look of vulnerability crosses her face; the new Marie is in the house. I can't tell if Clem notices. "It makes it even more scary," Marie says.

"So do you have a right to say, 'Clem, that doesn't feel very good when you say that'?" Coché asks, employing Marie's pet concept of "rights."

Marie sighs. "Usually by that time he walks away or cuts it off or stops somehow."

"Clem," Coché says, "if Marie says to you, 'That felt insulting, or please don't leave, I need to talk to you,' can you stay connected for a little longer? Or can you say, 'Marie, I can't—it's too hard for me. I'm leaving now.'"

"Depending on the situation," he replies. "If I feel you're being too unreasonable"—he gestures toward his wife—"and it's not going anywhere, then I'll leave."

"Can you say, 'I need to leave now'?" Coché asks, as opposed to just turning on your heel.

"Yes," he says, fading.

"Can you do that?" she repeats.

"Yes." He puts iron in his voice.

"Let me just give you a sentence: 'I don't want to continue the conversation now. It's too hard for me.'" Clem nods—but then Marie frets that they can't do this stuff at home.

"This is a testing ground for you," Coché checks her. "The goal is not for you to walk out of here and do this perfectly. The goal is for you to allow this to be a safe harbor so you can practice some of this."

"All right, then," Marie says, grinning. "Can I try?" She doesn't wait for an answer. She looks across to Clem. "I feel minimized when you present one of the biggest situations in my entire career as 'shopping time.'"

What she's referring to is the source of the argument that prompted Clem to indict her as permanently unhappy: The Saturday afternoon before, while Marie took a nap, he went on an excursion with their daughter. That was fine, except Clem stayed away and had dinner with the girl without calling Marie, leaving her with no car to do what Clem called "her shopping." In fact, she had to run errands to prepare for her first work trip to Africa. It does seem like a big deal: All the while she has been attending the couples group, she's been trying to revive her professional life and her efforts finally are being rewarded.

Marie's tone isn't damning, but Clem slips into *his* past, his past with her, and perhaps, too, with his own family or origin: He's not going to break solidarity with his perpetually reamed dad. "Well, I've been asking to go shopping for years," he whines.

"Wait, stop," Marie says, again without resentment. "I said, 'I don't like how it's been minimized as just shopping as opposed to preparing for one of the biggest events in my career.'" She's trying, but this could easily go south.

"Can I help?" Coché asks.

"Sure," Marie replies pleasantly. No wonder Clem looks confused.

"I'm Marie," Coché says. She claps her hands together in her lap and faces Clem. "'Clem, I don't think you intended to insult me, but it felt that way when you categorized my career preparation as shopping. I didn't feel like you were taking me seriously enough . . . You know, I appreciate that we're talking more, but there might be a way to talk better.'"

"Uh, I hear that you're saying that I didn't treat this as—as important as it was for you," Clem replies valiantly to his pretend wife.

"'Thank you for listening,'" says Coché, still being Marie. "'That really means a lot to me'—I bet it does." Now she's addressing Marie.

"Yes, it does," Marie answers.

"So then you want to say that."

"That means a lot to me," Marie says, locking onto her husband's face. "I feel closer to you when I feel like you understand the significance [of the trip] to me. So thank you."

"Okay," Clem says. He needs time.

Before lunch, Coché says she wants to return to Michael, to how he was "compartmentalizing" his feelings about his grandfather's death. Everybody does it to get through the day, she says, but the expression of emotion doesn't have to be all or nothing.

Okay, Michael says, "but the funeral isn't going to be until the end of next week. It just seemed easier if I waited until I actually got there."

"But here you are, in feelingsville," Coché says. "So what you might want is a way to bring up some of the feelings without losing your sense of composure altogether, or a way to move into talking about how you feel, and then away."

"Yeah, I want to have some way of saying, 'Okay, enough for now.'"

"I'll just ask you: Can you describe a little about your grandfather," Marie intervenes, "because it seems like he was important to you?" Her tone is curious and kind. She's sitting next to Rachael and Michael, in the rolling desk chair Coché usually takes.

"It's difficult talking about it," Michael says. "Rachael had a great relationship with her grandfather [who died a few years ago], so if I start talking about it, she just tears up." It's that again: the tyranny of Rachael's tears, and the mirthless laugh rattling under Michael's words.

"Then just face *me*," Marie commands Michael. Forget the wife at your shoulder for a moment. To see Michael without obstruction, Marie rolls her chair a foot toward the center of the room. Rachael chuckles appreciatively.

"So tell me about your grandfather," Marie begins anew, peering over the tops of her gold-rimmed glasses.

"He was a really—he was a good guy, a gentle soul." This, in contrast to the forbidding specimen of a father the group has heard about. "I never knew him to be bigoted or biased or . . . He loved to garden, to cook, he liked to have parties and get the family together. And my father and my aunts, you know, really loved him . . . and me, too." Michael is beginning to cry.

Rachael is as well—not, I think, because of her own grandfather but in sympathy for her husband. Marie rolls closer to the couple and reaches for Rachael's hand. She clasps it between both of hers without breaking eye contact with Michael. The group is transfixed.

What's making this especially painful for Michael, it turns out, is that his grandfather spent several years with "locked-in syndrome." He was completely paralyzed—he couldn't speak or move and was fed through a tube—and excruciatingly aware of it. "I'd talk to him, tell him what's going on, and he heard exactly what I was saying." The scene is horrible to imagine, and it's Clem who has tears in his eyes now. "I wish I could've been with him when he died," Michael pleads, gulping for breath. His head is tilted weakly to one side, and he regards Marie with something like gratitude, or trust. She's still holding Rachael's hand.

"When people come to me," says the small-town pastor who is the utterly human narrator of Marilynne Robinson's novel *Gilead* "whatever they say, I am struck by a kind of incandescence in them, the 'I' whose predicate can be 'love' or 'fear' or 'want,' and whose object can be 'someone' or 'nothing' and it won't really matter, because the loveliness is just in that presence, shaped around 'I' like a flame on a wick, emanating itself in grief and guilt and joy and whatever else . . .

"To see this aspect of life is a privilege of the ministry which is seldom mentioned," this wise man observes. And a privilege of a therapy group, I'd say.

As promised, Coché helped Michael move out of his spasm of sorrow: "How about saying to yourself, 'I'll come back and visit this place again, but now let's have lunch'?"

Michael laughed: "Okay, let's have lunch." No big deal, except for someone who has spent years keeping his feelings at stiff arm's length.

When the group reassembles, Michael offers to read a letter he promised to bring last time. In it, he for the first time revealed to another person his attraction to men, though he'd been aware of it when he was as young as nine or ten. "It was like falling off a cliff to actually put it down in writing, because I never admitted it. I mean, I told no one, not even a pen pal, like it didn't exist." He wearily pushes the hair off his forehead.

"If you didn't want to read the letter now," Marie says softly, "because of your grandfather—would you tell us?"

Michael hesitates, then turns to Rachael. "Do you want to talk about sexual orientation or the family?" he asks.

"What do you think is more important?" she asks.

"Well, given that—"

"—we're about to go home for a funeral," Rachael says, completing his sentence.

They settle on considering the family "acrimony" that Michael expects when he goes home for the funeral, a decision that Coché seems to approve. Apparently, Michael's aunts and uncles are furious at his father for secretly disregarding medical advice and prolonging their dad's life with blood transfusions. Not that Michael will feel sorry for his father if he's shunned or taken to task, he says. "I'm not close to my father—I guess I always found him kind of scar—" He stops.

"Part of the reason that I always had trouble with my sexual orientation," he tries again, "is my father is very bigoted." Michael is going to take up the theme, after all. The downside of the large family gatherings his grandfather loved was that they tended to deteriorate into shouting matches about "blacks, homosexuals, horrible things, just very ugly," Michael says, shuddering. "And I was like, okay, I'm gonna remove myself from that. Because God forbid my father finds out I feel the way I do." He stops once more. "I'd lose the love of my entire family."

A half a year ago, Michael said something similar when Coché asked him how it felt to hear that Rachael's father compared his grieving daughter to a cow. "It's my nightmare, too, that my parents wouldn't love me," he'd replied. Then it sounded like a narcissistic non sequitur; now it's making some sense.

"It wasn't like I didn't have attraction to women," Michael continues, "so I could just subserviate [the homosexual] part. And I blocked myself doing a lot of things, like, I really love plants, gardening"—like his grandfather—"but I didn't pursue that in school, because, no, that's kind of gay. So a lot of things I've done in life, I've done them not because I wanted to but because they wouldn't give me away."

The pieces of Michael are coming together. The group is getting why he's so well trained in the art of emotion nullification, why he's clung to a dull job, on the one hand, and pursued the adventures of an adolescent, on the other. When Michael stamped down a basic part of himself into a tiny nub, motorcycles and mammoth roller coasters became his inalienable human rights. I'm overplaying the causality here, I'm sure, but as I look across at Michael's crumpled face, I feel nearly as furious at his father as I did at Rachael's. What vicious nonsense was foisted on this man, and with such a tragic result. I'm not as skeptical anymore, either, about Michael's interest in opening lines of communication with Rachael about his sexuality: He wants the woman he loves to know him as he is, not as the facsimile he has toiled to present.

"What's it like to talk about it?" Coché asks Michael.

"It's sort of—it's uncomfortable. It's not *sort of* uncomfortable—it's very uncomfortable." Michael makes a real effort these days to catch his penchant to play down any unpleasantness. "It almost feels dirty, like bestiality, or child pornography or something." *Oh Lord.* But it's not just that, Michael adds. "It's like I'm labeling myself, and I'll be immediately pigeonholed." He has said that he's somewhat more attracted to men than to women—at the beach, for example, he'll notice the fine male forms before the female—and he fears that Rachael and the group will assume he's gay rather than bisexual, which is what he considers himself. They'll assume that he can't really want to spend his life with a woman—isn't that what all those closeted gay guys did in the fifties, took their wedding vows, then saw the light and bolted?

All of this occurs to me, I admit, sitting in the group. I feel great sympathy for Michael, but equally great apprehension for Rachael.

Coché doesn't seem particularly bothered by the multitudes Michael contains—she'll tell me that she thinks he truly wants to confine gay sex to his fantasy life, which seems feasible to her. For that matter, Rachael seems pretty tranquil. She's loosely holding hands with Michael across the middle of the love seat.

"There's a richness of experience and fantasy that can encompass a whole lot of things within a marital framework," Coché says to Michael, "only a small percentage of which you've given yourself permission to acknowledge in the face of your family." She pauses. "So if this works out exactly the way you want it, where will you be as a couple?"

"I won't have to feel rejection [from Rachael], or, on the flip side, like I'm pushing her away, if I can just make her comfortable with how it is."

"Are *you* comfortable with how it is?" Coché asks.

"No, not entirely."

"So maybe we want to do that piece."

"I think I'm more comfortable than you are," Rachael says. Not this again.

"That's probably true, I guess." Michael sighs.

"I don't get a sense that you feel threatened with this issue *at all*," Marie says to Rachael.

Now, that seems impossible to me—and Rachael, an honest broker, shades in the picture. "Actually, I was confused about [Michael's sexuality]," she says, explaining that before they got married, Coché urged them to thoroughly air the matter. They didn't. "I'd say, 'Let's talk about this,'" Rachael continues, "and he'd say, 'Oh, I don't want to.'"

And the group learns another new fact that raises the putative threat level on Rachael and Michael: They married when they did, less than a year after they started dating, because her visa was about to expire. "It was the only way to continue our relationship, because Rachael would have been deported," Michael says. He wasn't really ready, he adds, but "things were going well, sooo . . ."

It is in this unsettled state that the couple joined the group, though neither of them hazarded mention back then of their hasty wedding or, of course, Michael's bisexuality. (I remember Coché's snappy rejoinder when I suggested that Michael and Rachael, happy as they seemed, just signed up for the group for basic marriage education: "Believe me, nobody makes this kind of commitment just to get a few pointers.")

Over the year, however, outside of the group, Rachael says she and Michael have ventured into the minefield. "My original reaction was: What are you doing with me if you're more attracted to men than women? You're sitting on the wrong side of the fence. So that was hard, but as we talked about it, it seemed okay." She starts crying. "And I think a lot of it is we've been very close lately—"

"What are the tears about?" Coché asks.

"I'm not sure why I'm crying."

"I guess I'm wondering if it's because you have a lot of room in your heart for individual difference," Coché says, looking sympathetically at Rachael. The younger woman is dear to her, I think again, like a daughter. "And you love him very much and want him to have permission to be who he is, so you don't really want to be worrying about it. And on another level, it's kind of scary."

It was a mouthful, but Coché has captured the Rachael the group knows: a genuinely tolerant woman and an absolutely besotted wife. "Yeah," Rachael says glumly.

Once again, the group has to leave this topic. They have to get to Bella and Joe—what happened with them, anyway? There will be a next time, however, for Rachael and Michael. I'm glad, because I keep thinking about a conversation I had with a gay therapist and author named Joe Kort. I phoned him at his office in Maine after coming across an article he wrote in *The Psychotherapy Networker* called "Gay Guise: What to Do When Your Client Has Sex with Men but Is Straight." In it, Kort argues that his profession, as well as the homosexual community, is too quick to jump to the conclusion that gay behavior equals a gay man.

"Historically, therapists helped clients 'recover' and find their innate heterosexuality, much to the harm of many gays and lesbians," Kort wrote. "During the last three decades, in reaction to these prejudiced and destructive attitudes, we've seen the pendulum swing so far the other way that it's now become almost a therapeutic credo, not to mention a requirement of political correctness, to assume that men who have sex with men are 'in denial,' and that the clinician's job is to help them recognize and accept their 'true' homosexual orientation."

That bias has become automatic, Kort says when I talk to him, because we lump together sexual orientation/identity with sexual fantasy and sexual behavior. Yet the three often exist relatively independently of one another, a separation that we don't have much trouble accepting for heterosexuals. "If a man loves gangbanging fantasies," Kort says affably,

THE HUSBANDS AND WIVES CLUB | 257

"that doesn't mean he wants to marry a woman who likes to get gang-banged." (It's official: The virgin-whore dichotomy will never die.)

"And while a man's interest in gangbanging fantasies and videos may get stronger and stronger," Kort adds, "he's not going to leave his wife to go do that. So why would we think [Michael] will? Men can be homosexual and hetero-*emotional.* So they're romantically, affectively, relationally attracted solely to women—and they can be sexual with those women—but their sexual desires are primarily toward men."

But isn't that a huge loss for the man? I ask.

"For the man, the deeper loss would be living the gay life," Kort replies. "People just can't tolerate that a man could be primarily rela-tional—you know, like a woman—and fall in love with a *person* and make her a priority over his sexual interest." We think it's inconceivable, to coin a phrase, for a man *not* to think with his dick. Even lesbians get a pass on the rigid sexual classification system, Kort says. "We're not hounding Anne Heche, saying, 'Lesbian, lesbian, lesbian.'" (Heche is the actress who had a long relationship with the talk-show host Ellen DeGeneres before marrying a man.) "We're not trying to catch Anne Heche with a woman."

Bastardization of the language aside, Kort's "hetero-emotional" man sounds a lot like Michael. His increasing suppleness, his ability to countenance his own black feelings and his wife's, has drawn the couple closer, which has, in turn, made them more important to each other. (Their increasing interdependence, and the dread of loss that invokes, is what I think Rachael was referring to earlier when she told Coché that she was crying because the couple had been "very close lately.") I've also heard Michael say recently, outside of the context of his sexuality, that no one, *no one,* has ever known as much about him as Rachael—and still loved him, the implication being that what he has with her is sin-gular. On top of that, when we talk privately, Michael volunteers that he never had a good "emotional experience" with a man. (Oh, and in case it's still not clear, Rachael and Michael are both enthusiastic about their sex life.)

Which is not to wrap them up and stick on a bow, as Coché likes to say. After Kort unfurls his gangbang analogy, he pulls back a lit-tle. Sometimes, he says, a married man's sexual identity *does* change to

match up with his sexual fantasies. In fact, Kort says, he's treating a couple now, in their mid-twenties, who fit Rachael and Michael's description, and while "in this time in their life, they're who they say the are, I
told them, 'The way men discover their identity is when they fall in love
with a man . . .' This husband has to be vigilant about falling in love
with another man—it's never happened, he can't conceive of it, but a lot
of gay men couldn't either, until it happened."

Does "this husband" or Michael have to be more vigilant about falling in love with a man, I ask, than a heterosexual guy has to be about
falling in love with another woman?

No, Kort says. Michael wouldn't have to be any more careful than a
standard-issue heterosexual, unless he felt he was "cutting off his identity, pining for community and relationship with other gay men."

So it's irrelevant when someone's dominant sexual interest isn't getting any real-life play? I press.

Then Kort hedges again. He can get on a soapbox, but he really is
thoughtful. He hates to use this comparison, Kort says, but marrying
Michael could be likened to taking a recovering alcoholic as a mate. "I
tell people, 'He may have slips, he may go back to that life.' The addict
has to know that's a possibility, and so does the spouse."

Now it seems like the therapist is going too far: Michael, as far as I
and the group know, hardly had been "addicted" to gay sex. This isn't
Kort's fault, though. It's mine: I'm acting like a lawyer cross-examining
a client, trying to get the poor guy to commit to a single "right" answer
when there isn't necessarily one.

In *Parallel Lives,* Rose, literary critic that she is, says one of her primary motivations for writing the book was to broaden the repertoire of
"plots" for couples. So while John Stuart Mill's contemporaries considered him the ultimate in henpecked husbands (and he and his wife probably never consummated their union), the couple was relatively happy, in
the shared "delusion" that theirs was a marriage of equals. "Mill's mind
approved equality but his soul craved domination," writes Rose (who
gives equal treatment to the psychological and political). Meanwhile,
his wife "liked the feeling of mastery" while theoretically gravitating
toward equality. Is Harriet Taylor any worse off, Rose implicitly asks,
than Catherine Hogarth, who had ten children with Charles Dickens

before being deserted by him? Neither marriage is enviable, perhaps, but at least the nineteenth-century couples obliterate our assumptions of what's proper or good, give us a fresh piece of paper on which to write. "We feel anxious and unhappy," Rose says, "because the callowness and conventionality of the plots we impose on ourselves are a betrayal of our inner richness and complexity."

Her project is one that Kort, as well as Miller, who also wants us to add to the number of models for long-lasting relationships, surely would commend. And Michael and Rachael are two of its test subjects, you might say: a couple who are attempting to write a marital plot that allows them to live contentedly as man and wife without cheating complexity.

CHAPTER 15

─────────────

The Adventure of Marie and Clem

Joe was determined, if petrified. About two weeks before the twelfth group, he got up in the morning and fixed himself a bowl of oatmeal. It had been his favorite breakfast since boyhood, and it might start becoming necessary again. Bella was still asleep; three months pregnant, she was tired all the time.

Careful not to wake her—out of habit and also because he preferred not to have to answer any questions about where he was going, what he was doing—he showered and shaved and ripped open a plastic dry-cleaning bag. There it was: his favorite navy blue "power suit." He put on a crisp white button-down, then pulled on the suit pants. They still fit, even though he'd gained some weight around the middle and had had little occasion to dress up since he'd traded the formality of a law firm for the casual chaos of managing a restaurant. He slipped into the jacket; it felt good. The suit made his broad shoulders look even broader—whatever it took.

He got a stack of résumés, which he'd updated to reflect his short tenure at the restaurant, and put them in a leather file folder he found in the bottom of the closet, a relic of Bella's corporate life or his, he couldn't remember. Then he softly closed the door of the basement apartment and walked out into the squinty, bright spring day. Just a block away, there was a long strip of trendy restaurants and bars, and he was going to hit every one: Were there any waitstaff or bartending positions available? It occurred to him that trolling for restaurant work in a dark suit, brandishing a legal résumé, gave him a Willy Loman-ish aspect. So be it. He felt comfortable in the suit, and at least it would make him stand out. Usually, he stopped at a Starbucks for coffee, but he bypassed it in favor of a café that served jasmine tea. He wanted this day to be different; he'd started it with oatmeal, but now something new had to happen. His luck had to change.

This is one of the efforts Joe made between this session and last to find work, he tells the group, and for the second time today, they're mesmerized. The picture he's painted is almost as riveting as watching Marie wheel over to hold Rachael's hand. Joe also applied to be a baggage handler at the airport, he says, to teach English as a second language, and to tutor high school students for the SATs. And his scorched-earth campaign paid off: He's been hired to pore over legal documents eight hours a day, five days a week, searching for tiny technical flaws—a gig a temp agency found him. In addition, the law firm that was yesterday's big news, the one that hired him to work on contingency, threw him a case. He's working that in the evenings. "What I got to—what I was avoiding is I need to do whatever it is I need to do to support my family," he says. Joe sounds so . . . realistic. This isn't a person the group has heard from before.

Of course in the last session, Bella told Joe that as a condition of staying married, he had to get a job that was "paying the bills, giving [him] confidence" and stop lying to himself and her. So did he just capitulate to his wife . . . again? The vibe the group is getting off Joe certainly doesn't feel like appeasement (and, after all, he didn't exactly give in to Bella in the past; he just pretended to and then worked around her). He seems resolute, tougher somehow—no "dependent little boy" for him. The group has seen him bluff the stiff-upper-lip thing, granted, but his expressions aren't as exaggerated this time. And he looks tired, red around the eyes, appropriately for someone who is working two jobs. Joe tells people he had to get beyond his simultaneously self-pitying and cocky attitude, beyond the thought that kept occurring to him: "I can't believe with my experience and my education, I'm now going to be bartending.

"But oh, that's right," Joe says, flashing a smile. "I couldn't even get a job as a bartender." (The legal temp job materialized a week after his failed mission.) The change in Joe is as modest as it is awe-inspiring. He's just Joe, in blue jeans and a button-down, flopped on the couch next to his wife. But it seems like he has literally come into himself, occupying the skin he's in rather than the skin he wished he had.

Murray Bowen might say that what has happened is that Joe has come into *more* self, added a parcel of the stuff on the lifelong quest. I imagine Bowen listening to Joe's story, taking an insouciant drag on his cigarette, and drawling, "Damn, now ain't that something." Joe reacted to Bella's differentiating move in precisely the way Bowen predicts: He countered with his own. And Joe did so in a way that bore two marks of a fruitful effort: First, it must be done "for self alone," Bowen preaches. When Coché directly asks Joe if he did what he did "to please" Bella, he says, "No, it was something I needed to do for myself." (Undoubtedly, Joe knows this is the right answer, but dupe that I may be, he sounds genuine.) Second, Bella is surprised to hear about the lengths to which Joe went to find work; the first she heard of it was in the group. "To discuss the plan with another *who is part of the system* invites certain failure," Bowen maintained.

The group gives Joe raves for how grounded he sounds, how rightfully proud of himself. "You made it happen," says Rachael. "It's fantastic, and you seem so much happier."

"I have complete confidence in you," Marie adds. "Complete confidence."

"Yeah, this is the family where we bite the bullet and just make reality work, whatever we need to do," Coché says. "This is really different from the family where everything has to look good, whether it's good or not."

Until recently, Bella adds, she had not really digested how Joe dealt with pressure—by avoidance. "It's not my style," she says "but I really got, well, if I were avoiding, I wouldn't look at [bank statements]" either. Bella sounds less scared of strange Joe, even tolerant of the difference between them.

But not so fast. "So let's talk about the really tough stuff," Coché says, turning to Bella. The therapist has had several phone consultations with the couple, individually and together, over the past month. While

Joe was busy avoiding how dire their financial situation was, Coché asks, "was there anything you were avoiding, Bella, at least just a little bit?"

"I don't call it 'avoiding,'" Bella says, stiffening. Her response indicates why Coché's question teemed with qualifiers.

"I know," Coché says apologetically. "I set it up in a way that sounded negative."

"No, it's okay," Bella says, relaxing again.

After Joe quit the restaurant in disgust over the porn incident, Bella says she began to notice that not only did she and Tara have different values ("My business partner, [her creed] is 'Make money off of everyone you know,'" Bella said earlier in the day, "and I'm like, *no!*") but that their "partnership" was in name only. "With no Joe to blame," with his side of the triangle removed, Bella came to believe that all her friend wanted was a worker bee who wouldn't challenge her authority. This is a complete one-eighty for Bella. Six months ago, Coché tried to get her to consider whether Tara and she had the "same values," the "same sense of what's enough," to which Bella peremptorily replied: "Oh, my business partner and I are very similar, very aligned."

"I just want to draw your attention to two things," Coché says now. "Although you don't think of yourself as somebody whose coping mechanisms center around avoidance, I think all of us—and you, Bella—have blind spots." Secondly, the therapist says, we tend to disregard the people closest to us, such as, ahem, Joe, when they try to point out what we're missing.

Bella pauses, her eyes on Coché. While she's gained some pregnancy weight, she is looking good, wearing jeans and bronzy high-heeled sandals, her toenails painted red. "All right, everybody," she says cheerfully, "I was wrong."

The group laughs. Bella is not going to get uppity on them again.

On the one hand, Bella continues, she doesn't regret taking the risk to join Tara, because it got her out of the velvet coffin of her corporate job. But on the other, it has become plain that she was too eager to buy into the whole shebang. She is in the process of extricating herself from the restaurant, as well as the broader real estate venture, and the couple is putting their town house up for sale in a few weeks.

She and Joe also have agreed that he'll assume sole financial responsibility for the family in their baby's first year. That may seem like Bella is unfairly letting herself off the hook she hung them on, but for her to truly depend on another human being, especially one named Joe, would be an achievement. And Joe seems pleased, very pleased, to be the sole breadwinner. He's been thinking a lot about the law job he had before the couple moved, he says. The work may not have been scintillating, but there was "purposefulness" to it. "I was doing something for a reason." And supporting his wife, and soon his child, definitely falls into that category.

Coché nods her approval. Many jobs—like many marriages—don't consistently provide the "wows," she says, "but they do provide the whys and wherefores: I'm doing this for a reason, my children know I'm doing this for a reason." For the existentialist psychologist, the cultivation of meaning is the foundation for living. "You're all struggling with some individual preferences that can be hard to mesh with being married," Coché adds, calling Michael's sexual desires and Marie's intellectual ones back into the room. "And there needs to be a way for you to feel you're not giving yourself up by remaining in the relationship."

Coché's statement has Bowenian echoes, but then so do these lines from Rilke: "A complete sharing between two people is an impossibility, and whenever it seems, nevertheless, to exist, it is a narrowing, a mutual agreement which robs either one member or both of his fullest freedom and development. But once the realization is accepted that, even between the closest human beings, infinite distances continue to exist, then a wonderful living side by side can grow up, if they succeed in loving the distance between them which makes it possible for each to see the other whole and against a wide sky!"

These are stirring words (like countless other brides and grooms, my husband and I had them read at our wedding), but they're ontological as much as prescriptive. Which is to say I don't want to leave the impression that differentiation is the royal road to happiness for couples, the best or only road. When Rachael and Michael had their "attachment conversation" months ago, the one in which he sensitively acknowledged how he'd hurt her in the past, it seemed like the right step for them. The same goes for Bella and Joe at an earlier juncture in the group, when he told her about his feelings of loss after their miscarriage—the birthday party to which no one came. Both of the feeling-laden exchanges came at Coché's instigation, and the mutual understanding they engendered seemed to steer the two couples in the right direction.

Schnarch, likely, would snort at this (and Bowen, too, though he wasn't a snorter). Their disdain would not be for "mutual understanding" but for the notion that empathic conversations such as the ones Sue Johnson advocates, and Coché orchestrates at times, are useful toward that end. At a conference some time ago, Schnarch critiqued a videotaped vignette of a counseling session conducted by a therapist of the Johnson variety named Harville Hendrix (who has his own popular books and own couples therapy curriculum). In the tape, Hendrix tells a wife who has been physically abused by her husband to vent, while the man is asked to listen sympathetically. As the woman gets more upset and angry, Hendrix urges her on, and as she breaks down in tears, he soothes and cajoles with, "So deep, so deep, go with the pain, stay with it."

And how did Schnarch tell the audience he'd handle this pair? "I would turn to the wife while she's crying and say, 'You're telling me you hate him, and you're angry at him, then why are you stroking his ego? Your tears show him he can control you. You're also showing him he can do it again, because you still want his understanding.'" Such an intervention has an immediate, powerful impact, according to Schnarch. "The woman stops crying, draws herself up, and it scares the shit out of the guy because she's no longer a victim. What you're seeing, in short order, is the process of differentiation."

By pulling for people's strength, by "getting what's best in them to stand up," Schnarch says, he sets the stage for authentic intimacy. "As you become more differentiated, you recognize that those you love are separate people—just like you. What they want for themselves becomes as important to you as what you want for yourself."

This is an assertion more than an explanation, but it has common-sensical appeal: You have to love yourself to love others. Put differently, it's not the sustenance of close relationships that is doubted by advocates of differentiation; it's the avenue to achieve them that is at issue. Only a person with a well-defined self can truly meet another for Schnarch and

Bowen. Interpersonal independence is both men's preoccupation. For Johnson, and for Bowlby who inspired her, connection *is* self, or helps build it. We are the sum of our attachment systems, Bowlby believed (which is really a more radical notion for Western, individualist culture than the belief that emotional fusion is the enemy). Dependence should be respected as a natural part of bonding.

Again, though, neither doctrine carries the day for me. On the ground, in the group, in marriage, both seem beneficial at different times, for different couples—*and* for different therapists. Johnson tells me that some years ago she tried employing the paradoxical interventions of Erickson and Haley, "and they sort of worked," but she couldn't keep it up. As potent as they may have been in those two guys' hands, Johnson could not be therapist as wisewoman, enigmatically apportioning out the magic words. "I do think one of the reasons we need different models in couples therapy is not only because clients are different," Johnson says, "but because *therapists* are different."

A caveat: If you read this and think *Schnarch is the therapist for me,* or *Johnson, she's the one,* you may be right, but you may want to reconsider. Looking back on my wedding, I suspect my husband and I gravitated toward the Rilke quote because we were already adept at walking next to each other, with ample space in between: Passionately pursuing our own interests was something we'd each been doing for thirty-five years. I see my husband and me in a couple Michael Miller describes in *Intimate Terrorism:* "Like many people who possess high energy and whose native talents have been developed and affirmed in their youth, they [were] both aggressive, emotionally volatile, and quick on the draw." I suspect there are a fair number of couples like us: What we struggle with—very concretely—is how to touch across the divide. Now, I know Bowen would say we were each just short on "self" and therefore feared the engulfment of drawing too close. Perhaps, but if connection is what you seek, all that defining oneself, holding on to oneself, just doesn't embolden.

I'm underground, waiting for the subway with my husband, the father of my two daughters. We're about to go our separate ways, I on one train, he on another. His hair looks curly the way I like it. I want to say something to him, acknowledge him. Now he's opening the *New*

York Post; now I'm fishing in my bag for the *Times.* This is how it goes in marriage, "Well, if you're gonna"—fill in the blank—"then I am, too, dammit!" But his hair looks curly the way I like it; I want to feel his mouth on mine.

I have to make myself touch my husband. I'm such a connoisseur of his faults—why do I let my other tastes for him atrophy? I brush casually against his bare forearm, like an animal approaching a potential mate, like a schoolboy pulling a girl's braids. He doesn't seem to notice. Am I going to have to make the first move? I must speak, act. I have to. "Tim?"

One late-spring evening, with the group reaching its end, I arrange to meet Clem and Marie at their home. They live two hours away by car, and during the drive, I keep thinking of the session in which Bella and Joe bottomed out, Michael introduced his sexuality, and Marie confessed her longing to talk to Clem about what mattered to her. Taking in the five alternately anxious and implacable, eager and exhausted faces circling her, Coché remarked that couples can often "bond within wider ranges" than they believe possible. For example, she suggested, perhaps Clem could become more of an intellectual partner for Marie than she assumed was possible?

"I don't think it's in him," Marie said, "and in a way, if it [were] in him, I'd lose Clem." It still touches me to remember that, to hear Marie treasuring Clem, but in the car I'm thinking about the constraints she— and Clem, I'll come to apprehend more acutely—impose on themselves and their marriage. Specifically, I'm seeing the couple through the eyes of the psychoanalyst Stephen Mitchell, whose short but rich book *Can Love Last? The Fate of Romance over Time,* I read for the third time in the days before I left to visit Marie and Clem.

I first heard of Mitchell at a conference dedicated to his memory in 2001—at age fifty-four, at the height of his career, he'd suddenly died of a heart attack and had left behind an auditorium's worth of devastated admirers and friends. A clinician and a brilliant teacher, he was a key founder of modern "relational" psychoanalysis, the movement that manages to encompass the work of such diverse thinkers as Sullivan, Klein, Winnicott, and Bowlby, among others. Mitchell himself had become part of this august group, owing to the fecundity of his mind and, most spectacularly for my purposes, the layers of meaning he added to the psychoanalytic understanding of marriage.

In *Can Love Last?*, published posthumously, Mitchell turned upside down the conventional wisdom about the sources of ordinary marital malaise. His first step in the project, which draws on physics, neurobiology, and philosophy as well as psychoanalytic case studies, is to ask readers to reexamine their assumptions. "Where they love, they have no desire; where they desire, they cannot love," Freud famously said, and we blithely, if secretly, accept this as the dismal truth. But the formulation implicitly treats sexual craving as synonymous with romance, though they're really not the same, and the latter is what long-marrieds are likely to end up missing the most. "Romance requires love *and* desire," Mitchell writes. "Desire without love can be diverting and stimulating, but desire without love lacks the intensity and the sense of high stakes that deepen romantic passion. Love without desire can be tender, intimate, and secure, but love without desire lacks adventure, edge, the sense of risk that fuels romantic passion."

The opposing needs for safety and adventure—or "home versus freedom"—are part of being human, he goes on, but because the conflict between the two is "difficult to contain" within one person, we tend to make our spouse the repository for our security needs. Good old Clem, good old Marie. Yet in current thinking, neither self nor reality are fixed entities. It is the nature of both, Mitchell says, to be "inaccessible, fluid, discontinuous." So if we assume our spouse has a self—I know, it's a stretch—and we assume *change* is inherent to self, "How is it," he asks, "that in his or her primary relationship this man or this woman manages to feel so safe?" How do we pull it off?

Mitchell's answer is that we *make* our spouses safe; in a world defined by impermanence, "home and security are generated through an act of imagination," no less so—and this is the crucial move—than the early idealizations that we dismiss as nonsense once we realize who the blokes and dames we married *really* are. And why do we denude the ones we love? "The degrading of romance may have less to do with familiarity than the increasing danger of allowing oneself episodic, passionate idealization in a relationship that one depends on for security and dependability." Again, we can't hold the tension between the two, we can't tolerate the ambiguity.

For a relationship to last with a degree of romance intact, "what is valuable," Mitchell argues, "is not a continual objective take on reality but the ability to move in and out of different perspectives." After all, he says with a wink, "there is no good reason to assume that the other (that would be your husband or wife) is any less conflictual, any less multiplicitous, any less contextual than oneself." In contrast to Miller, who argues that couples would do well to abandon attempts "to recapture original glory" and search for a new model of coupledom, Mitchell is rehabilitating idealization as something to dip in and out of. "With all due respect, Mrs. Grant," says Mary Crawford, the practical, if jaded sister of Fanny's rejected suitor in *Mansfield Park,* "there is not one in a hundred of either sex who is not taken in when they marry." To which Mitchell might reply, "And isn't it wonderful to be taken in?" Rather than concede idealization to the foolishly hormonal—or the psychologically immature, like Freud did—we might better regard it as "a process of bringing alive features of the other that are hidden and masked in ordinary, everyday interaction."

I'm still occupied by thoughts like these as I turn onto Marie and Clem's quiet residential block. They seem to have pulled back the blanket of anger between them, at least halfway, but what's underneath it? What is next for them? As I approach the couple's house, heart pounding, I'm remembering how Coché cautioned Marie against "extreme black-and-white thinking." I peer through the screen door. It seems so *regular* in there, just like Bella and Joe's restaurant. Marie has her back to me, stirring something at the stove. She's barefoot, wearing her smocked jean jumper over a short-sleeved yellow polo shirt. At my quick, embarrassed knock, she turns and breaks into a smile. She looks genuinely happy to see me.

Clem appears moments later, clambering down the steps from the second floor. "Laurie had a late lunch, so we'll eat later, okay?" Marie tells him respectfully. It feels as strange to him to have me in their house as I feel being there. Marie is the unruffled one.

"Oh, that's fine," Clem replies a little shrilly. He smiles accommodatingly, though, never not accommodating, this man. His own short-sleeved polo, newer than Marie's and a deeply saturated periwinkle color, matches his eyes. Marie suggests that we sit on the screened-in front porch to talk on this mild May evening, and Clem offers me a beer, which I accept gratefully. He pours cans of Coors into frosty mugs straight from the freezer.

As I did with the other couples, I start by asking them how they met, what attracted them to each other. "Well," Marie begins, which surprises me, "he was really into weight lifting in college. You still are." She glances at Clem with a glimmer of admiration. "You're very physically attractive. You're an attractive man, so definitely that, uh . . . We had Biology II together, and it was a huge lecture hall, and you arrived late, and I was sitting there, and I saw him come in. So uh, you were wearing that yellow jacket, the one that—"

"It looks like just a basic golf jacket," Clem says, dousing the romantic scene.

But Marie won't let him, not quite yet. "You arrived late, yeah, I remember that." She pauses, her mind traveling back. "Not that you arrived late," that's not what I remember, Marie clarifies. She doesn't want to cast herself as the responsible, studious one, with Clem the tardy ne'er-do-well, not again. What she remembers is noticing him, she says, the bright yellow vision of him.

Marie's focus on the physical seems so out of character. This is the woman who got spooked when her husband gave her the "bump" at the workshop led by the Pilates instructor, who cried her first year in the group when she massaged Clem's shoulders. This year, she announced in her singular, slashing style that the "best hugs were the ones she never got," because she found them so suffocating. She felt the same about Clem's breath on her face in bed. Not long ago, I mused to Coché that perhaps because of her childhood, perhaps because of inborn temperament, Marie wasn't wired to enjoy sex, or any physical contact whatsoever. "I have no idea," Coché replied, "but I have had women her age, if they get with the right partner, they rediscover—or discover—sexuality. Who knows, maybe Marie could do it with Clem?" She sounded like she believed this was a possibility.

Clem vaguely remembers the scene in which he was the object of Marie's desire—she's told him about it, apparently—but as was the case in the group, he seems to struggle to absorb or acknowledge his wife's appreciation (which must make appreciating him lonely). He answers the question of what drew him to Marie by saying that the two "palled around" with the same people, until Clem ferried the whole group to a farm "this fraternity rented out and hired several bands."

"I needed a ride," Marie interjects, just in case I was entertaining the happy thought that she sought him out for a lift. She can be forgiven, however. To hear Clem speak of their courtship without mentioning anything singular about her, anything special . . . "You ain't a beauty, but hey, you're all right," Springsteen sings, one of the more devastating lyrics in all music, if you ask me.

"I had seven and a half cases of beer in the back of my truck," Clem continues, "and [Marie and I] started going out." Then he softens a little. "Yeah, and when you turned nineteen," he says to his wife, "I came to see you and gave you a flower and a kiss."

Clem was more enthusiastic when I first came in, and he pointed to the flowers on the kitchen table, hot-pink and orange Gerber daisies. A patient whom Marie helped at work gave them to her, he told me. "I'm so proud of her. You can tell what a great job she does." At least a half-dozen times in the group, Clem noted, almost reverentially, how smart his wife was, how organized: He's comfortable with her as his competent if critical mother.

As we talk on, I can't get over how alike these two are, how hooked they are on safety, as Mitchell would put it. One moment, Clem is yearning for Marie to "roll over and kiss" him in bed. The next, he sits up straighter in his chair and announces that Marie meets the top requirement he had for a wife: She'd never "stray or look at other men or have an affair. Marie's true to me, and that's one of the things I wanted, and that's what I got, so . . ." Later, at my questioning, he says that the only circumstance that would make him leave her would be if she were to have an affair.

So you'd be willing to merely share the same house with Marie and forgo the intimacy you've spent years crusading for? I ask.

"I see—I see—I see it getting better," he stutters.

What if it doesn't? I ask.

"I'm unwilling to relent on—on . . ." He scowls slightly at me, then bursts forth, "She's my Marie, and no one else is going to have her, and I'm going to stay with Marie."

Whoa. His intentions are honorable, I suppose, but I wish I didn't think he was bound to "his Marie" mostly by fear of the unknown. I wish Clem would risk believing that there are parts of her that are a mystery to him and that he can't be sure what she's capable of. The cost of the absolute knowingness, which is a fantasy, anyway, is so high. "While betrayal makes us too real to each other, its impossibility makes us invisible," writes Adam Phillips, whose book of aphorisms about monogamy is Mitchell's *Can Love Last?*—the condensed version.

As for Marie, she is funny, self-deprecating, and meditative this evening, like she has been in the last sessions of the group. Her feet rest on the white wicker coffee table in front of her, her jean jumper falls between her knees. Yet I wonder, too, whether she is willing to take the leap to idealize her husband, to believe that there is new terrain to be discovered. Out of deference to Marie's fascination with the Civil War, Clem says he has planned a summer trip to visit some battle sites with her. If Marie would dare allow it, maybe Clem *could* get caught up in the history of the era. Maybe he could be more of an intellectual partner than she thinks. And maybe, after watching her husband traverse the grassy fields of Antietam, she'd even want to sleep with him, if she could bear him being anything other than gentle, dependable Clem.

But that may remain *my* fantasy. When I ask Marie in what circumstances she finds herself wanting to have sex with Clem, she doesn't answer. In the interminable seconds that follow, she and I stare at each other. I'm not looking away; then I'd have to see Clem. How must this feel to him? (Well, maybe no worse than hearing your romance reduced to seven and a half cases of beer.) Then, too, a journalistic mentor once told me that the best way to get an answer out of someone is to resist the impulse to fill in silences with chatter. I'm amazed Marie can be mute for so long. Maybe with this much time, she actually will call up a memory of desire.

"I don't know how to answer that," she says, finally.

"You don't know the answer," I keep on, "or you're just embarrassed to talk about it?"

"I don't know the answer." I think we all sigh, Marie, Clem, and me.

And yet . . . yet. As we sit on the screened-in porch, watching the light drain from the sky, something else Mitchell said occurs to me: "When patients complain of dead and lifeless marriages, it is often possible to show them how precious the deadness is to them." The line is a wry critique of the "security operations" couples mount to fend off emotional risk, definitely, but it's not only that. If you take seriously Mitchell's assertion that the human need for safety/predictability is no less valid than that for adventure/danger, you hear the double-entendre: how truly precious deadness can be. How precious it is here in Clem and Marie's mint-green shingled two-story, purchased two decades ago as a falling down wreck. Through the succeeding years, the couple worked to make it livable while raising two daughters and holding down full-time jobs.

After all that scrimping and sawing, there is this sturdy house with shelves built by Clem and white wicker furniture on the porch and a vase of fresh flowers on the table. There are the lovely, smart girls, one of whom darted through the kitchen in shorts and headphones shortly after I arrived, headed for a run. There is the garden that Clem showed me, "Marie's pride and joy," and the shiny used luxury car that Marie said Clem had "always wanted" and recently managed to buy on eBay. There is the one thing that has always been good in their marriage, the couple says, as we sit there, drinking our second beers as the seagulls squawk, and the dusk turns to darkness: No matter what, they can count on each other for advice and support when either is battered by the outside world.

Will anything truly and irrevocably change for the better between Marie and Clem? I hope so. They both still say they want that. But if not, they have this house, those girls, the way they crack up at the same old family stories, her memory of how handsome he looked when she first laid eyes on him in a crowded lecture hall, his memory of the kiss they shared on her nineteenth birthday. They have this house, those girls, and the memory of how they once were each other's best or only answer.

EPILOGUE

Therapy *Worked*?

My year with the group officially finishes in May 2007, but I don't stop shuttling to Philadelphia once a month. I can't. Marie and Clem, Bella and Joe, Michael and Rachael—they all reenrolled, and my curiosity about their fates, and the outcome of therapy in general, is too great. It also would seem rude not to come back, as if I didn't care about these people who'd bared themselves in front of me for twelve months. In my role as half fellow spouse, half-observer, I became part of the group. They felt it, and so did I.

I also decide to contact Leigh and Aaron. Not only had they left the group on a disturbing note, with Aaron's "dirty Goldbergs" epithet, but for most of the year they seemed to be in an indeterminate holding pattern. I'm not sure how they perceive their marriage overall, or their ten-year tenure in the group. And I have no idea what has ensued in the months since their departure.

Put another way, I lack a story about what keeps them together, or frankly, what keeps Leigh with Aaron. Unlike the other couples, whom I've come to view as mutually flawed and mutually resplendent, Leigh always seemed the more desirable of the two. She was caring, intelligent, attractive, and exuded integrity. Aaron was a handsome man, and it wasn't that he was *not* necessarily caring, intelligent, and honest, but in the milieu of the group, you couldn't necessarily tell what was inside of him. Which is to say nothing of his sexual dysfunction.

I arrange to meet with the couple in Coché's office, first Aaron, then a month later, Leigh. At their request, Coché is along both times to chaperone. Reporter that I am, part of me wants to get them *alone*, as if I could pry out some secret, but Coché's presence comforts Leigh and Aaron and probably allows them to speak more freely. And I'm not trying to get them to break and reveal what a rotten shrink they think Coché is. If there is one thing I know, Leigh and Aaron both respect the therapist enormously. (During the interviews, she will sit off to the side pretending to read some papers, intervening only rarely.)

During my talk with Aaron I'm touched, as ever, by what a well-meaning man he is—which of course may be one reason Leigh cast her (second) lot with him—but he's no easier to reach than usual, sticking to his rote explanations of the couple's troubles, their progress, and so on. I do manage to learn a few new details: that Leigh's "comparing" him to her late husband "was not easy to take," and that if Coché or Slowinski had pushed him to move any faster, he probably would've fled therapy and Leigh.

Aaron holds a paper in his lap during our interview—reminding me that in his early years with the group, he took constant notes—and as we're wrapping up, I ask him if there is anything he hasn't gotten across to me. There is.

"Over the course of our first couple months dating," Aaron says, half-reading his paper, "I said to myself, 'This woman, Leigh, she really is *interested* in me. She's not being, you know, overly critical. She really cares about me.'" He still sounds a little dazed by his luck. He finishes with a flourish: "I feel that everyone wants to be loved, and I feel that this may have been the first time—when I met Leigh and obviously to this day—that I felt truly loved."

Aaron searches my face: Do I understand the gravity of what he is saying? I think I do. He waited more than half of his life, in Raymond Carver's words, "To call myself beloved/To feel myself beloved on this earth." With all his quirks and sexual handicaps, it has occurred to me several times that Aaron could easily have ended up living out his days in puttering, muttering loneliness. (I imagine him in a frowzy SRO, but he's too well-off for that.) I've never forgotten the image of Aaron's parents ordering him into the kitchen to take his meals, like a servant. But as I said, I knew why Aaron married Leigh.

I begin to get a better grasp on the reverse when I speak with Leigh. The couple's first date, recall, had been at a crowded New Year's Eve party, and it was only on their second that they had a chance to talk. She judged him "very, very interesting—he read the *New York Times*," she declares. Not only could Aaron "carry on a conversation," unlike the handful of other men she'd dated since her first husband died, but he loved college basketball, which she has watched at big family parties since girlhood. "Aaron's like a running commentator—he's fabulous to watch a ball game with," she says, grinning. "It was very comfortable for me—I hadn't found much of that before him." Also important for Leigh: Aaron was financially set, with a decent job and family money to cushion him. Coché sums up Leigh's situation with the coolness of a social scientist: "Socially and developmentally, Aaron was an attractive match for her."

Then came the couple's first attempt to sleep together. Aaron, "frozen with fear, arms at his sides," breaking out in shingles the next day; Leigh, stunned. That's when she told Aaron that unless he got help, she was going to stop dating him. "And I really didn't think it was going to go further, because I had my issues, but [sex] wasn't one of them," she says, choking up at the memory.

I look at Leigh then, tears in her eyes, wearing a pumpkin orange sweater—one that looks so soft, I want to touch it—and for the first time I really notice the age spots on her face, the way she has a slight tic, blinking her left eye. When she met Aaron ten years ago, she was a middle-income widow with one teenager at home and three kids in college, not exactly a prime catch in the harsh marital market for women over a certain age. As Coché has said to me, in so many words: We forget marriage isn't just about who we'll have but who will have *us*. Now I think of Leigh needing to be had, not only Aaron.

To Leigh's surprise, Aaron agreed to go to therapy—to join the group and visit Julian Slowinski—and the couple's relationship took on a momentum of its own. Another woman probably would've seen the "handwriting on the wall and moved on," Leigh says. "But Julian kept saying, 'We can work more on this.' I wasn't going to start dating somebody else. It would've been like having an affair!"

Does Leigh ever blame the therapists or the group for keeping her with a man who was wrong for her? I ask.

Not really, Leigh says. "Judith was telling me that I couldn't fix it, but I didn't listen to her." (What I probably said, Coché interrupts, is that "Aaron might be able to make some progress, but [your relationship] might never be what you hoped.") From a distance, Leigh says she can see how Aaron became "one more rescuable project," like her father and younger brother before him, who basically fell apart after her mother died, leaving Leigh as the practical and emotional center of the family.

But the more I think about it, the more I resist the impulse to pathologize Leigh's stick-to-itiveness. Yes, staying with an impotent boyfriend when you say you *need* sex, thrive on it, could be seen as a kind of unhealthy dependence, or "*co*dependence," to be pop-psychologically precise. Differentiators Bowen and Schnarch surely would have none of it, but I think there is something admirable (and adaptive for monogamy?) about a person whose sense of self is staked on caretaking and nursing the relationships she has.

"I'm so loving and affectionate, I thought Aaron would just relax and find sex reinforcing," Leigh recalls thinking in the couple's first few years. "Because why wouldn't anyone want to be loved? Looks like anyone would want that." She laughs at her naïveté but I hear it straight, and I think she's right: Who *wouldn't* want that?

And on some level, Coché says, "Aaron understood that there was something terribly, terribly wrong. My sense is that he had a real appreciation of what Leigh gave him and a tremendous dedication to making [a more regular sex life] *the* goal of his existence." He also managed to tolerate Leigh's measuring him against her first husband, which I've attributed to his general imperviousness. Coché says I'm selling him short, however. "He can imagine what it's like to lose a brilliant husband too young, when you have four children, whereas a lot of men would say, 'I don't care who you were married to—get him out of our life!' Aaron is bigger than that."

Ultimately, too, Aaron wasn't the only one who had to change, Coché says. Leigh had to tamp down her understandable anger and hand-wringing, if she wanted to get what she said she did. "Leigh's reactions—horribly upset, disgruntled, sort of bewildered—were very natural, but as [those negative feelings] began to show, they colored the interaction and became part of the problem, rather than part of the solution," Coché says. It was then that the group, in its earlier iterations, began to turn up the pressure, as in: "'Yo, Leigh, if you say it that way, how can Aaron possibly listen to it?'"

Occasionally during this trying time, Leigh also recognized that Aaron was pushing her in one direction she actually wanted to go. Coming, as she did, out of the tumult of her childhood, of having to become the grown-up in her family at thirteen, her first husband was a welcome safe harbor, she says: He loved her, protected her, and reigned supreme. She'd started to chafe under that arrangement before he died, but she found herself expecting Aaron to duplicate it. "I kept wanting him to be more in charge, to be an adult," she says. Instead, by virtue of his strengths *and* limitations, he taught her to be "more of an equal partner," to share power and responsibility. "It's one of the most wonderful things we have," Leigh says.

So how is the couple getting on now, a year out of the group? I finally inquire. I know they're seeing Coché together, and also individually, once a month. "Things are so much better now, just the whole tenor of our marriage," Leigh says. The sudden eruptions of anger—which Coché explains as the result of Aaron's coping with conflict by "being a good boy" until he can't contain himself anymore—have virtually disappeared. "And I'm at a different place now in terms of what I need from him," Leigh adds. "Like last night he had dinner waiting for me when I came home, and he calls me during the day to see how I am. We cheer together at basketball games."

Wait—after eleven years, is she saying she's given up on sex?

"No, but I'm not expecting things to be natural, because they can't be. Even now when we make love, it has to be in a very controlled environment: lights off, covers up, on *my* side of the bed—God forbid, we'd be on his side. Always the same routine. I'd like him to soften and be able to relax more in touching—we're working on it with Judith—but . . ." In other words, if nothing more changes, she can abide it.

Seeing Coché two-on-one has been productive, Leigh continues. "Aaron doesn't get away with anything with Judith. A few times she's called him on the carpet, and he can't just retreat into the group." Which is what she thinks happened their last year. Aaron saw himself "as a graduate, and wasn't going to do any work," and neither the group nor she—buying into her husband's we've-come-a-long-way-baby routine—challenged him.

Coché says that she could see that Aaron was on automatic pilot, and she tried drawing him out several times early on (remember the incest comment?), but in the end she let him, and Leigh, set the tone. And Leigh didn't make much noise, Coché thinks, because the first part of the year she was pretty content with Aaron, and then, when all of a sudden she wasn't, she resisted being the troublemaker *one more time*. The deadline pressure—the group was ending, and what was Leigh going to do with this man?—forced her hand.

That their last round in the group wasn't a rousing success doesn't contravene that in prior years the group was integral to their progress, Coché says. Aaron, who'd been a lone ranger for nearly two decades when he met Leigh, was sustained by the presence and input of other men who were gobsmacked by their women, the therapist says, if not for the same reasons. He—and Leigh—also had an especially fertile relationship with a couple who left the group a couple of years before I sat in. "Both wives were frustrated with men who lived in their heads, who were too black-and-white," Coché says, and the other husband, quick and sharp-tongued, was a master at "teasing Aaron into a position of looking at himself."

A year later, as I'm working on the final draft of the book, I call Leigh again. This time, she's practically exultant. Their marriage, she tells me is "the best it's ever been—it really is.

"I am so much more flexible in letting Aaron give to me *as he can*," she goes on. "I mean, he's a phenomenal listener, you know. I've been going through a little bit of a medical emergency, and he has been bringing in dinner or cooking dinner, doing the laundry, all these things—and not complaining, not judging, not keeping points: I'm doing this, so you have to do that. There's a calmness between us."

She thinks the meditation she started practicing a year ago has contributed to the new mood—Aaron is trying it, too—as have the couple's continued monthly trips to Coché: once for her, once for him, and once together.

Now I'm anticipating the status-quo report on their sex life, the one that will undercut her enthusiasm: *It is what it is.* But, no. It sounds as if, and I can hardly believe it, the couple's lovemaking has become something akin to "natural." What's made the biggest difference, Leigh says, "are the things you don't think about, like him becoming warm when we're holding each other—Aaron's body used to be ice-cold. He never changed temperature, never went through the subtle signs of being aroused, but now his body is just responding to me. And he's enjoying it. I can just sense it." In a way that recalls the attachment research, Aaron has stopped trying to merely affect his wife; he's begun to let *her* affect him. They may still be using the vibrator more than she'd prefer, but Aaron is "really there," Leigh continues. Oh, and Aaron also initiates sex now, "and not just the night before we see Judith." Leigh lets out a big laugh. "I'm in a so much better place with all this now, you can tell."

It would be easy to mock Leigh and Aaron, or pity them. *Twelve* years of therapy in order to have decent sex, twelve years to get the marriage they (or she) want. It's true that in New York, where I live, you can be in psychoanalysis for a decade and lay claim to being a member of the intelligentsia, a searcher, but a *couple* who goes to such lengths to stay together, who allows outsiders to pierce the marital unit year after year? Get a divorce already or have an affair. The only instance in which such a lengthy go at marriage therapy might be tolerable is when children are involved, but Leigh and Aaron didn't have any together. And for those who choose to persevere, please, please keep a stiff upper lip about it. As one writer snarkily put it, *"Couples therapy:* Is there any phrase in the English language that lands with such a depressing thud? Surely a thousand other acts would be more restorative for a troubled husband and wife. Flying a kite. Cooking a gourmet meal. Having sex."

"Having sex." If only Leigh and Aaron could have. Some couples, alas, are unable to heed that brisk advice. They find themselves seeking help, then perhaps relying on it.

People will have different opinions about whether therapy "worked" for Leigh and Aaron. They themselves think it did, and Coché agrees. While it's true that they will never have the chemistry that Mark and Sue Ellen have, the therapist says, or even the memory of it, "what they've created is what I'd call the 'good enough marriage,' one that deepens over time, one that feels more and more whole and more and more important."

Yet the couple's sex life took on the shine it has now only when Leigh let up to an extent on the therapeutic project, stopped even half expecting that Aaron could be molded into her ideal lover. That raises the question of whether therapy has been, in Coché's formulation, more part of the problem than the solution. Adam Phillips writes, "In our erotic lives, trying is always trying too hard; we have to become lazy again about effort, because the good things only come when it stops—affection, curiosity, desire, unworrying attention." That sounds right, but then, if Leigh and Aaron hadn't tried really, really hard for some time, wouldn't they have forever remained two mannequins in bed, with twelve inches between them? Is becoming lazy about effort hard work? Perhaps Phillips's epigram can be given another twist: Only with effort can we eventually become lazy about it.

I'll let Leigh have the last word. In her good-bye to the group, she expressed heartfelt gratitude to Aaron for hanging in there with her, lo these many years. Though still shaky from her earlier acknowledgment of his shower outburst, Leigh spoke with emotion and conviction when she turned to Aaron and said: "I really thank you, in spite of all the arguing, and the aggravation it's caused you, the stomach upset and everything else. I've never felt so loved by anyone." She paused. "Because you had to work so hard."

Michael and Rachael

As the second year of the group begins, there is no denying the mutual tenderness and respect flowing back and forth between Michael and Rachael. The year before, he'd simultaneously—and probably not coincidentally—developed some compassion for his wife and for himself, for the sacrifices he'd made in the name of keeping his parents' love. No longer did Michael insist on living in an emotion-free zone where he determined the rules of engagement.

So it comes as a mild shock when Rachael says, in the second session of the new year, that Michael refuses to discuss their having children together. "Every time I talk to him, you know, 'Do you want to have kids or whatever,'" Rachael says, "the subject gets changed."

Rachael was moved to address the impasse, she says, by watching Bella and Joe with their new daughter, who was born soon after the second group began and sits by her parents' side, usually placidly, in her car seat. "It's been so long since I've seen a little baby, and it was kind of like, Wow, that looks great. So now I want to work with it." She glances at Michael and titters nervously. He looks like he's gritting his teeth.

"She says I change the subject all the time—yeah, I do," Michael admits. "I don't want to get into it. If it happens, great, but I don't want to go through the whole marking the calendar, and timing everything, and taking temperatures, and taking semen samples out to be spun."

The story that unfolds is that Michael and his first wife climbed the infertility treatment ladder, up to the rung of in vitro fertilization, with no success. Doctors were not sure where the problem lay, but testing showed that while Michael's sperm count was in the fertile range, it was on the low end. After the couple split, Michael's ex-wife got pregnant, twice, which hit him hard. Before that, he says, "There was no solid proof" that he was the infertile one.

"You don't know that for sure," Rachael murmurs.

"Oh, I think it's pretty clear," Michael replies, as in *I know you mean well but please don't patronize me.* He and Rachael have been having unprotected sex, a good bit of it, for more than two years, and nothing.

With the group's urging, and over the course of two days—this is a weekend-long meeting—Michael reveals that, irrationally or not, he's certain he's infertile (even though he got his first wife pregnant once early in their marriage), and that maybe the homosexual part of him has been "internalized" by the hand of God. This is just one more instance, he says, where he feels like a failure as a man. And to adopt a child, an idea Rachael has proposed, would just be a constant reminder of his lack. "I had to go borrow someone else's kid," he says.

There is another layer of complexity: Michael wants Rachael to just get knocked up because he doesn't want to have to actually *decide* to have children. He is afraid to be a father because he's convinced that he'll subject his children to the same kind of dehumanizing tantrums his own father did.

Buffeted by feelings of fear and inadequacy, it seems that Michael has fallen into his old caustic-controlling two-step. Rachael says if she makes even the most nominal effort to get pregnant—once she put a pillow under her butt during sex; elevation is supposed to aid fertilization—he derides her for believing "silly old wives' tales" or informs her: "It's not going to happen. Don't even *think* about it."

But unlike in the past, Michael quickly lets down his defenses in the group, and by midway through the second day, he has aired acute shame over his perceived lack of "virility," to use Joe's word, and over his inability to give Rachael what "she deserves." As they did months before, after Rachael confronted Michael about his contempt for her "manipulative-female" tears, each shows empathy for the other, which seems to open lines of communication over what might be next for them. A stab at fertility treatments? Adoption? Coming to grips with childlessness?

For all the grace the couple displays, and the continued progress they're making, I still feel scooped out when the Sunday-afternoon session ends. Michael suffered his homosexuality for more than three decades, and now, when he's finally accepting himself, he can't get the woman he loves pregnant? The cosmic unfairness of it is killing.

In the next group, in January, Michael delivers the news: He and Rachael are going to have a baby! God is not dead, or merciless, after all. They both seem euphoric, and Rachael's pregnancy proceeds without incident. Their child, a girl, is born on September 2, nine months to the day after Michael confessed his "infertility" to the group. Rachael was either pregnant that weekend, or conceived within days of the dam breaking on the topic.

When Coché wondered aloud whether couples could "generate a tsunami" of passion for each other if they never had it, her question had almost seemed rhetorical. You're either blessed with what Mark and Sue

Ellen had from the get-go, or you're not, which doesn't mean you can't have a good marriage; it just won't be predicated on that heady experience. But in the final *final* session of the group—the second year is coming to a close, and no one is returning—I note, with pleasure, that tsunamis do strike out of season.

Rachael and Michael's daughter is two months old by this time, and not only has the couple's elation at being parents persisted, but Michael now seems as "in love" with Rachael as she always has been with him. "I'm still—I love you more all the time," he stutters, sweetly flummoxed by the strength of his affection. He looks into Rachael's eyes. "I just—I don't know where it comes from."

They've both told me repeatedly that they don't think they'd be nearly as happy were it not for the personal and marital deconstruction, then rebuilding, that the group encouraged. They've even wondered whether they'd still be married without the group.

"Wow," Coché says to Michael's profession of love for Rachael. The therapist chuckles deeply. "That is so *wonderful.*" I agree.

Rachael's eyes are glossy with tears. So are Michael's.

Bella and Joe

Having a child also seems to have brought purpose and contentment to Bella and Joe. It's interesting that both new-parent couples, at least so far, have seen an uptick in happiness; a preponderance of studies show that contrary to expectation, marital quality drops, often precipitously, when children enter the mix. The reasons Bella and Joe (like Rachael and Michael) are the exception to the rule are probably that neither of them was actually ambivalent about becoming a parent, and they hashed out the changes in their respective roles before the baby was born—factors that, according to close analysis of the data, prevent the decline in marital satisfaction.

Bella and Joe's second year in the group is relatively quiet. They've put their town house on the market and moved into Joe's mother's apartment to save money, which isn't half bad since his mother spends most of her time in her vacation home. For them, this round of the group is akin to an extended career-coaching session, the issue being how Joe might best thrive—and survive—in his new job as an in-house lawyer. The position is perfect for him, except it's only temporary, unless Joe is able to convince the higher-ups they can't do without him. By the end of the year, he seems to have pulled it off: His boss has suggested that he'll be able to stay indefinitely (and despite the cratering economy, he still has the job as of June 2009). Joe is massively relieved to have the steady paycheck, and Bella is hardly chafing to get back on the fast track. Again and again, she says she loves raising her daughter, and though she expects to eventually return to work, she wants to find something that is more creative than corporate.

Those concrete accomplishments notwithstanding, I understand why Michael, joined by Rachael, says in the final group session that Bella and Joe didn't seem to go beyond the superficial this year. Though the couple does seem to be "working as a team," which was a goal for both of them, there is still something elusive in Bella's all-is-well comportment. The group knows, after all, how good she and Joe are at hiding things. And there was an incident midway through the year when Joe started to say something and Bella signaled for him to stop—whatever the topic was, it was to be for Coché's ears only.

Joe and Bella think, unsurprisingly, that Michael is wrong, that they've haven't avoided the "hard stuff." They may not have had as much to discuss in the group this year, they say, because they were applying what they learned last year at home. Bella brings it back to her daughter. "I've been so happy," she says, "just so happy."

Marie and Clem

When I walk up the strip of driveway next to Marie and Clem's house, what strikes me on this, my second visit, is a large boat resting on a trailer hitch. I know Clem has owned boats, fixes them up, but this is the first one I've seen. It commands the small yard with its curvy, sky-blue bow and rather majestic, pointed prow, jutting toward the screened back door.

This time, I don't have a moment to peer timorously into the house.

Marie greets me at the door, her hair in shoulder-length curls, wet from the shower. I'll find out later that for the first time in her life she's getting real haircuts, not just having inches chopped off; the curls sprang with the layering around her face and the jettisoning of all that heavy length.

I follow Marie into the kitchen, and we hug—I'm not sure who takes whom into whose arms. At one time, I would've been positive it was me. But Marie has changed so remarkably since then—even, from what I've gleaned from afar, since the second group wrapped half a year ago—that all I can say is that she and I found ourselves hugging.

Clem appears, smiling broadly, and the three of us quickly take seats at the kitchen table, around a plate of bagels and cream cheese.

"So," I ask, "how are things going?" I'm grinning, but I try to sound matter-of-fact. "Studied nonchalance," I'd call it, were I writing about myself.

I'm eager because I already know part of the answer to the question, and the news had me cursing with incredulity. Coché first informed me of the development (she had permission from the couple to issue an update): Marie now wanted to have sex *all the time.* "For real," Coché told me.

Clem doesn't jump right to that subject, because it would not be seemly, perhaps, and it never was only about *that,* not only. "Things have been going great for the last six months or a year," he says. "The gears are finally meshing, like German gears that are just smooth and uh." The "uh" is buoyant, there is air underneath it, and Clem laughs, a real laugh, kind of embarrassed but real. Michael and Rachael were the anxious laughers in the group, not Clem.

Did you ever imagine your marriage would get better? I ask.

"A year ago, no," Clem trills. "It was hard to keep, keep going. And just"—he beams at Marie; she smiles in return—". . . you've been so awesome to be with. And so much fun lately, and now that you're happy with your job, you're so much more engaged." Marie has traveled to six countries in Africa and South America over the last two years for what has become a full-time job training locals to set up and run health clinics.

"You know, you're letting me touch you more, you're touching the girls more," Clem continues. "You're riding your bike, going to the beach. Like Marie says to me"—Clem turns back toward me— "'Let's go down to the beach and read a book for an hour.' And it was just so relaxing to spend time and feel that she *wants* to spend time with me. A month ago, she said, 'Let's go out to dinner,' and she dressed up nice, and we went out to dinner." This is the first I'd heard Clem run on about how his marriage hummed rather than coughed and sputtered.

"Yeah," Marie concurs. "It's working out great."

"The sex is great," Clem says, finally. We all laugh.

In the last session of the second group, Marie had announced—to my (and the group's) astonishment—that she wanted to "restructure" the couple's sex life. "I want a different sex life." Until this point, sex for Marie was, at best, a means to show consideration for Clem, at worst an onerous duty that left her feeling "hunted." To hear that she had an independent desire for it—*Sheesh*, as Coché would say.

The changes she wanted probably would require "exploration," Marie went on, and she wasn't sure whether she or Clem would need "external help" at some point. They'd just have to see. Clem, not unreasonably, was disconcerted by the talk of restructuring. "In what way?" he asked his wife. "I mean, just more variety?"

"I have things that I fantasize about, and I would like to incorporate it into reality," Marie replied quietly. "That's what I would like to do."

Rachael cracked a joke, and Marie addressed the worry in Clem's eyes. He apparently had been upset by pictures she showed him of a party to celebrate the opening of her first health clinic. In one of the photos, she was dancing with a gaggle of men, but if the angle of the shot had been slightly different, Marie assured Clem, with the group listening in, he'd have seen "four women dancing, too." He absolutely did not have to worry about her cheating on him, she said.

In her third year with the group (my second), Marie accomplished the major goal she'd set for herself: She became a fully dimensional member of an intimate cluster of people, a kind of family. She attended to the other members, encouraged and supported them, without losing her incisiveness. And she wasn't a cactus anymore, or a sensitive fern, stabbing or folding up when wounded or threatened; she let herself trust Bella and Joe and Michael and Rachael. With them, and Clem to an extent, she managed to articulate why she was hurt, frustrated, or angry, then move on. Clem continued to try to be more direct, and his effort, together with Marie's softened demeanor, made the conversations the couple had in the group more productive.

That said, the pair still carried to the group scenes from their life that demonstrated how possessive their old selves were. There was a Christmas trip with their daughters to Washington, D.C., that was especially brutal. The contours were familiar, and the details, inevitably, banal. The family's second day in D.C., they'd planned to go to the Holocaust Museum; the evening before, Marie reminded Clem that they had to leave the hotel by 9:30 A.M. to get tickets. No problem, Clem said. No problem, he said again in the morning, while pulling the covers over his head as his eldest daughter followed suit. Marie dragged her family out of bed with time to spare, but then wandered through the museum silent and hateful because, once again, a promise had been broken, and she was the bad guy. Clem put on a happy face for his girls. That evening, Marie starting crying and saying she was tired of Clem's patting her on the head, then blowing her off; Clem, having downed a bottle of champagne with his eldest daughter in the hotel hot tub, hollered, "I just can't take it anymore" and left, in such a way that Marie and the girls were sure he was going to ask her for a divorce. Marie called her parents and told them the family wouldn't be coming to their house the next day for Christmas Eve because—and she decided to tell them the truth—Clem was preparing to leave her.

Here is how the aftermath of this fight was different, how progress in long, disturbed marriages is measured in teaspoonfuls. On Christmas Eve, the family drove home in a gray funk. That evening Clem asked Marie to go for a walk in the dark. He told her that he *did* want their marriage to work. She told him she wanted that, too, but she did not want to be placated and dismissed anymore; if they couldn't fix that, she would move on. It was the first time in twenty-three years of marriage *she'd* breathed a word of divorce. Then Marie and Clem decided to speak with their daughters, rather than act as if nothing had happened. They'd explain, in general, some of the issues plaguing their marriage and their intent to surmount them. The couple also wanted to address the alliance that sometimes arose between Clem and his eldest, against Marie. So over Chinese takeout (they'd expected to be at Marie's mother's for Christmas Eve), the couple and their girls all talked, and they all cried.

On Christmas day, Clem and Marie talked some more, for hour upon hour, and it was hard, because Marie felt like she couldn't "get anything back from" Clem, and then, after a while, he "went further," and they got somewhere.

All this Clem and Marie told the group, and worked through some of the underlying causes once more: how Clem lays all their problems at Marie's feet, how he is so hopped up with fear when he anticipates her judgment and ire that he'll agree to anything without even hearing, without even being *able* to hear, what she is asking. What is new in the second year is the intensity at which Clem is drawn into the discussion.

Different from last year, too, Marie showed vulnerability to Clem; she was someone who could be injured by him, someone who wanted his love, not just his respect for her diligence and intelligence. When he's "dishonest" with her, Marie told her husband at one point during the Holocaust Museum debriefing, "It hurts me." She paused, and then spoke in pensive bursts. "I tried so many ways . . . and each one comes up the same. You know, I'm frustrated . . . And if I could find a way, I would do it. I'm searching, I'm looking, because I love you. I just can't seem to find it . . . and I would love to find it . . . I want you to be my partner. I don't want to be an authority, I want a partner. I want *you*."

Now, back at the kitchen table, Marie compares her decision to become "sexual and sensual" to the flash of light that is the trope of the saved Christian. "I had a moment where I could make a conscious decision, and I chose it. This is what I want, and I'm gonna go after it. Judith always said that changing, actually, doesn't take a lot of time. It's getting to the point where you're ready to change that takes time."

Fundamental for her, she says, was "moving out of a victim mind frame," a place she'd never acknowledged occupying before. "That's probably what took me so long, because that role, it does feel very comforting and familiar to me, safe—so why the hell would I want to leave it? It's perverse, I know, because it's so destructive." Then, "I was shutting Clem out, and I needed to allow him in."

But what did she *do*, I ask, once the switch was flipped? How did she execute?

Marie had "glimpses" over the years of what it felt like to desire and feel desirable, she says, and she had to "grab" them, "form them and shape them." And then talk to Clem about what had lain dormant between them: "Okay, we haven't had much sex [over the years], and I know *you* haven't had much sex, but this is what I want when we're making love, this is where I think I can plug in." It wasn't just a matter of technique, she says, of please put your hand here or there. It was more the atmospherics, a question of how Clem approached her, "which made if difficult for the poor guy," Marie says fondly, "because sometimes I couldn't express it well." For example, she'd never forgotten a particular touch from their early dating. "Just the way he stroked my jawline," she says, "and when I looked into his eyes, I saw such desire. It didn't feel like there was this 'Can I get to third base?'"—a desperate eagerness that is a condition of adolescence *and* sex-starved marriages, certainly—"it was just like he was really turned on, to *me*." Marie giggles. "Not that I can get him to re-create it. Lord knows I've tried."

An exact repeat isn't the point, anyway, she says. Sharing images, snippets from their past, just puts them on the right path. "It was a lot more trial and error than I'd anticipated. Sometimes we'd almost have to go forward, and I'd say 'I'm not sure *what* I want, but I know this is not it.'"

Sitting at Marie's side, Clem has been listening to her intently, but calmly. I wonder out loud whether he was discombobulated by his wife's newfound lust.

"I was like, 'Wow, this is so strange: Marie wants sex more than I do,'" Clem says delightedly. He sighs with feigned exhaustion. "I went to work with circles under my eyes; I can't *go* three times a day at this age!" Clem sounds more joyous than I've ever heard him.

"But there was a period where you were wondering about your adequacy as a lover," Marie reminds him gently. "We did have to cross that hurdle."

"Yes," Clem says, sobering up. "It was a little sudden: Say, I wanted to have sex once a day and Marie wanted it more." (I guess that thrice daily wasn't an exaggeration; Marie attributes her enormous desire, by the way, to the years of self-imposed deprivation.) "And I was feeling a little inadequate. I was the one always chasing Marie; it was sort of weird to be chased."

Having felt sexually deficient herself, Marie was sensitive to Clem's feelings and tried to "validate" him, she says, assure him that he was the man she wanted.

"Yeah," Clem continues, "I guess I was feeling like she feels better about herself, she's traveling, and Oh, I'm going to lose her. Maybe she'll want someone younger, who can, you know, satisfy her."

"Oh, you're my cougar," Marie jokes, rubbing Clem's arm. They both laugh.

"So we talked about it," Clem says, "and I have no doubt that I'm important to Marie. And when she's over in Africa, she's working, and if she's dancing and joking around with other people, she's dancing and joking around. Even if she's flirting a little bit, it probably makes her feel good, and she's not gonna follow through on anything."

In fact, Marie is leaving the next day, Sunday, for a weeklong conference (in another state, not on another continent). "You saw the boat in the driveway?" Clem continues. "It has a cabin in it, and Marie said to me, 'When I come back on Saturday, make sure to have the boat ready.'" Clem's voice rises teasingly, imitating Marie. He apparently has been redoing the cabin's interior: new carpet, seats, the works. "So we can go out and have a nice romantic evening, put the boat on the marshes, and have some cocktails, or a bottle of wine."

"That's great," I gush. I can't wipe the smile off my face. This is the same Marie who couldn't hide her scorn for boating, prompting Coché to grumble to me once, "Would it kill her to go out on a boat with the man?" This is the same Clem who spouted, "Marie's true to me, and that's one of the things I wanted, and that's what I got"—period, the end. These two are affirming my faith not in God but in therapy, in marriage, in the human potential for change, in mystery (so maybe in God), and in their own magnificently ordinary extraordinariness.

As they talk on—to me, to each other—I'm enchanted by them: Marie, lightly tanned, thinner, in a royal-purple T-shirt, her curly hair drying. Clem with those blue eyes, his hair a freshly trimmed brownish red (he's had it colored, which at first pierced my heart—an effort to remain young for his wife? But later, when Marie says, "Doesn't Clem look great? Can you believe he's going to turn fifty," I sigh with relief. It's all right).

Marie keeps floating changes she made that allowed her to embrace Clem as her husband: the self-confidence she acquired by succeeding at a challenging, exciting new job; the relinquishing of disappointment in how Clem had failed her; and, when I ask, having her adored daughters leave the house for college.

"They can be used as a very convenient shield to hide behind," Marie says. Then she apes her own sanctimony. "I'm a devoted mother, so therefore I don't have to relate to *him*." And speaking of her children, Marie says, she also realized she wanted Clem to de-domesticate his dealings with her. "There's a lot of times where I've been demanding, 'No, you can't touch me the way you touch the girls. I am your lover. You need to touch me as a lover, not as a daughter. I am somebody *else* in your life, and you need to carve out a niche for me.'"

Marie hasn't lost her ferocity, thankfully, in my opinion. And now that it's directed toward her wanting Clem's husbandly attentions—he always complained that Marie put him "low on the totem pole," but what must have hurt more was that she appeared indifferent to where he put her—it's a whole different matter.

"Once you brought it to my attention," Clem says, referring to Marie's hierarchy of touch, "it was like, yeah, I can do that. Okay."

As for Clem, what he keeps returning to is how he doesn't run around with his friends much these days, how he'd rather hang out with Marie. He also plans to work on their house again. Marie has complained through the years, he says, that the place was "horrible," that she'd never have a nice house. "I want to spend time fixing it up, getting it looking real nice, because I'm so happy with our marriage."

"That's great that you want to do that, go for it," Marie says to Clem. "But the irony is, I don't care anymore. I cared about the house because I thought that's what marriage was: having a nice house."

So much for that house, and those girls.

Bibliography

Abraham, Laurie. "The Landscape of Desire." *Mirabella*, November 1999.

Boo, Kate. "The Marriage Cure: Is Wedlock Really a Way Out of Poverty?" *New Yorker*, August 18/25, 2003.

Bowen, Murray. *Family Therapy in Clinical Practice*. Lanham, Maryland: Jason Aronson Publishers Inc., 1978.

Carrere, Sybil, Kim T. Buehlman, John Gottman, James A. Coan, and Lionel Ruckstuhl. "Predicting Marital Stability and Divorce in Newlywed Couples." *Journal of Family Psychology* 14:1 (2000): 42–58.

Cassidy, Jude, and Phillip R. Shaver, eds. *Handbook of Attachment, 2d ed, Theory, Research, and Clinical Applications*. New York: Guilford Press, 2008.

Cavell, Stanley. *Pursuits of Happiness: The Hollywood Comedy of Remarriage*. Cambridge, Mass.: Harvard University Press, 1981.

Coché, Judith, "Resistance in Existential-Strategic Marital Therapy." *Journal of Family Psychology*. 3:3 (1990): 236–250.

Coché, Judith, and Erich Coché. *Couples Group Psychotherapy*. New York: Brunner/Mazel, Inc., 1990.

Coontz, Stephanie. *Marriage, a History: From Obedience to Intimacy, or How Love Conquered Marriage*. New York: Viking, 2005.

———. "Till Children Do Us Part," *New York Times*, February 4, 2009.

Dicks, Henry. *Marital Tensions*. New York: Basic Books, 1967.

Doherty, William J. "Bad Couples Therapy: How to Avoid Doing It." *Psychotherapy Networker*, November/December 2002, p. 26.

Edge, The Third Culture. "The Mathematics of Love: A Talk with John Gottman." April 14, 2004. www.edge.org/3rd_culture/gottman05/gottman05_index.html.

Epstein, Mark. *Going to Pieces Without Falling Apart: A Buddhist Perspective on Wholeness*. New York: Broadway Books, 1998.

———. *Psychotherapy Without the Self: A Buddhist Perspective*. New Haven, Conn.: Yale University Press, 2007.

Feld, Barbara G. "An Object Relations Perspective on Couples Group Therapy." *International Journal of Group Psychotherapy* 47:3 (1997): 315–332.

Frankl, Victor E. *Man's Search for Meaning*. Boston: Beacon Square Press, 1959.

Fraley, Chris R., and Phillip R. Shaver. "Airport Separations: A Naturalistic Study of Adult Attachment Dynamics in Separating Couples." *Journal of Personality and Social Psychology* 75:5 (1998): 1198–1212.

Gillath, Omri, Mario Mikulincer, Gurit E. Birnbaum, and Phillip R. Shaver. "When Sex Primes Love: Subliminal Sexual Priming Motivates Relationship Goal Pursuit." *Personality and Social Psychology Bulletin* 34 (2008): 1057–1069.

Gladwell, Malcom. *Blink: The Power of Thinking Without Thinking*. New York: Little, Brown and Company, 2005.

Goldner, Virginia. " 'Let's Do It Again': Further Reflections on Eros and Attachment." *Psychoanalytic Dialogues* 16:6 (November 2006): 619–637.

Gottman, John, and Nan Silver. *The Seven Principles for Making Marriage Work: A Practical Guide from the Country's Foremost Relationship Expert*. New York: Crown Publishers Inc., 1999.

Gottman, John. *Marital Interaction: Experimental Investigations*. New York: Academic Press, 1979.

———. "Temporal Form: Toward a New Language for Describing Relationships." *Journal of Marriage and the Family* 4:4 (November 1982): 943–962.

———. *What Predicts Divorce?* Mahwah, NJ: Lawrence Erlbaum and Associates, 1994.

Gottman, John M., and Clifford I. Notarius. "Decade Review: Observing Marital Interaction," *Journal of Marriage and the Family* 62:4 (November 2000): 927–947.

Gottman, John, James Coan, Sybil Carrere, and Catherine Swanson. "Predicting Marital Happiness and Marital Stability from Newlywed Interactions." *Journal of Marriage and the Family* 60:1 (February 1998): 5–22.

Gottman, John M., Sybil Carrere, Catherine Swanson, and James A. Coan. "Reply to 'From Basic Research to Interventions.'" *Journal of Marriage and the Family* 62:1 (February 2000): 265–273.

Gurman, Alan S., ed. *Clinical Handbook of Couple Therapy.* New York: Guilford Press, 2008.

Haley, Jay. "Marriage Therapy." *Archives of General Psychiatry* 8 (March 1963): 213–234.

———. *Uncommon Therapy: The Psychiatric Techniques of Milton H. Erickson, MD.* New York: W. W. Norton & Company, 1986.

Hazan, Cindy, and Phillip Shaver. "Love and Work: An Attachment-Theoretical Perspective." *Journal of Personality and Social Psychology* 59:2 (1990): 270–280.

———. "Romantic Love Conceptualized as an Attachment Process." *Journal of Personality and Social Psychology* 52:3 (1987): 511–524.

Heyman, Richard E., and Amy M. Smith Slip. "The Hazards of Predicting Divorce Without Crossvalidation." *Journal of Marriage and the Family* 63:2 (May 2001): 473–479.

Jayson, Sharon. "Hearts Divide Over Marital Therapy." *USA Today*, June 21, 2005.

Johnson, Sue. *Hold Me Tight: Seven Conversations for a Lifetime of Love.* New York: Little, Brown and Company, 2008.

Johnson, Susan. "Are You There for Me?" *Psychotherapy Networker,* September/October 2006, p. 41.

Kiecolt-Glaser, Janice K., and Tamara L. Newton. "Marriage and Health: His and Hers." *Psychological Bulletin* 127:4 (2001): 472–503.

Kipnis, Laura. *Against Love: A Polemic.* New York: Vintage Books, 2003.

Kramer, Peter D. *Should You Leave?* New York: Penguin Group, 1997.

Kunce, Linda J., and Phillip R. Shaver. "An Attachment-Theoretical Approach to Caregiving in Romantic Relationships." *Advances in Personal Relationships* 5 (1994): 205–237.

Lewis, Thomas, Fari Amini, and Richard Lannon. *A General Theory of Love.* New York: Vintage Books, 2000.

Maugh, Thomas H., II. "Study's Advice to Husbands; Accept Wife's Influence; Marriage: Data Showing Compliance Is Best Cast Doubt on 'Active Listening,' a Common Counseling Approach." *Los Angeles Times,* February 21, 1998.

Miller, Michael Vincent. *Intimate Terrorism: The Crisis of Love in an Age of Disillusion.* New York: W. W. Norton & Company, 1995.

Mitchell, Stephen A. *Can Love Last? The Fate of Romance over Time.* New York: W. W. Norton & Company, 2001.

Mitchell, Stephen A., and Margaret J. Black. *Freud and Beyond: A History of Modern Psychoanalytic Technique.* New York: Basic Books, 1995.

Mikulincer, Mario, and Phillip R. Shaver. *Attachment in Adulthood: Structure, Dynamics, and Change.* New York: Guilford Press, 2007.

"The Most Influential Therapists of the Past Quarter-Century," *Psychotherapy Networker,* March/April 2007.

Noller, Patricia, and Judith A. Feeney, eds. *Understanding Marriage: Developments in the Study of Couple Interaction.* Cambridge, U.K.: Cambridge University Press, 2002.

Phillips, Adam. *Monogamy.* New York: Pantheon Books, 1996.

———. *Winnicott.* Cambridge, Mass.: Harvard University Press, 1988.

Prager, Karen J. and Linda J. Roberts "Deep Intimate Connection: Self and Intimacy in Couple Relationships." In Debra Mashek and Arthur Aron (eds.), *Handbook of Closeness and Intimacy.* Mahwah, NJ: Lawrence Erlbaum Associates, 2004.

Roberts, Linda J. "Fire and Ice in Marital Communication: Hostile and Distancing Behaviors as Predictors of Marital Distress." *Journal of Marriage and the Family* 62:3 (August 2000): 693–707.

Roiphe, Katie. *Uncommon Arrangements: Seven Portraits of Married Life in London Literary Circles, 1910–1939.* New York: The Dial Press, 1997.

Rose, Phyllis. *Parallel Lives: Five Victorian Marriages.* New York: Alfred A. Knopf, 1983.

Russo, Francine. "Can the Government Prevent Divorce?" *Atlantic Monthly,* October 1997.

Schnarch, David. *Passionate Marriage: Keeping Love & Intimacy Alive in Committed Relationships.* New York: Henry Holt and Company, Inc., 1997.

Shaver, Phillip R., and Mario Mikulincer. "Attachment Theory and Research: Resurrection of the Psychodynamic Approach to Personality." *Journal of Research in Personality* 39:1 (2005): 22–45.

Sillars, Alan, Linda J. Roberts, Kenneth E. Leonard, and Tim Dun. "Cognition During Marital Conflict: The Relationship of Thought and Talk." *Journal of Social and Personal Relationships* 17:4–5 (2000): 479–502.

Stanley, Scott M. "Making a Case for Premarital Education." *Family Relations* 50:3 (2001): 272–280.

———. Thomas N. Bradbury, and Howard J. Markham. "Structural Flaws in the Bridge from Basic Research on Marriage to Intervention for Couples." *Journal of Marriage and Family* 62:1 (February 2000): 256–264.

Sullivan, Harry S. *The Interpersonal Theory of Psychiatry.* New York: W. W. Norton & Company, Inc., 1953.

Walsh, Froma, ed. *Normal Family Processes: Growing Diversity and Complexity,* 3d ed. New York: Guilford Books, 2003.

Weiss, Philip. "Is This Marriage on the Rocks?" *New York Times Magazine,* May 7, 2000.

Winnicott, D. W. *Through Paediatrics to Psycho-Analysis: Collected Papers.* New York: Brunner-Routledge, 1992.

Yalom, Irvin D. *The Theory and Practice of Group Psychotherapy,* 4th ed. New York: Basic Books, 1995.

Acknowledgments

My deepest appreciation goes to therapist Judith Coché, who trusted me—and herself—enough to allow me to sit in on the group. Coché was brave to put her skills on the line and also to recognize that therapy could be written about responsibly. I know the process was scary for her at times—she did not have veto power over what I said about her or her clients—but she was unfailingly enthusiastic and generous with her time.

I'm equally and profoundly beholden to Rachael and Michael, Bella and Joe, Marie and Clem, Sue Ellen and Mark, and Leigh and Aaron. They warmly welcomed me into the group and were as honest with me as people can be. They made my professional life fascinating, and no matter what went on in a particular session, I left feeling oddly happy. It was the recognition of my connection to other people, of the common humanity that binds us, that moved me. I thank the group for that unexpected gift.

Aside from Coché and her clients, this book includes the fruits of conversations with dozens of clinical therapists and academic researchers. For their patience and wisdom, I especially want to acknowledge Margaret Black, William Doherty, Jay Efran, Mark Epstein, Janice Kiecolt-Glaser, Cindy Hazan, Richard Heyman, Susan Johnson, Michael Kerr, Joe Kort, Jay Lebow, Valerie Manusov, Michael Vincent Miller, Linda Roberts, David Schnarch, Phillip Shaver, and Scott Stanley. Thanks, too, to my editor at Touchstone, Zachary Schisgal, for taking the book very seriously and championing it among his colleagues.

For assigning and expertly editing the magazine story that led to the book, I'm indebted to *New York Times Magazine* editor Ilena Silverman. After the piece was published, I credit my agent Eric Simonoff for persuading me that this was an article that actually should become a book (unlike so many, the implication being). This was the first project for which he represented me, and he had my back from beginning to end.

ELLE editor-in-chief Roberta Myers has been my boss, and friend, for close to fifteen years. Every writer has a few people she writes for, the readers in her mind, and Robbie is chief among them for me. She is a great conceptual and line editor, and no one has been more supportive of my writing, literally and figuratively. Without hesitation, she gave me a year-long leave from my position at *ELLE* to write the book, then enthusiastically took me back in the worst environment for publishing in memory.

Because I have many friends who are writers and editors themselves, I've received some incredible help. Peggy Orenstein was a huge cheer-leader for the book, starting with the proposal and ending with her careful, insightful read of the entire manuscript. Dani Shapiro gave me a succinct, spot-on critique of the first chapter. Her words got me going in the right direction and, pinned to my office bulletin board, buttressed me along the way.

Daphne Merkin generously edited the manuscript, and her suggestions were, like her own writing, elegant and erudite. My office buddy and dear friend Rachael Combe did the same and caught slips in logic or consistency that I (and everybody else) completely missed.

On this front, too, it is my incredible luck that my best friend since college is the widely respected and beloved editor Lisa Chase. Big-deal authors pay her to edit their books, but I got her services—everything from brilliant organizational suggestions to cuts that made a so-so sentence sing—for free. As my closest friend, she is also the first person I call if I need to cry or gloat or just get solid advice. Like Lisa, my sister Shelley Abraham and my parents, Kaye Price and Harold Abraham, believe in me and love me unreservedly, which makes—has always made—meeting challenges more possible.

Finally, I wrote my last book living alone in a one-bedroom apartment, my boyfriend a three-hour plane flight away. Now I'm a mother to Edie, 9, and Tess, 5, and I worried before starting that I'd constantly feel torn between caring for them and finding the time and concentration to write. I'm happy to report that the balance worked. Undoubtedly, that is because I have wonderful, loving girls who've given my life new purpose. Thank you very much, ladies, as we say around our house. It's also because my husband, Tim, is the rare father who actually shares childcare, who thinks that it's important to be intimately involved in the day-to-day details of his daughters' lives. At the same time, he's always urged me to do work that is meaningful and is willing to sacrifice to that end. I am grateful to Tim for his consistent support, and for his love.

Printed in the United States
By Bookmasters